A Sense of the Sacred

ALSO BY ADELE GETTY

Goddess: Mother of Living Nature

A·SENSE
OF·THE
SACRED

Finding Our Spiritual Lives Through Ceremony

ADELE GETTY

Taylor Publishing Company
Dallas, Texas

Published by Taylor Publishing Company
1550 West Mockingbird Lane
Dallas, Texas 75235

Library of Congress Cataloging-in-Publication Data

Getty, Adele.
    A sense of the sacred : finding our spiritual lives through ceremony / Adele Getty.
        p.   cm.
    Includes bibliographical references (p. 201) and index.
    ISBN 0-87833-946-9
    1. Rites and ceremonies. 2. Spiritual life. I. Title.
B600.G48   1997
291.3'8—DC21   97-8997
                                                            CIP

Printed in the United States of America

10 9 8 7 6 5 4 3 2 1

This book has been printed on acid-free recycled paper.

CONTENTS

FOREWORD

Francis Huxley

A sense of the sacred is, I often think, not all that different from a sense of occasion. Occasions come in all sorts: good and bad, sad and happy, mad and sane, some that only Ronald Firbank's Mrs. Shamefoot can do justice to: "the world is disgracefully managed, one hardly knows to whom to complain," and others that take on a life of their own to general satisfaction.

It was at such an event that I first met Adele, in 1984 at the Ojai Foundation. The occasion, as she later describes here, was an arduous jamboree of teachings, regimens, disciplines, and ceremonial practices from all over, and the official advice on how to deal with this abundance was to take what was on offer as a set of tools rather than a set of beliefs. Reassuring advice for the occasion, I thought, seeing that most of us were starting from scratch where this kind of ceremonial life is concerned, and found it easier to believe everything in general rather than something in particular.

All the same, one must believe in something if one is to enjoy oneself at such events, even if it's only that it's possible to do so. Why else should one get involved? So that being settled, the real question is what makes ceremony enjoyable? To answer this I should first say that this book is about ceremony, even though (as you will soon read) the dream that set Adele on this way told her to teach ritual. Why this change of name, when the dictionary definitions of the words hardly differ? Adele tells me that she made the change after hearing American Indian medicine men speak against mechanical ritual and in praise of heartfelt ceremony. I can appreciate this distinction, for to my ears also 'ritual' often sounds more regimented, heavier, more esoteric than 'ceremony,' which I find implies a certain grace, even if it is only that of good manners. The distinction is not easy to maintain, but having seen Adele and her fellow ceremonialists in acton, it comes out rather like the difference between speaking by the book and speaking as the spirit moves one. Why not a bit of both? Well, that depends on whether everyone taking part can read from the same book without feeling imposed upon. If they can't, quite the best thing is to let the spirit speak for itself: and it's my belief that that is the joy of the occasion.

It is here of course, that one's sense of the occasion becomes part of the sense of the sacred. This is another of those things that hardly need be explained, if only because whatever the sacred feels like, its presence makes everything self-evident as it comes. However, seeing that it can come in many different guises—it can touch lightly or deeply, alone or together, in peace or in tragedy—there is one thing I have found useful to say about it, that it is indeed a presence.

It is also a light, as Adele reminds us in this book by putting the question: In whose light do we stand in when we do what we do? I had brought this question with me to Ojai, for it was fresh in my mind and I found it very interesting. It had come to me when I found myself being bored, impatient, unimaginative, and bad in my timing—I was practicing psychotherapy then—and was asking myself what to do about it. I found the answer when I found a small figure of Kuan Yin whose simple beauty pleased me so much that I was soon telling it my troubles aloud. From there it was but a step to keep her image in mind when I was about my business, and the results refreshed me so well that I wondered how it was that I had not done this before, and what others did when suffering the same disorder. So I asked them, and that was the question: In whose light do you attend others?

It was wonderful to come across one or two who answered without hesitation, for the question took quite a few by surprise. But these too came up with some fine answers, though there were a couple that gave me pause. "In nobody's light" was one, for I doubted that I would ask counsel from anyone who could say such a thing unless, perhaps, he were a devotee of Zen Buddhism, and "In my own light" another, for if that were so I would rather be somewhere else.

At this moment I realize that I'd been open to this question for quite some time, from my anthropological days when I kept company with those who found their light in jaguars, giant centipedes, poisonous toads, bears, Bernard Shaw, cemetery spirits, the blacksmith god, the love goddess, the late emperor Nero (now reformed), and Kali, to mention a few; and glad enough I had been to realize what this meant more at the beginning than the end of their proceedings, which could sometimes be dubious. In our world, of course, one is unlikely to run into such people, but even so I like to keep the question "in whose light?" in mind, especially when I take part in a ceremonial gathering, the kind Adele describes in this book. So of course does she, because the general purpose of such gatherings is to establish a common presence of mind to everyone's refreshment, no matter what particulars are on the agenda; and without a guiding light it is easy enough to lose one's way.

This may sound complicated, but the practicalities involved are, as you will find, simple enough—indeed, by the time you finish the book, they'll appear to be not very different from common sense. What makes the difference is that this common sense has made room in itself for a sense of presence, the sense of occasion, the sense of the sacred itself, all of which are much less difficult to recognize than you might think. The only problem is how to make them your own, and I have little to say on this subject that Adele doesn't say to better purpose. So I shall leave you to enjoy her book for itself, with one last remark in the spirit of all the occasions she brings to our notice. It comes from that wonderful old fellow Lao Tze: "Of second-rate leaders," he says, "people respectfully say that 'he has done this, he has done that.' Of first-rate leaders, they do not say this, they say 'we have done it all ourselves.'"

ACKNOWLEDGMENTS

This book is the result of a dream that changed my life. In 1978 I was in graduate school and working as a teaching assistant. For the previous two years I had been teaching statistics, research methodology, test and measurements, personality theory, and computer applications in psychology. Early one morning in March, I was startled awake by an old woman, who was both fierce and kind, and she gave me two messages. The first was a poem, a litany of the names of Goddess for the Goddess. At that time I knew very little about the Goddess, but became determined to discover all that I could. My first book, *Goddess: Mother of Living Nature*, was my way of saying thank you for this visitation by the Eternal Feminine. The second message of the old woman was a command. She shook a gnarled finger at me and said, "Teach ritual." I was shaken and a bit horrified by this imperative. I wrote the dream in a journal and in the morning went to the college to find my advisor, George Jackson.

When I showed George my journal, his response was simply, "You must do this." I was shocked: I did not want to teach ritual—it would be too embarrassing, too unacademic. George insisted that I write up a proposal to the department about teaching a fall semester class entitled, "Ritual and the Imaginal Process." He even helped me write it. When my class was accepted, my life changed immediately. I began to meet anthropologists and medicine men who took seriously the ideas of ceremony and initiation. George suggested that I use *The Way of the Sacred*, by British anthropologist Francis Huxley, as the class text. Six years later I met Francis and we married.

In those years of discovery I met a number of people who were influ-

ential in my life and work. The late Don Jose, a Huichol shaman, continues to be a guiding light. To the American Indians who discouraged me
from trying to become an Indian, I owe much appreciation. In particular I
am grateful to the late Sun Bear, who first introduced me to the Medicine
Wheels; Heyemeyohst Storm, who taught me not to give my power away;
and Harley Swiftdeer and the late Rolling Thunder.

I especially would like to thank Steven Foster, Meredith Little, and
the late Virginia Hine from Rites of Passage for having faith in me and
employing me as a Vision Quest guide.

Over the years, many people helped to shape the content of this
book; I thank them for their influence, support, and insight: Andra Akers,
Jose and Loyddine Arguelles, Prem Das, Nancy Goddard, Rosemary
Gladstar, Robert Greenway, Joan Halifax, Kat Harrison, James Hillman,
George Jackson, the late R.D. Laing, the late Eve Loewe, Mescalito,
Terrence McKenna, John Michell, Lou Montgomery, Gabrielle Roth,
Theodore Roszak, Brant Secunda, Shawnadese, Sunwater, the late Gordon
Tappan, Wabun, and my great-grandmother Adele.

I am especially grateful to the following institutes and organizations,
and the people behind them, for supporting my work: Rites of Passage, the
Ojai Foundation, Hollyhock Farm, and Women's Alliance.

To the members of The Circle, my ever-growing ceremonial family,
our work together over the last twenty years has been of prime importance.
This book would not be possible without your wisdom.

A special thanks to Colleen Kelley—and our years of teaching
together, Robert Ott for his keen sense of ceremony, and Rupert Sheldrake
and Jill Purce—for our long evenings together filled with good conversation. To Charlotte Kelly and all the women of Women's Alliance, to the
members of Casas las Barrancas, my community: Cal Peacock, Scott
Pitman, Annie Rafter, Tertit Ring, Linda Tellington-Jones, Knut Fjortoft,
Sandra Wilson—thank you.

And above all to my husband Francis Huxley for his unending and
generous support, his keen insights, and his eye to keep this work "in the
light."

Finally, I would like to thank my agent, Howard Sandum, for having
faith in this book, and Holly McGuire, my editor, who provided support
and a very helpful critique of this work.

A Sense of the Sacred

·1·

THE BURNING OF
THE GARDEN

> God has made the soul so cunningly and so secretly that no one knows
> truly what she is.—MEISTER ECKHART

A SENSE OF THE SACRED

The deep common need to overcome separateness, find atone-
ment with one another, transcend individual limits, and
achieve union with God, Nature, and the Universe is as
ancient as humanity. However, separation from the primordial oneness is
an inescapable part of the human adventure. In the past, the sense of at-
one-ness was supported by the tribe or the community through ceremony,
prayer, and celebration. Important moments in life were marked as rites of
passages, with the entire community acknowledging the change in status
or the achievements of an individual. The absence of proper initiation is at
the root of much of the heartbreak that passes for family life in the twentieth century. As Joseph Campbell stated, "If you want to find out what it
means to have a society without any rituals, read the news of the day,
including the destructive and violent acts by people who don't know how
to behave in a civilized world."

The decay and disappearance of the sacred from ordinary life parallels the appearance of the dysfunctional family. This spiritual decay gives
rise to a number of other developments, such as rationalism, agnosticism,
atheism, scientific materialism, and the urgent needs of the ego, id, and
superego that Freud addressed with his theory of psychoanalysis.

After living in London for some years, I returned to California and noted that almost everyone I met was in a recovery program. When I thought about what they were recovering from, I realized that it was the profanity of everyday existence, and the loss of the sacred. It is as if the fabric of life has dropped a stitch, and we must now go back, and weave it into the tapestry before it is too late. Mutuality, connection, and participation are keys to the sacred, and through them meaning can be restored to contemporary lives.

We are desperate for connection in the form of kind, loving, family bonds, and a supportive sense of community. Ceremony offers a way to move into a state of conscious engagement with the spirit of life. The idea of reintroducing initiatory procedures, and simple but elegant ceremonial symbolism into modern life strikes a chord with most people. Human beings are refreshed by a sense of magic and any spiritual formality that honestly increases meaning and connection in our lives. Through an understanding of the ceremonial initiatory process it becomes possible for family and friends to communicate in a more effective way and to live their lives in the light of the Spirit.

Life presents many challenges, among them birth, puberty, marriage, divorce, blended families, career choices, sexuality, substance abuse, psychological emergencies, and death. We often find ourselves muddling through these transitions in the most painful way. Labeling a mid-life crisis as a crisis is not enough. The underlying malaise of emptiness that permeates contemporary life calls us forth in search of meaning. People are hungry for something more than just a label, or the "talking cure" of the therapeutic hour. Those who attend workshops often find themselves inspired by the end of the weekend, only to find that when they return home to family, jobs, and community the "feel-good-fix" of the weekend dissolves overnight. Cultivating the soul in ordinary life empowers people to take charge of the sacred in their daily lives, not as a profession, but as a way of being and sharing the way of the sacred with family and friends.

In spite of all that we have learned recently about patterns of self-destructive behavior in the individual, the family, and the culture, we have yet to go beyond diagnosis, and see the root of the problem as the absence of the sacred. The acknowledgment of life-passages through ceremonial activity, proper initiation, animism, and shamanic techniques are essential as we witness the death of our cultural and religious roots.

On Speaking Terms with Nature

Of all the pantheon, Great Mother Nature has been the hardest to kill.
—C.S. Lewis

There comes a time when every civilization begins to disintegrate. The crumbling generally begins from within and works its way out to the surface of society for all to see. This rise and fall, this ebb and flow, appears to be a natural movement within evolutionary social dynamics and has been documented many times through the ages. In *Re-visioning Psychology*, archetypal depth psychologist James Hillman states: "The push for progress has left many corpses in its wake. Totems, idols, and the personages of myth were the first to be mocked and scorned. Then followed images of every sort—gods, demons, saints, the forces of Nature, the qualities of character, the substantives of metaphysics." Whenever this state of progress-over-spirituality occurs in a culture it is a sure sign that a mythological era is coming to an end. The life blood of the old myths grows cold, heroes are only partially remembered, Gods and Goddesses lie fallow, and people begin to sleep a dreamless sleep. To lose our mythological sense cripples our capacity to dream, and dooms us to live soul-less lives. Myth is by its nature a wondrous story of archetypal dimensions; myth has both a personal and a transpersonal function. It cannot be removed from life without inflicting a crisis of meaning, for without it there is no way to bind together our fragmented experiences.

Hillman's use of the phrase the "substantives of metaphysics" is important. *Substantive*, means "having a real existence; actual or essential." *Consubstantiality* means to be "made of the same stuff." It is what the theologian Martin Buber meant when he spoke of the "I-and-Thou" relationship and what the Hindu greeting *Namasté*—"I honor the God within you"—means. Living Nature is real, just as we are real. Consubstantiality urges us to recognize that we and the rest of creation are one and the same. To deny this reality gives us license to burn the garden in which we live side by side with all of creation—the garden in which all things are born, live, and die.

There is a growing awareness in this country for the need to re-sacralize our lives and reconsecrate our souls. As rationalism proves itself to be a partial truth, a new era of myth-making is being seeded into the fertile ground of our collective mind. People are once again choosing to anthropomorphize or personify their environment. Hillman in *Re-visioning Psychology* feels that "personifying not only aids discrimination; it offers another avenue of loving, of imagining things in a personal form so that we can find access to them with our hearts." To personify is to make animate, to see all of creation as alive and imbued with Spirit. Doing this allows our soul to develop, for the soul is the vital animating principle in all life. Soul connects the plant, animal, and human worlds. This is particularly timely, when we stop to consider the state of the Earth. As human beings, we have not only broken faith with ourselves, we have broken faith with our ancestral inheritance. Any individual or species who dares to destroy its own habitat or the habitat of another surely brings about its own demise. To commit murder or suicide as an individual is madness, to do it as a species is unspeakable.

The absence of meaning that permeates the modern world can be remedied through a new relationship to one another and Nature. Indigenous cultures have long maintained an animistic world view. They are in active relationship with the animals they hunt and the spirits of their ancestors. They make offerings to the spirits of the place in which they live, honor their taboos, and experience life as a mutually interconnecting web. These activities are more than a metaphor. It is how they truly experience the world in which they live. Nature is seen as alive, not just with generation but with Spirit and Soul, and it is this confluence of Man and Nature that actually animates creation.

The Western world, at least since the Enlightenment, has long wanted to deny this view of Living Nature. The very word *animism* was popularized by E.B. Tyler, the founder of British anthropology. A contemporary of Darwin, Tyler observed that native and rural peoples everywhere shared this view of interconnected reality. (Initially he wanted to name it "spiritualism," but unfortunately this term had already been picked up by the Victorian Fox sisters, who were actively engaged in table-knocking seances). The introduction of the word *animism* at a time when the theory of evolution was coming into its own was an attempt to keep alive the memory of our ancient kinship to all creation.

Conceptually, animism was not unknown to our Western heritage. Beginning with the pre-Socratics, the philosopher Thales, declared that "all things are full of Gods." The Greeks called this force *psyche*, which means "soul;" in Latin the word was *anima*, and it too means "soul." Throughout the monasteries of Europe and in medieval universities the philosophical teachings on Nature were animistic: everything had a soul. Behind this vital, sensitive force that flowed through everything was the *anima mundi*, the soul of the world, and humankind was seen as a microcosm of the larger cosmic whole.

In his classic work *The Golden Bough*, scholar James Frazer showed how even the roots of our Judeo-Christian tradition contain elements of old pagan and animistic traditions. The birth of Christ takes place in the presence of animals at the nativity; his public life is preceded by his "vision quest" of forty days and nights on the mountain; and the Crucifixion and Resurrection hearken back to the first tale of resurrection—from ancient Sumeria—where the Queen of Heaven, Inanna, is hung on hooks until dead, and rises after three days to join the living. The celebration of both Passover and Easter can be traced back to the feast of the Goddess Esther, which was celebrated on the first Sunday following the first full moon after the spring equinox.

More recently, climatologist James Lovelock has upset the scientific world with his Gaia hypothesis. This is a complex theory that brings the geology of the Earth, the atmosphere, the oceans, and all biological activity together to form Gaia, an ancient Greek name for the Earth Mother. According to Lovelock Gaia "is a self-regulating entity with the capacity to keep our planet healthy by controlling the chemical and physical environment." Rational materialists object to the idea of the Earth being alive, because if the Earth is alive, she must then have a soul, and consequently a purpose. Modern science is strongly opposed to life having a purpose, for purpose implies that there may be a God behind evolutionary development. No matter what the scientists proclaim, the Gaia hypothesis speaks to something deep within the soul of humanity, and it is almost impossible to read a book on modern science, the nature of consciousness, or ecology without seeing it mentioned. The theory is permeated with anthropomorphic and animistic implications.

Ever since the scientific Enlightenment, animism has been viewed as an embarrassment to the Western mind. It was something "quaint" that primitive people practiced, an artifact from the past. But recently scholars from many different fields have been breaking the code of silence concerning animism. Dr. Rupert Sheldrake, a biochemist from Cambridge,

England, and author of *The Rebirth of Nature—The Greening of Science and God* has entitled Part Three of his book: "The Revival of Animism."

6   Addressing the ongoing debate concerning animism he states: "The old dream of progressive humanism is fading fast. There are still those who dream of the conquest of the biosphere by the technosphere, the human control of biological evolution through genetic engineering, and so on. But attitudes are changing around, and within, many of us: there is a shift from humanism to animism, from an intensely man-centered view to a view of a living world."

Thomas Moore, a leading lecturer in archetypal psychology, and author of the best-seller, *Care of the Soul*, returns the reader's mind again and again to the animistic view as he explores the "loss of soul" in modern life. Philosopher David Abram in his recently published book, *The Spell of the Sensuous*, discusses animistic shamanism: "The deeply mysterious powers and entities with whom the shaman enters into a rapport are ultimately the same forces—the same plants, animals, forests, and winds—that to literate, 'civilized' Europeans are just so much scenery, the pleasant backdrop of our more pressing human concerns." Again animism is a recurrent theme throughout the book.

Eco-psychologist Theodore Roszak, while discussing the Gaia hypothesis in his book *The Voice of the Earth*, says: "In time, with enough help from artists and visionary philosophers, this body of fact and theory may mature into an ecologically grounded form of animism. We will find ourselves once again on talking terms with Nature."

SEEING THROUGH MYTH

There is a joke among anthropologists that "myth is other peoples' religion." Unfortunately, since the Enlightenment even our own religious heritage has been turned into a myth or at best a parable. In an unpublished manuscript, social anthropologist Virginia Hine states: "Myth in its real sense is not mere fantasy or the opposite of reality. Myth is the belief system, the world view, the *zeitgeist* which shapes the structure of any society."

One current myth of modern society has us living in a nightmare world of the dead. Nature is inanimate and exists solely for our purpose. Material goods are the primary source of status and well being, and it is assumed that more technology will correct the mistakes of previous technology. The mind is now likened to a computer chip, and virtual realities and simulations of Nature are promoted as if they were superior to original creation. The myth of the coming future is saturated with apocalyptic visions, degenerate humanity, and fascist extraterrestrials who treat humankind with the same consideration that we give to laboratory rats.

We are urged to believe in the myth of developmental psychology—that mental disorders are the result of what our parents did to us. People are encouraged to accept this myth as true, as a fact, to never question its validity. This is truly a novel idea. Never before this century have people blamed their parents for the problems in their lives. In the past people looked for the source of their difficulties in the milieu in which they lived. If you were mentally disturbed or physically ill, you would examine what taboos you might have broken, or who might have put a hex on you, or what God or Spirit you may have offended. Illnesses of all sorts were a community event.

These modern myths are completely inadequate and incapable of dealing with any form of psychic or spiritual reality. The absence of meaning and connection generated by living in this disjointed and technologically sterilized nightmare is at the core of our search for "family values." The collective narcissism that has grown out of the past century is symptomatic of the large scale fear and denial that faces a world on the brink of disaster. To live for the moment, create your own reality, and define your boundaries are part of its credo. No other people have ever lived so totally as if they only had one life to live. Historically, people have lived connected to their ancestors, not just to their own "past lives," and through the succession of generations they were connected to future beings as well.

Given this current state of affairs, all is not lost, for we come out of a rich mythological background. The world's great religious traditions guide and teach us how to live full lives. The fairy tales and mythic stories of every culture teach us about the nature of good and evil, and the consequences of our actions. A recent poll in *Newsweek* states that 58% of the population would like to experience spiritual growth. Millions of Americans are quietly searching for a sense of the sacred. "Junk values," while seeming to thrive through the media, are uniting the Left and the Right to stand up together in favor of family values. The family unit desperately needs to be re-sanctified, but the challenge is how to bring a sense of the sacred into the ordinary.

One way to initiate this process is to begin to pick up the pieces left along the roadside from the past. The first task is to gather the debris and sort out the hidden treasures among the weeds. We must pick through the bones of our past, gather the gems and stones, the fur, the feathers, the disregarded parts of our psyches, and we must plant new seeds for the future, tending and nurturing the delicate new shoots. Yet we must be aware that culture is constantly shape shifting: It is the nature of the beast. Our perceptions, too, continually change, as does our language. Changes in metaphor indicate changes in our view of reality. The kinds of stories we tell reveal the borders of the roads we travel, and what is a road but a way to get from here to there? Before it was a road, it was a track, and before it was a track, it was a path through the forest made by animals, and animals have been telling us how to get from here to there for a very long time.

PSYCHE AND EROS

"Perhaps it would not be too much to say that the most crucial problems of the individual and of society turn upon the way the psyche functions in regard to spirit and matter."—CARL JUNG

We are by nature a species who create, recite, and receive stories. This capability may be the most meaningful thing that differentiates us from the rest of the animals. I cannot imagine a time when we did not sit around the campfire telling or listening to a story. Recently, storytelling has been reserved for children in the form of fairy tales, but now stories and their magic have been reclaimed by adults—Robert Bly, Clarissa Pinkola Estes, and a multitude of others. Professional storytellers are a sought-after commodity. Even in our technologically driven world, the longing, the fascination, and the comfort of a good tale continues as we huddle around the glow of the television.

In the past, stories were handed from storyteller to storyteller, from campfire to campfire. In time, certain stories were committed to the written word, and the written word passed from culture to culture, all the while changing languages, changing form, and changing meaning. Fairy tales, fables, and stories follow humanity from civilization to civilization, like the wild beasts of the night that follow and circle the encampment. Therapists, linguists, and mythologists now mine the stories of our past,

unearthing hints about how to live in the present. Tales that were interpreted one way a hundred years ago suddenly take on new significance
today. It's as if each story that has come down to us through antiquity has
become an Immortal like the Gods of old.

One such tale is the story of Psyche and Eros. Described as "floating
in star matter," this tale is thought to be the oldest, most famous, and most
delightful of fairy tales. Folklorists have traced the tale throughout the
world. It is the seed out of which grows Cinderella, Sleeping Beauty,
Beauty and the Beast, and Blue Beard's Castle. It comes to us embedded in
The Golden Ass, a classical work by Apuleius:

> Once upon a time there lived in a certain place a King and
> Queen. They had two beautiful daughters and a third daughter,
> Psyche, who was so extraordinary that human speech was incapable
> of describing her beauty. In fact, people were struck dumb at her
> loveliness, so much so that they began to worship her as the Earthly
> manifestation of the great Goddess Venus. This of course did not go
> over well with Venus. She summoned her son the notorious Cupid,
> or Eros, to avenge her jealousy by making Psyche fall in love with
> an unhappy, poor, and lowly man.
>
> Meanwhile Psyche seemed destined to remain unapproachable.
> Her two sisters were married off to kings, but no one dared to ask for
> the hand of Psyche. She was miserable and in her heart bewailed
> her own beauty. Her father, suspecting that perhaps a God had been
> offended, consulted the oracle of the region. The oracle decreed
> that Psyche was to have no mortal husband, but instead was to be
> offered up on the nearest mountain top, dressed in funeral robes, to
> a frightful dragon.
>
> The kingdom mourned, the family wailed, and all the people
> escorted the bride to meet her doom. All too soon, trembling
> Psyche was alone on the summit of the mountain. Suddenly the
> West Wind began to breathe around her and ever so gently catch
> her garments and lift her up, carrying her gently over the cliff and
> down to a flowering valley, wet with dew.
>
> Psyche fell asleep and upon awakening, arose from her grassy bed
> to behold a grove of giant trees and crystal clear waters flowing
> beside a wondrous palace that could only have been built by a God.
> The walls were carved with wild beasts and animals of all sorts. The

walkways were paved with gems and jewels and the walls were carved in silver and gold. Overcome by beauty Psyche forgot her fear and entered the palace. A voice spoke out of nowhere, and told her to go to her chamber and refresh herself and then prepare for a royal banquet. Psyche did as she was instructed. She slept, bathed and feasted and eventually returned to her bed. That night a lover came, made her his bride, and departed before the first light of dawn. From then onwards the palace became her home, the serving voices her only companions, and what had been frightening now became a delight. Though she could not see her husband, she came to know him by touch, and by the sweet sound of his voice in the night.

One night her husband told her that her sisters would seek her out, and that if she should hear their cries to ignore them, for to do otherwise would cause him much suffering and bring about her demise.

In the comfort of the night Psyche agreed to do as her unseen husband requested, but in the light of day and alone, Psyche was overcome with grief. The following night Psyche convinced her husband to allow her sisters to visit her. He consented but made Psyche promise not fall prey to her sisters, who might very well try to make Psyche betray him. Psyche protested that she would never betray him, that she loved him more than life itself.

The next day the sisters visited the mountain top where they believed Psyche had met her doom. The sound of their grief echoed off the rocks and stones. Psyche called out to the West Wind to carry her sisters safely down into the valley, and there the sisters were reunited. At first they were overjoyed to see one another, but soon the sisters began to glance with envious eyes at the beauty and luxury in which Psyche lived. They became curious about her husband, suspected him of being a God, and turned green with jealously at the thought of Psyche living like a Goddess.

The sisters suspected that Psyche did not in fact know what her husband looked like, and convinced her that he was a horrible monster who must be slain. That night as he lay sleeping she lit an oil lamp, and saw for the first time his sleeping winged body, his bow and quiver. In her ecstasy she accidentally pricked herself on one of his arrows. (This is how Psyche came to fall in love with Love itself.) She started and accidentally spilled a drop of hot oil on the sleeping Eros, who awakened in burning pain and fled from Psyche's betrayal.

Overwhelmed by the despair of losing her love, Psyche threw herself into the river. But the river, in homage to Eros, threw her out of his waters and onto a bank of sweet smelling herbs, where she met the Old God Pan. The God of Wild Nature was teaching the mountain Goddess Echo how to speak the language of all things. The goat-footed God took one look at Psyche and knew that Psyche was love-sick; he urged her to pray to none other than the mightiest of Gods, Eros. Psyche took seriously the wise counsel, and continued on her way.

By chance Psyche found herself in the town of one of her sisters. After greetings were exchanged, Psyche told her sister how she had followed her counsel, and how Eros had fled, adding that Eros had proclaimed that he would now marry none other than Psyche's sister. The sister immediately took leave, returned to the craggy mountain top, and threw herself off the cliff. This time there was no West Wind to carry her downward; she tumbled to her death, and her remains were devoured by the birds and beasts.

Once more Psyche is led to another town. She finds her other sister, repeats the story, and that sister in turn rushes off in hope of becoming the bride of Love. She too met her doom, her remains feeding the wild animals.

Meanwhile Venus is informed by a white sea bird of the fate of her son Eros—his falling in love with Psyche and his painful burn. Furthermore the bird tells Venus that the world has fallen into disorder. There is no pleasure, no joy, and no love between couples or friends, and parents no longer love their children. Discord is everywhere.

Psyche continued on her search for her beloved and found herself in a temple of the Goddess Ceres, where she proceeded to set in order the unkempt sheaves of wheat, barley, and tools of the harvest, the scythes, sickles, and hooks. As she was tidying up Ceres arrived, and Psyche pled for help in the name of the one who provides the rites of harvest, and the ceremonies of the land. Although

Ceres felt pity for Psyche, she dared not side with her over her kinswoman Venus, and in the end asked Psyche to leave her temple.

Psyche then came upon a tree decorated with talismans of gold dedicated to the Goddess Juno, who came down from heaven on the back of a lion. Psyche begged Juno to deliver her from danger and protect her as she is with child. But Juno, although inclined by nature to help, cannot violate the deeper bonds of her kinship to Venus.

Psyche decided her only hope was to find Venus and submit to her wrath. Venus in her fury had Psyche beaten by her servants, Sorrow and Sadness. Then casting barley, lentils, chick peas, beans, and poppy seeds together on the ground she commanded Psyche to sort the heap of seeds by nightfall. Overwhelmed by her task, Psyche does nothing, but an ant takes pity and gathers other ants to come to her aid. Working diligently they swiftly sort the seeds and vanish before Venus returned. Venus suspected that somehow Eros has helped Psyche, and threw her a meager crust of bread before retiring for the night.

Just before dawn Venus called Psyche to her, and pointed to a forest along the bank of a river. She told Psyche, "There wander a flock of sheep with golden fleece. I bid you to gather me some of their wool." Psyche willingly made haste, not to gather the wool, but to take the moment to throw herself into the river. But a green reed growing in the sacred waters murmured its song of inspiration. "Oh, Psyche do not pollute my waters with your death and do not approach the golden sheep at this hour, for they can destroy you with their fury. Wait until they have calmed themselves in the river, and hide here in the shade of the plane tree, then you can gather their golden fleece from the bushes and the briars." The true and gentle words of the reed saved Psyche from destruction, and she returned to Venus with the precious fleece.

Again, Venus is neither amused nor satisfied, for she still suspected that Eros was helping Psyche. She gave Psyche yet another task. "Go to yonder mountain top and to the black stream that feeds the River of the Dead. Take this crystal urn and fill it with the icy water and quickly return it to me." Psyche swiftly found her way to the mountain top, and at the source of the stream found a spring guarded by the most terrifying dragons, with very long necks and eyes that never slept. Even the waters warned of danger, saying such things as "flee, flee or die," "Beware! Take warning." At this point Psyche's fear took her beyond tears, and although present in body, her senses and spirit abandoned her. Just in time the Royal Bird of the God Jupiter appeared. The Eagle told Psyche that to even touch a drop of the water would be her end. Then carrying off the urn, he flew past the dragons, filled the urn and returned it to Psyche, who joyfully presented it to Venus.

By this time Venus began to suspect that perhaps Psyche was a sorceress and she devised one last task for her. "Take this box and go to the underworld and ask Persephone to fill it with beauty so I can anoint myself with it before I go to the Theater for the Gods." Psyche felt that this surely would be her end, for no one returned from the land of the dead except Persephone herself. She went to a high tower with the thought of throwing herself down, when the tower spoke to her saying, "Why do you wish to kill yourself? Do not give up at this your last danger. Instead go to the hill of Tenarus and there you will find a threshold and a path leading to hell. But do not go with empty hands, carry cakes made of barley and honey, and in your mouth place two coins. Along the way you will meet a lame ass and his lame driver, who will ask you to pick up some sticks that he has dropped. Pass on by and do not speak a word. Soon you will come to the River of the Dead. There Charon will ferry you to the Land of the Dead; the price will be one of your coins. Drop the coin out your mouth into his hand. As you cross the river you will see an old man floating in the water with raised hands asking you to help him into the boat; do not be moved by pity to help him. When you have crossed the river, old weaving women will ask you for help, but ignore them for to touch their web will mean your end. And remember not to lose even one of your barley cakes.

"At the gate of Persephone you will meet a huge hound with three heads who barks day and night at the dead. Give him one of the cakes, and you shall enter the house of Persephone. She will welcome you, and offer you a rich feast, but sit only on the ground, ask for simple bread, and eat it only. Then deliver the message from Venus, telling Persephone why you have come. When you have received some of her beauty, return the way you have come. Give your second cake to the dog on your way out. Give your last coin to the ferry man after you cross the river, and return by the same path to the land of the living. Most importantly do not look into the box, and do not let your curiosity seek to view the treasure of divine beauty." So spoke the far-seeing tower.

Psyche did all that she was instructed to do, and soon found herself blessed by the light of day. Possessed by an overwhelming curiosity to have just a little of the divine beauty, Psyche opened the box, but saw no beauty. Instead out of the box came a deadly sleep that left Psyche lying on the ground as a sleeping corpse.

Meanwhile Eros had recovered from his wound, and could no longer bear the absence of Psyche. He slipped out the window and flew with great haste to Psyche's side. There he wiped the sleep from her face and placed it back in the box. Then with a gentle prick of his arrow he awoke Psyche, bemoaning her curiosity, and urging her to complete the task his mother had demanded, while he would tend to the rest. So off he flew, and Psyche hurried to bring Persephone's gift to Venus.

Eros flew straight away to Heaven and pleaded his cause before Jupiter. In the end, Jupiter had Psyche brought to heaven, where he gave her ambrosia to drink, making her an Immortal and thereby appeasing Venus's horror of a lowly marriage for her son. In the presence of all the Gods, Psyche and Eros were united in a marriage that will endure forever. Soon a daughter was born to them, known to us mortals as Pleasure.

THE SOUL OF THE WORLD

That the story of Psyche and Eros has persisted for thousands of years tells us something about its importance. At its most simplistic level it is a classic love story: girl meets boy, girl loses boy, girl gets boy, and lives happily ever after.

The Jungians have excavated another level in terms of the archetypal feminine. They speak of the story in terms of the myth of the Eternal Feminine, her initiation into individuation or self-hood, the sacred marriage between the feminine and masculine, and of the different aspects of the feminine that emerge as the result of the journey into the underworld.

Most importantly they address the transformation into wholeness that comes about as the result of Psyche—or Soul—diving deep into Death and emerging as a Divine Being.

The interpretation of Psyche and Eros holds many possibilities. My intention in retelling the story is to see it as a lesson in how to anthropomorphize. In light of the sacred, animism, or the Gaia hypothesis, the story becomes a message from Psyche as the Soul of the World, illustrating what Hillman refers to as "personifying." The Greek tale of the *Golden Ass*, with its embedded story of Psyche and Eros appeared during the same historical period in which Plutarch, in his essay "On the Failure of the Oracles," declared "the Great God Pan is dead!" a cry that was heard throughout the antique world. The synchronicity of this moment was a crucial event in the Human-Nature relationship. As long as Pan was alive, Nature was alive. If Pan was gone so was Echo, and our capacity to speak with Nature. The land, the plants, the animals, the trees, rivers, and rocks became only scenery. No longer was Nature filled with Gods. How could the Oracles speak their truths if we no longer had the ears to hear them, or the eyes to see them?

The journey of Psyche is made possible because Psyche is inextricably participating in a sensuous world. The ensouled reality of Psyche is a place where everything has a face, a voice, things speak to her, and she is never surprised by this act. We too never question this reality. The Palace is decorated with carvings of Animals and Plants. The very Walls speak to her. Her tasks are made possible only with the aid of a number of helpers. From the beginning the forces of Nature are communicating with Psyche, like the West Wind, who carries her to the Valley, and the River, who refuses to allow her to drown herself in his Water. After Eros flees, the first person she meets is Pan, accompanied by Echo, who wisely advises her to make petitions to Eros. It is the old God of Nature who sets Psyche on her course. Her first task of sorting the grain is made possible by the help of the Ant People. The Whispering Reed tells her how to gather the fleece of the Golden Sheep in order to complete her second task. Venus's third demand, to fill a Crystal Vessel from the Spring that flows to the underworld, is accomplished with the aid of Jupiter's Royal Eagle.

Up until this moment all of Psyche's helpers have either been Plants Animals, or forces of Nature, like the Wind, or the River. For her final task, the journey into the underworld, the helper is a Tower, who gives Psyche explicit directions on what to do and what not to do. The Tower, reminds us that it is not only Nature that has Soul, but that man made things also have Soul. Her salvation is made possible by her instinctual ability to notice and respond to an animated world.

We can let ourselves imagine that Psyche is all these things, a girl in love, an archetypal embodiment of the feminine, and the Soul of Gaia. As the Gaian soul, Psyche is offering us another way of seeing the world. Just at the time when Pan is being declared dead, and the Oracles have failed to perform their duty, along comes Psyche saying, "Look how natural it is to be communicating and participating with all of creation. Not only is it natural, it is essential for my survival." The foundation of all culture is based upon this universal relatedness. The role of Eros as the heavenly embodiment of the masculine is also recast as he comes down to Earth. Only when grounded through his love for a mortal woman does the winged God of Love mature from capricious Cupid into the beloved. The love between Psyche and Eros is consummated in the dark, with Psyche unable to see what her lover looks like until she glimpses him by candlelight. She then recognizes him as a God. This coming together of the winged God of the Sky and the earthly Feminine principle is, of course, the sacred marriage of Heaven and Earth. The soul is delighted and enlivened by this connection.

A story like Psyche and Eros is meant to stimulate our imaginations, and guide us into cultivating the field of relationships and connections. The marriage of Psyche and Eros restores the love between family and friends, and parents once again love their children.

Theologian Father Thomas Berry, in his book *The Dreams of the Earth*, reminds us that in our Western tradition, luminaries such as Hildegard of Bingen and St. Francis of Assisi encourage us to partake of communion with the natural world. The bestiaries of the medieval period and the seasonal liturgies of the Christian church engage us with the animals and Nature, while the symbolic and moral impact of St. Francis, Hildegard, or seasonal liturgies teach us how to care for one another.

American Indians, with their ceremonial dances and songs, evoke in us an ancient memory of our connection to the natural world. One of the great gifts of the Four Corners area is the seasonal ceremonies in which the Deer, Antelope, Eagle, and Buffalo are invoked into the world. The Hopi's rattlesnake dance calls in the rain so the corn may grow and the people may live. Among the Plains Indians, the annual Sun Dance renews both the spirit of the people and the world. In the Northwest, totem poles reveal the creation stories as totemic kinship tales from the animal world. The traditional stories of Coyote and Raven are mythic tales that humorously guide and instruct the people how to live a sane and happy life.

Visitors to the Southwest who witness the holy dances of the Pueblo cultures, often have their hearts broken open as the ancestral memories of another way of being floods into them. I am always struck by the number of people who weep upon first encountering these seasonal rites of relationship; the intimacy of these moments evokes a sense of respect, mutuality, and participation in our Earthly reality. Inside the natural world, we begin to participate in a truly sacred community. When we alienate ourselves or destroy this world, we alienate and destroy ourselves. Our personal and collective psyche suffers irreparable damage, and we lose our sense of aesthetic, moral, and emotional grounding. We become bereft of fellow feeling, and incapable of passing on to the next generation a sustainable sense of the world. The Soul of the World can only be healthy if humanity agrees to participate in a living, rather than a dead, world. Then perhaps we too might give birth to a universal Pleasure.

·2·

The Quest for Meaning

Our Everchanging Relationship to the Sacred

Our everchanging relationship to the sacred is an ongoing thread that weaves itself throughout all of the cultures of the world. From the most idyllic moments of native peoples, to the darkest hours that have confronted modern humanity, a sense of the holiness of life has sustained us, for it is a perennial impulse to seek communion with the Godhead. When we reflect upon who we are as a people, it is possible to mark certain historical moments as turning points either towards or away from a coherent integrated perception of the sacred. By looking at the evolution of culture we begin to have a sense of our shifting relationship to the sacred. We can question our collective understanding of what the sacred means, and how that knowledge impacts our relationship to our loved ones, our community, and the Earth itself.

Long before the written word, before agriculture, before organized religion, before even simple village life, we were a spiritual people. The bones of our ancestors tell a tale that stretches back in time for tens of thousands of years. In France, Switzerland, and Spain, Paleolithic caves reveal the story of our ancient past. Imagine the great ice fields slowly retreating, new lands appearing, and small bands of people migrating with the seasons, following the great herds of animals, intermingling with the people they met. Fifty thousand years ago, our European ancestors made the hillside caves their home. Outside, the great herds of bison, reindeer, horses, mammoth, and woolly rhinoceros roamed the valley floor. The cave bears, saber-toothed tiger, and wolf hunted. The streams and rivers were abundant with fish, the land was lush with edible plants, berries, fruit, and nuts. Overhead, the sun and moon and stars moved across the sky, the seasons turned, the birds disappeared and returned, and the cyclical nature of life was woven into the fabric of our being.

The diary they left for us was well hidden, for it was not until this century that these great Paleolithic caves were discovered, to the astonishment of the modern world. In southwest France, near the village of Les Eyzies, a series of caves were discovered that contained paintings of exquisite beauty. The paintings of animals portrayed on the walls of Lascaux are perhaps the most beautiful renderings of animals known to humanity. They date back to 35,000 years B.C. The artifacts unearthed in these caves shattered our previous view of the Paleolithic. The archeological record is part of our inheritance, informing us that our ancestors were not the primitive brutes portrayed by Hollywood, but highly skilled artists and craftspeople, whose spirituality was in harmony with Nature, and who believed in an afterlife.

In all of the ancient caves, from France to Russia to the Mediterranean, an abundance of primarily female figurines were found. These figures, now simply known as The Great Goddess, represented the Feminine as the vessel for the great mystery of life. She gave birth, bled with the cycles of the moon, suckled the young with her milk, and welcomed the dead back into her womb-like caves. This image of the Divine Feminine continued through the Neolithic Revolution that heralded both agriculture and the domestication of animals. Scholars now state with assurance that our early ancestors worshipped a feminine deity, whom they call the Earth Mother. But the Earth Mother was not a singular deity—she existed in company with the Male principle and with the spirits of all animals, plants, and forces of Nature.

Among the artifacts of this period we find a carved reindeer antler that is a lunar calendar marking conception, gestation, and birth. It dates back 32,000 years ago. We also find that early trade routes were already established, for the caves contain cowry shells from the sea, and red ochre from distant lands. The people ritually buried their dead, often near the hearth of the cave, implying a form of ancestor worship. The bodies were painted with ochres and left with talismans and amulets, a clear indication of a belief in an afterlife, as well as a belief in the power of magic to guard and protect the soul on its journey. The caves also abound with paintings of animals and plants and signify a sacred relationship of kinship that exist-ed between all. With the end of the last Ice Age, around ten to twelve thousand years ago, people left the relative safety of the caves for perma-nent settlements and the abundance of the fertile valleys. With this cultur-al step forward our understanding of the sacred began to transform.

SETTLING DOWN

Between 10,000 and 5,000 B.C., the hunters and gatherers of the caves began to create the beginnings of what we now think of as "civiliza-tion." The development of early agricultural practices required an acute observation of Nature. The gathering of seeds, the sowing, harvesting, and winnowing of grain, and the storage of food gave way to farming and ani-mal husbandry. Through the act of domesticating plants and animals our ancestors began to lose their dependence on hunting and foraging.

As the first permanent villages established themselves, the ease of hunting diminished as concentric zones around the settlements were hunt-ed out. The very nature of villages altered the numbers of wild and domes-ticated species. Out of the act of settling down arose a sense of place. Natural configurations in the landscape such as stones, caves, and springs were viewed as guardian spirits. The lay of the land was (and is still) likened to the body of a woman, and out of this metaphor, the concept of the Great Goddess as Earth Mother came into being as a religious symbol. It was into the body of the Earth Mother that the seeds were planted, and her fecund nature generated life and food. The forces of Nature were seen as living entities that required regular attention in the form of offerings, prayers, and seasonal rites.

At the same time, our relationship to possessions was radically chang-ing. A true surplus of goods was possible for the first time, for in the past, we could only possess what we could carry on our backs. With permanent set-tlements, arts and crafts such as weaving, pottery, and early architecture came into being. All of these ongoing developments created a profound shift in how we viewed a spirited world. The literal inner and outer worlds began to be seen as opposing forces. Eventually, farmers saw themselves as separate, and above, the shiftless life style of the nomad or pastoralist, even as the wandering tribes came to recognize the bounty of harvest time, as the season for raiding parties.

PEACEFUL CULTURES

Throughout India, Eastern Europe, the Mediterranean, the Middle East, and Northern Africa, early civilizations were flourishing. For over a thousand years various cultural centers, such as Catal Hüyük in Turkey, Mohenjo-daro in India, or the biblical city of Jericho, existed as unfortified settlements, showing no signs of war, plunder, or invasion. Such early civilizations boggle the mind when trying to imagine a thousand years of peace.

The archeological remains paint a consistent picture. For instance, the city of Jericho, dated at 9550 B.C., was founded at the site of a sacred spring. Initially an unfortified settlement, Jericho was built in the shape of a crescent moon, while all of the houses were constructed in the form of beehives. The archaeologists found images of the Goddess in every house, and a nearby temple unearthed a stone carved with breasts.

In Turkey, the site of Catal Hüyük flowered between 6500 and 5700 B.C. It predates the more famous cities of Mesopotamia by two thousand years. First excavated in the early 1960s by James Mellaart, Catal Hüyük startled the scholarly world. The city existed for almost 900 years without any signs of warfare or weaponry, and was eventually deserted after a fire. Archeologists excavated 139 rooms, 48 of these shrines to the Goddess. The walls were adorned with large reliefs of the Goddess giving birth to bulls and other horned animals. Although the Goddess was primary, the artifacts show a balance between the feminine and masculine forces, and the essential nature of partnership and connection. A figure of an embracing man and woman was found, along with a terra-cotta figure of a large woman seated upon a throne giving birth, while stroking two leopards.

It was here that the earliest representation of the Goddess as Maiden, Mother, and Crone appears, and this Trinitarian view of the divine continues into modern times as the Father, Son, and Holy Ghost. In terms of the sacred, this splitting apart of the Godhead into its different aspects indicates that the old collective unified mind of the past was acquiring a more individualized perspective. The story unearthed at Catal Hüyük, when seen in the light of the sacred, was a tale of an idyllic life. Humanity was betwixt and between the old hunter/gatherer times and the emerging new city-states. The Great Round was giving way to something linear, and yet the wild and the tame, the masculine and feminine, were still coexisting peacefully.

One highly evolved culture was Crete, where the sacred mysteries were apparently an open secret, for the people of Crete lived in what the Navaho would call a Beauty Way. The classical Cretan civilization existed for at least four thousand years. During that time, the people of Crete developed metallurgy, architecture, engraving, irrigation, paved roads, viaducts, cities with sanitary installations, fountains, weaving, pottery, and plastered limestone frescoes. Trade, industry, animal breeding, and a mercantile sailing fleet made and kept Crete economically strong. The city of Knossos was populated by a hundred thousand inhabitants.

From Riane Eisler's research in *The Chalice and the Blade* we learn that Nicholas Platon, a former superintendent of antiquities in Crete, worked at excavating the island for almost fifty years. He describes "vast multi-storied palaces, villas, farmsteads, districts of populous, and well organized cities, harbor installations, networks of roads crossing the island from end to end, organized places of worship, and planned burial grounds." The art contained fabulous frescoes, fine jewelry, paintings of women, griffins, birds, and statues. The social structure was also unique in that there seemed to be an absence of poverty or autocratic rule. There are no signs of warfare.

Platon goes on to say that "the fear of death was almost obliterated by the ubiquitous joy of living. The worship of nature pervaded everything. The whole of life was pervaded by an ardent faith in the Goddess Nature, the source of all creation and harmony. This led to a love of peace, a horror of tyranny, and a respect for the law. Even among the ruling classes personal ambition seems to have been unknown; nowhere do we find the name of an author attached to a work of art, nor a record of the deeds of a ruler."

From the remnants of these peaceful cultures we can piece together the sacred as it existed in antiquity. Through art, architecture, ceremonial objects, and eventually the written word, we can interpret what the sense of the sacred meant to our early ancestors. From the archeological evidence of the Middle East and Greece we find a sense of mystery concerning the sowing and harvesting of wheat, barley, and rye. Rivers were viewed as a source of life and death, and springs were often referred to as holy wells, where miraculous healings and divine visitations occurred. A large pantheon of Goddesses and Gods was depicted with guardian animals such as the lion, bear, snake, cat, dog, eagle, and dolphin. The Goddess, and woman as her representative on Earth, was held in high esteem, and yet somehow the masculine was not diminished. This world view existed in a delicate state of balance, in which the pairs of opposites were in harmony. It was a time when wild Nature was still holy, animals bestowed a blessing, and every house had a hearth and an altar. For the next seventy centuries the deserts of the Near East would evolve into what we now call the cradle of civilization.

That generations of people lived and died, never knowing the horror of war, poverty, or starvation is an affront to our idea of progress. People who dare to speak about these idyllic cultures are labeled "idealists," a word that has its roots set in the Platonic ideal or idea, meaning a conception of something in its most excellent or perfect form. As the result of our recent mythology, we assume mankind has always been the "killer ape," accepting warfare as a sad fact of life. For inhabitants of the modern world it is easy to believe we are living as the crown of creation, and that never before have people lived so easily or in so much luxury. We hardly know how to react to archeological evidence indicating certain ancient cultures may have lived as well as we do now, or perhaps better. It doesn't really matter if they were the norm or not. What matters is that we have evidence of cultures who lived peaceably and well for hundreds or thousands of years. It is as if they have revealed themselves during this century in order to show us a possible way of imagining the world.

MAGICAL MYSTERY TRADITIONS

The classical traditions of Egypt, Greece, and Rome were engaged in a variety of mystery cults. Each contained large pantheons of Gods and Goddesses, elaborate public ceremonies, oracles, and practitioners of various magical arts. Gods and Goddesses of Egypt passed into Greece and eventually on to Rome. At every step of the way they were transformed along with the accompanying myths.

Egypt was a long-lived culture lasting thousands of years. The sacred kings and queens were thought to be divine, and through elaborate burial practices were reincarnated into the next generation of royalty. The vulture-headed Goddess Mut presided over the rites of the dead and weighed the deeds of the deceased. She was also synonymous with the cat Goddess Bast, who was the inspiration for Egypt's most celebrated sacred festival. As her representatives floated on barges down the river, hundreds of thousands of participants were said to line the banks of the Nile shaking rattles, drinking, dancing, and playing music. The sound of the orgiastic festivities was reported by the Greek Hesiod to be almost deafening.

Egypt was a land of magical rites and the most powerful magic was to acquire the true name of the Gods. With the correct invocation, magicians were said to be able to raise the dead, heal the sick, kill another human being, and transport themselves at will to other places. The fertility of the land and animals was also controlled through magical rites, and if the crops failed, the king or queen was held responsible. Repeated crop failure or blight could mean their death.

The Egyptian pantheon was abundant with Gods and Goddesses— modern people are still familiar with figures such as Isis, Osiris, and the Sun God Ra. Many of the deities invoked a totemic animal such as the dog-headed Anubis, cat-headed Bast, hawk-headed Horus, and the scorpion Goddess Serket. The mystery traditions of Egypt were rich in seasonal celebrations. The rustic ceremonies of the common person were performed year after year and rested on the direct observation of Nature, while the priestly caste followed a ceremonial astrological calendar that worked backwards from summer to spring to winter and autumn.

The most famous of Egyptian ceremonies was the Festival of Isis. Winged Isis was said to have established the healing arts, agriculture, law and justice, and kingship itself (her name means "throne"). Held at midsummer when the Nile River was beginning to rise, her festival honored Isis mourning the death of her husband, the corn-god Osiris—as her tears fell, the river rose.

The rising of the Nile coincided with a sign from heaven. The dog star Sirius, brightest star in the sky, appeared at dawn in the east. It was also called the star of Isis. The beginning of the Egyptian year was demarcated by this event, which was also the time to flood the fields in preparation for planting. This solemn event took place in November after the flooded Nile had retreated from the land. The planting ceremonies in both Egypt and Greece were enacted with mourning and tears. The seeds were returned to Earth as if they were the body of a loved one, with the women sitting on the ground, fasting and crying.

The harvest began in March and continued through the spring. The corn's growth symbolized the resurrection of Osiris from the dead, and the grain cutting was done with a somber mood, for every farmer was severing the corn-god from the Earth, while invoking the Goddess Isis. The priests would bury effigies of Osiris made of corn and earth, and when they dug them up the corn would be sprouting. This death and rebirth ritual where the God gives his body in order to feed the people continues to this day in the symbolism of the Eucharist.

Around the time of the winter solstice another ceremony took place commemorating dead Osiris and the great love Isis had for him. People set rows of oil lamps outside their houses, and throughout Egypt lamps burned all night long. This night of illumination is thought to be similar to our All Souls' Eve, when the souls of the dead return to their old homes. Families would leave food outside for the hungry ghosts and the lights would lead them back to the grave.

These ancient rites of cyclical renewal continued into Greece, where mystery cults flourished. Greece, too, had a large pantheon of deities, as well as oracles and a powerful priest caste. As in Egypt, the Greek new year was heralded by the predawn rising of the star Sirius. In Crete it was the time for making alcoholic drinks from fermented honey, grain, and grapes. This celebration was marked by a giant nocturnal bonfire lit in the Dictean cave, and was visible from miles around. This cave is where the Goddess Rhea gave birth to her son Zagreus the Hunter, also known as Orion. He is the ancient manifestation of the wine God Dionysus.

The worship of Dionysus, who suffered the same fate as Osiris, was always accompanied by raving, intoxication, dancing, Maenadic frenzy, and sacrificial death. Legends of Dionysiac frenzies speak of women running wild through the mountains and live bulls torn apart with hands and teeth alone. Both men and women were initiated into these Bacchic rites and, unlike most mystery religions, initiates were not bound to a particular sanctuary or priesthood. Processions into the mountains and the accompanying ecstatic frenzy were led by wandering priests who claimed to have been initiated into the orgiastic rites through private and direct succession.

In terms of the sacred, the most mysterious ancient rite took place at Eleusis. The Eleusinian Mystery was a yearly ceremonial initiation in which tens of thousands of people participated annually. As a mystery cult it was highly successful, for it endured for more than a thousand years. Initiates included Plato, Socrates, Herodotus, Hesiod, and the Homeric authors. It is safe to say that anyone of any importance made their way to Eleusis at least once in their life. More impressive is the fact that no one ever revealed what the mystery of the initiation actually was. From the Homeric *Hymn to Demeter* we learn how the Goddess Demeter teaches the traditional foundation of life by transforming the Eleusinian plain into a vast field of corn. In terms of the ceremony proper, we know that the candidates for initiation fasted in preparation and that there was a torchlit procession followed by an all-night vigil. The initiates sat veiled in silence under sheepskin-covered stools and there was ribald humor. Communion with the divinity took place after drinking barley or rye water from a holy chalice and ended with participants approaching the altar and being shown something magical that filled them with awe and appreciation toward life and the afterlife.

Needless to say there is much speculation about all of this. Some researchers have proposed that the rye was infected with mold (ergot) that induced a state of consciousness in the way LSD does. Others suspect a poppy-opium derivative. Early Christian writers suggest the magical item was nothing more than an ear of corn representing life, fertility, and rebirth. Whatever the sacred object was, no one ever broke the vow of secrecy.

The Romans also had their mystery cults. They had been engaged in a long struggle with Hannibal when the Sybylline oracle prophesied that if they would bring the meteoric head of Cybele from Phrygia to Rome they would have success in establishing a new civilization and push back the Carthaginians. In April the ancient stone was brought to Rome and installed in what is now St. Peter's Basilica. That year the harvest was larger than could be remembered and the following great spring festival of Cybele and her son/lover Attis was readily embraced. The eunuch priests of Cybele hearkened back to the servants of Artemis in Greece and Astarte in Syria. Like Egyptian Osiris and Greek Dionysus, Attis was also destined to die and be reborn.

The spectacle of Cybele's followers mourning the death of Attis was so contagious that many a Roman man was carried away by the pounding drums, clashing cymbals, and flutes of her priests. Rapt in the frenzy of the moment and seeing the eunuch priests slashing themselves with knives, the Romans would leap forward, grab a sword, and castrate themselves on the spot. The Day of Blood ceremony was the day that an effigy of the dead Attis was placed in his tomb, while devotees mourned. But come nightfall the tomb would be opened and Attis would be gone—risen from the dead.

The priests would anoint the lips of mourners and offer whispers of salvation in their ears. The following day was a time of jubilation and rebirth. All this took place around the spring equinox.

The mystery traditions of these three civilizations rose out of a polytheistic world view in which the rhythms of Nature took precedent. The image of death and rebirth was mirrored in the seasonal planting and harvest ceremonies—the success of the harvest was dependent upon the proper ceremonies being done in a sacred way. By the time of the Roman Empire rampant paganism was in a state of decay. The old Gods were either mocked and scorned by the educated or not responding to the prayers and offerings of those who still believed. In general, the pagan world of the Mediterranean had turned so barbarous and hideous with superstition and black magic its own death was inevitable. The stage was being set for a new God to arrive and a new view of the sacred.

THE ONE TRUE GOD

Historically coinciding with the cultures of Egypt, Greece, and Rome were the wandering Semites or Hebrews who brought with them an all-powerful God. Unlike the pantheons of Gods and Goddesses who co-existed together throughout the land, this new God demanded total allegiance as "the one and only true God." The Hebrew tribes slid into the no-man's land between the farmer and the pastoralist. They were not bound to a sense of place, and their God, who was a storm God, was also a traveler. The Hebrew God came to be known as Yahweh or Jehovah, and as recorded in Deuteronomy he issues a command:

> You must completely destroy all the places where the nations you dispossess have served their gods, on high mountains, on hills, under any spreading tree; you must tear down their altars, smash their pillars, cut down their sacred groves, set fire to the carved images of their gods and wipe their name from that place.

Eventually the One God successfully wrestled with the Gods and Goddesses of the ancient world, but for the intervening thousands of years, the concept of polytheism and the divine link between Man and Nature persisted, even in the face of advancing technologies. This is a key moment in terms of our cultural relationship to the sacred and deserves to be consciously understood. So many threads—religious, political, ecological, mythological, and philosophical—weave themselves together here into a radical moment of spiritual metamorphosis or epigenesis. It is the point of bifurcation between farmers and pastoralists, Cain and Abel, city and country, masculine and feminine, the Earth Mother and the Sky God, and polytheism and monotheism. It is as if the story of our relationship to the sacred is a broken pot, and by finding all of the shards we can piece it back together, thus making sense of how we arrived at the end of this millennium.

In his book *Nature And Madness*, Paul Shepard states that there is something about monotheism that human psychology finds intolerable. That in a pluralistic world of diversity, the monotheist feels lost and disconnected, that there is a sense of the "death of God." He quotes David Miller as saying "theology becomes irrelevant to faith, and philosophy irrelevant to everything." He goes on to say that in a polytheistic world there is a collection of forces and Gods, which keeps our psyche harmonized with the inner and outer worlds, and through this experience our "thoughts become divinized and the earth sacralized." Without this harmonization, what we are told we should believe in, and what we actually experience about the nature of reality becomes incongruent, leaving us adrift in a world that is irrationally dualistic.

CHRISTIANITY: THE THIRD FORCE

With the Roman Empire and the subsequent rise of Christianity, we can see the impulse toward the sacred returning. The Roman Empire took in all the lands surrounding the Mediterranean, in Europe, the middle East, and Africa, plus France, and Great Britain. On one end of the spectrum of the sacred there was Rome with all of its pagan rites, its pantheon of Gods and Goddesses, and its mad, corrupt decadence. On the other end of the spectrum were the Hebrews with their one God, their refusal to pay taxes, or accept Caesar as God, and their prohibition against idols or any representation of God.

In A.D. 70, the Roman general Titus completely destroyed Jerusalem. It was then rebuilt as a Roman city in the second century A.D. In the sixteenth century, the Muslim emperor Suleiman built the present day walls around the Old City. After the horror of World War II, the allied countries created the modern Zionist state of Israel, returning the Jews once again to their chosen home land.

Each conquest of Jerusalem has had a distinct impact on religion, and on our view of the sacred. It has passed from the hands of pagans to the high culture of Egypt, back to the pagans, to the Jews, to the pagan Romans, to Christians, to Muslims, up to the present moment when it is currently occupied by Christians, Jews, and Muslims. The historical struggle for religious dominance continues until this day with the Palestinian Holy Land as its epicenter.

With the birth of Jesus of Nazareth, and his later public life, a third force was introduced into the antique world. Christianity provided an alternative to Jewish orthodoxy and the absurd decadence of paganistic Rome. Sociologist Rodney Stark in his recent book *The Rise of Christianity*, suggests that the early Christians were converts from the educated and privileged classes. As Rome fell into decline, the elite left the city for the sanctuary of their country villas, and according to Stark Christian converts were the result of social networks of families and friends. For the first four centuries after Christ, Jews who could not abide the strict orthodoxy of Palestine, nor find comfort in the world of the Gentiles, could embrace Christianity as a middle way. After all Christianity did share the same background of the Old Testament as the Jews. One only had to accept Jesus as the Messiah, and the Gospels as true.

In A.D. 313, the Emperor Constantine with the Edict of Milan transformed the Roman Empire into the Holy Roman Empire, thus creating a vast Christian empire throughout Europe. Stark believes that women played a major role in converting their influential pagan husbands into Christians. Furthermore, Christianity was very appealing to women for it returned to women some of their previous status. Under Christianity women were no longer the property of men, and marriage was sanctified. At the end of the day, the old pagan Gods failed their people as plagues and epidemics struck. Generations of the educated and middle classes must have been horrified by the perverse, corrupt antics of the Caesars, and particularly the sixth Caesar, the Emperor Nero. Stories of Nero feasting while Christians were burnt, or fed to the lions, the infamous Roman orgy, the blatant greed and graft surely appalled all who were truly civilized. The sense of apocalyptic doom was widespread as the Roman Empire degenerated into societal madness. The teachings of Jesus Christ were clearly a breath of fresh air amidst the decay and stench of Rome. The Christian network created a social support system that cared for its persecuted members, offering a God who was a healer, one who preached love and forgiveness, rather than fear of the Lord, or a failed paganism of debauchery.

The Church of Rome was also very cunning in its ability to transform the old pagan deities into Christian saints, and the pagan feast days into Christian holy days. To this day, all of our Christian holy days can be traced back to their pagan counterparts.

In the fifth century the Neoplatonists and Gnostics were viewed as the primary threat to early Church dogma. In 415, the head of the Alexandrian library, a woman know as Hypatia, was murdered by the authority of Bishop Cyril, patriarch of Alexandria. Hypatia was the foremost philosopher, mathematician, physician, and astronomer of her day. She was an initiate of the Eleusinian Mysteries, as was everyone of any importance in those days. She was well loved by the people, and famous for her public discourses. Letters sent to her were addressed to the "Muse" and the "Oracle."

Her murder was no ordinary crime. While on her way to the library she was attacked by a group of monks, dragged into the Caesarium, stripped naked, flayed alive, and her remains burnt. This obviously did not go unnoticed by the populace. Shortly after Hypatia's murder, Bishop Cyril became responsible for the canonization of St. Catherine of the Wheel. Scholars can find no historical evidence for the existence of Catherine. Her life story, however, does have remarkable parallels to Hypatia's. Catherine was said to be a scholar and brilliant philosopher, she also lived at the same time and place as Hypatia. Her death was as a Christian martyr, and was as gruesome as Hypatia's. Catherine was reputedly placed between two wheels, "the Catherine Wheel," and simultaneously crushed and burnt. She was saved by a bolt of lightning, but her persecutors then beheaded her, whereupon angels appeared and carried her body off to Mount Sinai.

Cyril must have suffered a guilty conscience and perhaps fear for his own life, for scholars assume that he fabricated St. Catherine as a way to Christianize and canonize Hypatia, as well as appease the people of Alexandria. One of the philosophical debates of the time was whether or not women had souls. This was part of a larger argument in which Cyril argued against women's right to be priestesses in the Church of Rome. He had already declared the Gnostics to be heretics for supporting women in a tradition they traced back to Mary Magdalene. Strangely enough, at the Council of Ephesus, a place sacred to the old pagan Goddess Diana, Cyril went on to ensure that the feminine principle would forever be enshrined in the heart of Christian doctrine. We do not know what his motive was, perhaps it was political, perhaps it was personal, but he successfully argued to give Mary, the mother of Jesus, the title *theotokos*, which means God-bearer. From that moment on Mary became the church-sanctioned Mother of God, and once again a thread from the past, in the form of a benevolent feminine spirit, was woven into our sense of the sacred.

For the next thousand years the Church of Rome would spread itself throughout the western world, incorporating itself into government, king-ships, economics, and the arts. And yet in every country the common rural people continued to practice many of the old ways, in the form of fertility festivals, seasonal rites, herbal medicine, and a vast array of superstitions.

WE ARE ALL IN PIECES

Tis all in pieces, all coherence gone;
all just supply, and all Relation…
—JOHN DONNE

Beginning with the Renaissance of the fifteenth century, scientific rationalism emerged as a vision in the minds of such people as Francis Bacon, Copernicus, Galileo, Kepler, Newton, and Descartes. Their inspira-tion arose out of a desire to break away from the oppressive nature of the Church of Rome and all of its superstitious beliefs concerning God and cre-ation. It was Bacon who articulated a scientific utopian vision of the future in his *New Atlantis* (1624). He envisioned the power to control all of Nature, the creation of new life forms, and parks where animals would be kept for the sole purpose of vivisection experimentation.

His book became the bible for a materialistic view, and established a scientific priesthood who would make the world a better place. He saw sci-ence as a "masculine birth" that would create a "blessed race of Heroes and supermen, where Nature would be placed upon the rack and her secrets tortured out of her." This is the dark-rooted side of science.

It was Rene Descartes, famous for his revelation: "I think therefore I am," who formulated the idea that the entire universe was a huge machine working according to mathematical laws. He supplied the fundamental articles of faith for a mechanistic world view that continues to this day in biology and physics. Dreams, psychic phenomena, healing, and even the five senses are viewed as subjective experiences, and simply do not exist in an objective mathematical view.

In *Rebirth of Nature* Rupert Sheldrake describes in detail the impact of the scientific revolution on our relationship to Nature. Accordingly, all of Nature was perceived as being inanimate and lacking in soul, while scientists became the "lords and possessors of Nature." Quoting Descartes, Sheldrake says that animals did not feel anything because they were just machines: "their screams were no different than the sounds an organ makes when its keys are struck." The vitalists of the day opposed this idea, calling it "murderous" and "contrary to the common sense of mankind."

He goes on to remind us how the Cartesian model of duality, with its mind/body split saw the human being as a machine as well. Remember the homunculus—the little man who lives inside your brain and pulls all the levers? At first the human worked like a steam engine. Later the brain was manned by a telephone operator, or a movie projectionist. Now the body is a computer, with software, hardware, and a tiny computer programmer living somewhere inside our brain. The question of where the vital force comes from continues to haunt scientific thought up to the present day and is referred to as the "ghost in the machine," a term first used by philosopher Gilbert Ryle in a public lecture and later used by Arthur Koestler in his book of the same title.

Scientific rationalism, secular humanism, the mechanistic world view—call it what you may—dovetailed very neatly indeed with the Reformation, industrial revolution, materialism, and cultural imperialism. In England, during the time of the Reformation, Oliver Cromwell (1599–1658) headed a revolution against the Roman Catholic and Anglican churches, and became the Lord Protector of the Commonwealth. The Cromwellians pitched rocks through the stained glass windows of churches and cathedrals, destroyed statues of saints, and began knocking over as many ancient standing stones as they could find. In Avebury their attempt to destroy the ancient Druidic site ended when a barber was crushed by one of the falling monoliths. He was buried on site, with his barber tools still in his pocket; his remains now rest in the Avebury museum.

England had long maintained much of its ancient heritage in the form of seasonal festivals such as the May Pole Dance. A few years after the revolution, John Aubrey reported that prior to Cromwell, he had toured the countryside witnessing rural England's seasonal festivals, which could be traced back to pre-Christian times. On a new tour of the countryside he found that virtually all of the old ceremonial festivities had ceased. The ancient bonds to the land were being destroyed, and in their place urbanization and the Industrial Revolution would come calling.

SEVERED FROM THE SACRED

With the Enlightenment came progress and invention. At the same time the New World was opening up, feeding the suppressed hunger of the European common man for land. No one need live any longer under the feudal landlord. The newly available lands of America, Australia, and Africa meant that both the pioneer spirit for land and industry could be satisfied. Land meant freedom, power, and potential wealth. The cultivation of large scale wheat and grain crops in the New World was directly related to increasing population. England in 1800 had a population of 9 million people; a hundred years later the population had increased to 45 million. Villages became towns and towns became cities.

As the Industrial Revolution kicked into gear, there was a direct correlation between increased urbanization and industrialization. In one century we seemed to lose all sensitivity to the landscape and our environment. Factories mushroomed along river ways, railroads ran along the embankments, coal and slag heaps disfigured the hillsides, and rivers became sewers and garbage dumps.

The development of large scale mining and manufacturing operations coincided with the dismemberment of society, the destruction of the landscape, and the demise of the communal family environment. Agriculture creates order based on nature and the seasonal cycles. Industry creates order, too, but it is unnatural and manmade, with man deciding what hour we rise, go to bed, etc. Workers were forced to follow an artificial ordering of their days, thus depriving them of the most basic link with Nature and the Sacred. The "company town" was a place of exploitation and tyranny, where the factory and the slum went hand in hand.

Urbanization of large portions of the population forever altered the life of the family. According to Lewis Mumford in *The Myth of the Machine* by 1851 only one third of the population of England had been born where they now lived. In cities like Manchester, Birmingham, Liverpool, and London living conditions were appalling. The lack of living space, sanitation, and plumbing meant urban centers were a cess pool of suffering and want. Worker housing consisted of one-room barracks for an entire family. In Manchester there was one toilet for every 212 workers. In Liverpool, one sixth of the population lived in underground cellars. From the beginning of the 1800s infant mortality rates steadily rose in the industrial centers. In New York, by 1870, infant mortality was 240 deaths out of every 1000 live births.

People lived and died in view of the factories and mines in which they labored. Men, women, and children worked fourteen to sixteen hours a day, with no hope of rising above subsistence poverty. The daily life was one of toil, drudgery, filth, and exhaustion. There was always the threat of having your job eliminated by a new machine or technology. The family was fragmented by the need to find jobs; no longer was there an extended family to provide support.

The relationship of father and son was forever altered, for the sons no longer saw how their fathers worked. They were simply absent for large portions of the day. Never before had a majority of sons grown up not working side by side with their fathers. This fragmentation became complete with the advent of the modern family, where both parents often must work outside of the home. The absence of connection, love, and enjoyment of one another is a devastating environment for everyone, and the dysfunctions are many. Alcoholism, legal and illegal drugs, physical and sexual abuse, and neglect are national issues. The frustrations of modern life erupts daily with various forms of senseless violence; fanatical groups terrorize the world; and a resurgence of pro-Nazi and racist sympathies becomes a daily theme. In an attempt to force order on the chaos of modern life, Fundamentalism has arisen as anodyne to free thinking and self expression. All of these factors combined with the disconnection from the rural landscape, the loss of seasonal rhythms and celebrations, and the break-up of the extended family was a destructive blow to our collective experience of the sacred.

SCIENCE AND THE NEW FUNDAMENTALISM

Fundamentalists of all persuasions share a fanaticism in their beliefs. Whether expounding a literal belief in the holy books of religious tradition or traditional scientific dogma, in all fundamentalists the impulse is to control people's lives and how they think. This type of dogmatic, close-mindedness always seems to degenerate into intrigues and dirty tricks.

Nothing irritates the fundamentalist scientific establishment more than to come up against New Age, holistic thinkers, the Christian right, or one of their own who dares to break rank. To protect itself, the scientific establishment founded a scientific watchdog group known as the Committee for Scientific Investigation of Claims of the Paranormal—CSI-COP (pronounced "Psy Cop"). Their magazine, *The Skeptical Inquirer*, reportedly strives for open dialogue, CSICOP is another story entirely.

A number of years ago, French immunologist Jacques Benveniste was investigating the role of antibodies and antigens. He began to dilute the antibodies in an aqueous solution, and to his surprise the antibodies did not disappear when diluted 100,000 times. The water apparently retained a memory of the antibodies. Following good scientific methodology, he sent his experiment around to other labs for verification. They in turn replicated his work, which he then published in *Nature*, the most prestigious scientific journal in Europe.

Unintentionally, Benveniste had discovered substantial proof for homeopathy. Shortly thereafter, he was visited by John Maddox, the editor of *Nature*, the Amazing Randi, a sleight of hand magician; and Martin Gardner, who prides himself in being a debunker. None have any experience in immunology, but they are all members of CSICOP. Together they proceeded to make a hoax of Benveniste's experiment.

As a consequence of their visit, Benveniste lost his job. There followed a huge public outcry in France, as outraged scientists picked up his experiment and replicated his work. They found that the antibodies had a wavelike response to the dilutions, as weakening, and then returning stronger than before, exactly what homeopathy claims with its medicinal dilutions. Benveniste was attacked because he unintentionally discovered something contrary to the scientific model of reality. The hoax replication of John Maddox is unacceptable to the open minded. It smacks of the same religious fervor that was responsible for the witch burnings of the Inquisition.

CSICOP is not the only "ghost busting" organization. *Vegetarian Times* (August 1991) has identified the "quack busters," health care vigilantes who monitor health fraud. These organizations include the National Council Against Health Fraud, the American Council on Science and Health, and the Consumer Health Information Research Institute. All of these organizations share board members. Among their priorities and policies: The opposition to organic produce, nutritional medicine, vitamins, and herbal therapies; homeopathy, naturopathy, reflexology, and chiropractics; a disbelief in chronic fatigue syndrome and environmental illnesses; and the support of pesticides and food additives. The ACSH is backed by multinationals such as Exxon, Dow Chemicals, Procter and Gamble, Gerber Products, Burger King, the National Dairy Council, and American Meat Institute. ACSH recently advised that it is dangerous to limit fat in children's diets. This statement was printed in *Parenting Magazine*. When consumer protection takes on this kind of role, backed by special interest groups, it becomes both absurd and dangerous.

The truly skeptical are opened minded to any possibility, and not threatened by the irrational. The Enlightenment was supposed to liberate us from the superstitions and tyranny of the Church of Rome. In its place we now have a system of scientific fanaticism, determined to dictate to the world a rational but none-the-less one-sided view of reality. One of the sad results of scientific fundamentalism is that science has once again attracted the ire of the Christian right, rekindling the old battle between evolution and biblical creationism. In many parts of the country, school districts may choose to teach that God created the world in six days, not as a metaphor but as a fact. Whenever science becomes religion, religion likewise can turn around and become science. It is the children who lose in this particular battle. The failure of scientific rationalism is that it erodes away any sense of meaning or purpose to life. By making our belief in the Spirit an embarrassment, we are no longer certain how to act or how to raise our children, and religion becomes just another fairy tale, having no living context in a modern world.

Many scientists believe in a greater mystery and are eager to find a way to bridge the gap between rational materialism and the spiritual world. These scientists recognize how fundamentalist views compromise our capacity for genuine free thinking, fueling an adversarial world, already rife with antagonism. The fragmented technological culture of the present encourages us to feel incoherent and out of step with life. By reexamining our long and checkered relationship to the sacred, and by incorporating elements of the sacred into our daily lives and families, we can begin to remember that it matters who we are, how we treat one another, and how we live our collective lives. The manner in which we conceptualize the world and our relationship to all creatures and things, shapes the quality of the world in which we live.

HEAR NO EVIL, SEE NO EVIL

. . . never forget, when you hear the progress of the Enlightenment praised, that the Devil's cleverest ploy is to persuade you that he doesn't exist.—CHARLES BAUDELAIRE

Over the last two decades, thinkers like Fritjof Capra, Rupert Sheldrake, Joseph Campbell, James Hillman, Aldous Huxley, and Gregory Bateson have wondered if we did not throw the very "substantives of metaphysics" out with the arrival of rational reductionism. It is common knowledge that in America most people still believe in God and mistrust the scientific establishment. In the face of scientific fact they continue to pray and have their astrological charts done. The world may be an inanimate object to science, but to the common person the Earth is alive, animals feel pain, and a sense of spirit prevails. Three hundred years after the Enlightenment, people continue to believe and trust in the authenticity of their own experience of life, even if it runs counter to rational thought. Coming into the end of the twentieth century, the utopian dream of Bacon's *New Atlantis* begins to look more like an Orwellian nightmare.

Over the last four hundred years there has been a distinct separation between science and religion. The result is a science that has no spiritual values, and although religion and spirituality deal with the nature of the divine, neither science nor religion, outside of fundamentalists sects, have been willing to deal with the issue of evil. Evil requires a subjective value judgment, and labeling something or someone as evil is fraught with danger. All too often pointing a finger at evil has been a political ploy ending with the persecution and death of entire segments of the population. The burning of thousands of women during the Inquisition, the genocide of the Holocaust, and the current animosity towards Blacks, Jews, Arabs, and the gay community, speak to the dangers involved in labeling a group of people as evil.

Any question concerning the nature of evil also raises questions about God. In his book *People of the Lie*, Scott Peck defines evil as opposition to life, stating that it has to do with killing that is not required for biological survival. He goes on to say that murder is not restricted to the death of a physical body, killing of the spirit is evil, too. Any attempt to control others or strip of them of their capacity to think for themselves robs them of their humanity. This thievery is evil.

To defeat evil one must be willing and able to confront it with love. There must be a spiritual dimension to the confrontation. When a person or a culture falls into evil there is a consequent unwillingness to confront the conscience, whether individual or collective. This prohibits a person or group from submitting to a higher principle or living life under the auspices of a guiding spiritual light. Just as our historical relationship to the sacred has changed and moved back and forth across a wide continuum, our personal relationship to evil has changed as well.

Parents have a moral responsibility to reprimand and confront immoral acts in their children. Every child experiences certain moral crossroads: whether or not to lie, steal, cheat, bully, and abuse others to gain status or material goods. Parents who aid their children in such activities or protect them from accountability teach their children that such acts are acceptable.

We are not born evil but we can become evil as a result of the choices we make and how we exercise our own free will. Recently parents were found to be helping their children cheat in 4-H competitions by instructing their children to do such things as stick a water hose down the throats of their animals to increase their weight. That something as wholesome as the county fair should become a source of cruelty, greed, and unethical behavior is shocking. These same parents will shudder in despair if their child grows into a criminal or murderer, disavowing any responsibility for their outcome.

The psychiatrist R.D. Laing once told me about a potential client who came to see him, leaving Laing with the feeling of being in the presence of evil. The man was an anesthesiologist who was exceptionally gifted in his craft. Apparently medical insurance companies who insure anesthesiologists recognize that four or five patients a year will die as a result of complications from the anesthetic. They are prepared to support the doctor in any consequent malpractice suits. This particular anesthesiologist only lost one patient a year to accidental causes. He then chose two or three other patients, and killed them in the operating room, in the unwitting company of the surgeons and nurses.

As Laing listened to his story, he told the man that he would see him as a client if he promised not to kill anyone while in therapy with Laing. The man refused to make that promise. Laing realized what the man really wanted was the confidentiality of the therapist's room as a place where he could gloat over his capacity to get away with murder. Laing refused to see him any more. He could not press charges against him, since it was one man's word against another, and Laing's moral decision was based upon his refusal to become a receptacle for this man's murderous ego.

The problem of evil is certainly a personal moral dilemma, but it can also be a scientific one as well. I am not implying that science is evil, but it does seem that scientists should be held morally accountable for their creations and their actions. The human experiments on the Jews, gays, and Gypsies by the Nazis, secret CIA experiments with LSD, and the human guinea pigs who were dosed with radiation by medical researchers in the United States, speak to a moral crossroad that scientists must confront.

Scientists who enter into a Faustian bargain for power and glory often do so at the cost of jeopardizing not only individual lives but the life of the planet. Andrew Delbanco in his powerful book *The Death of Satan* quotes Richard Rorty from his book *Contingency, Irony, and Solidarity*, on science and its relationship to the sacred.

> Once upon a time we felt a need to worship something which lay beyond the visible world. Beginning in the seventeenth century we tried to substitute a love of trust for a love of God, treating the world described by science as a quasi divinity. Beginning at the end of the eighteenth century we tried to substitute a love of ourselves for a love of scientific truth, a worship of our own deep spiritual or poetic nature, treated as one more quasi divinity....[Now we are at] the point where we no longer worship anything, where we treat nothing as a quasi divinity, where we treat everything—our language, our conscience, our community—as a product of time and chance.

Evolutionary humanism was an attempt by the scientific community to do away with God and yet keep a sense of divinity about life. As humanist Sir Julian Huxley stated in his interesting book *Religion Without Revelation*: "A humanist evolution-centered religion too needs divinity, but divinity without God." He suggested we melt down the Gods and look to ordinary Nature as a source of inspiration and magical mystery. This is all well and good, but the humanism that Huxley espoused also requires that we clear-cut our language and psyche of all metaphors that anthropomorphize creation, including the mystical language of the sacred, and eliminate all God-like projections concerning our sense of the divine. Furthermore, after melting God down, we are then expected to resurrect our long history of believing in God into a secular humanism. Rather than believing that God created the world, we now get to create God, and God is us. The evolutionary thrust becomes the force that carries us upward as the human species attempts to transcend itself. Huxley tells us that man has been appointed managing director of the biggest business of all, the business of evolution, and that we can not refuse the job.

Huxley has many admirable thoughts concerning science, religion, and ceremony, in fact he is extremely reasonable and high minded in his concern for Nature, social systems, and life in general. He feels that only by taking control of our evolution we will fulfill our "transhuman destiny." Huxley's call to create new ceremonies around birth, marriage, and death were highly perceptive in terms of basic anthropology and visionary in outlook. Unfortunately, evolutionary humanism, as reasonable as it is, has been a failure in terms of converts.

Humanism believes that a strong moral fiber can exist without any spiritual language or metaphor. It does not allow for that which makes the imagination sing or the soul sigh in comfort, for our human evolutionary development has always occurred in the company of an incomprehensible Godhead. The vitalist or animistic view is quite likely part of our genetic memory. To cut ourselves off from Nature, but still acknowledge our evolutionary development is a contradiction in terms. The scientific urge to know everything by breaking the world down into smaller and smaller components of itself ultimately wounds our capacity to function as caring human beings, for it strips our lives of all meaning. When everything concerning the nature of reality is left to blind chance, the soul of the world suffers. The word *chance* is related to the old Roman Goddess Fortuna, who turned the karmic wheel of Fate. Rather than view our existence as the result of blind chance, humanity might be better served by acknowledging the hand of Providence.

When Nietzsche first declared that "God was dead" few realized that if God was dead so was his fallen angel the Devil. Delbanco quotes Susan Sontag as asking the question: "How can we find our moral bearings when we have a sense of evil but no longer the religious or philosophical language to talk intelligently about evil?" Sontag's question can also be asked of the sacred.

As we reconsider personifying our environment and our relationship to the spirit, we must also consider the demonic. To live in a world that is full of deities or in a world where one God reigns supreme automatically implies the existence of the counter force known to Christians as the Devil. I have yet to meet a traditional shaman who viewed the spirit world as made up of only benign beings. Every spiritual tradition from Paganism to Christianity recognizes the left-hand path. Since the Enlightenment, the concept of the Devil has been purged from our moral imagination, and yet evil seems to greet us daily via the newspapers and television newscasts. We have come to accept the horrors of the war in Bosnia, the madness of the slaughter in Rwanda, terrorist bombings, and children as murderer and murdered with a shrug.

Delbanco laments that "we have no language for connecting our inner lives with the horrors that pass before our eyes." Delbanco takes both the demonizing of the fundamental right and the liberal psychology of the educated to task. He feels that "the health of society depends upon our idea of evil, and we have an obligation to name evil and oppose it, in ourselves as well as others." We must not create euphemisms for evil. Recently when a gunman shot and killed kindergarten children in Scotland, the local minister promptly announced that the village "had been visited by evil." The psychology of the murderer's life was not permitted to become a rationale for his evil deed.

In a time of "political correctness" Delbanco quotes John Updike and one of his witches of Eastwick when she says that evil is not a word they like to use: "We prefer 'unfortunate' or 'lacking' or 'misguided' or 'disadvantaged.'" Many serial killers and murderers claim to hear voices that tell them to kill, some acknowledge the source as being the Devil. Part of us wants to say "sure, the Devil made you do it" and dismiss it as a feeble attempt for an insanity plea. But people have always heard voices and every religion has as its leaders those who have listened to the voice of God, from Moses, to Jesus, to Paul, the voices have guided the people. Likewise the voice of evil has also spoken and condemned many a poor soul. With the advent of rationalism and the social science of psychology all of the voices are now just aspects of a pathological illness. If we are to bring a sense of the sacred back into our lives, we must not dismiss evil through our psychology or through a postmodern analysis that simply deconstructs all realities of good and evil.

The return of the sacred requires that each one of us find a way to incorporate basic values back into our lives, our families, and our communities. We can learn from our past, and we can make a conscious effort to go beyond simple feelings of nostalgia or superstition to create a better future for the world.

THE PAST COMES CALLING

In the quest for meaning and the effort to examine how the pattern of the sacred evolves and changes, I have looked at a number of cultures and their belief systems. All of the information I have drawn from has come directly or indirectly from such disciplines as anthropology, biology, sociology, archeology, climatology, and history. The scientific approach makes it possible for us to acquire a better and more thorough understanding of our past, how we came to be, where we came from, and how civilization and its diverse ways evolved.

From the discovery of the Paleolithic caves, to archetypal psychology and the work of archeologists such as Maria Gimbutas and James Mellaart, to scholars such Riane Eisler, comes a new interpretation of what our past actually means. All of these discoveries have taken place in the last one hundred years and point us in the direction of rethinking who we are as human beings. The past has come calling at the end of the millennium, and it has the eerie feeling of not being by accident.

We can dispassionately view the sacred as it meanders from primitive life to high civilization, from paganism to monotheism to atheism with its subsequent consequences. We can be thankful to science for its many innovations, inventions and creature comforts and still question its supremacy over life. Over the last twenty years James Hillman and other

Jungians have worked their way into the mainstream, bringing with them the Gods and Goddesses of Greece, and the ancient tales of our heritage as human beings. Out of dreams, myths, fairy tales, magic, and of course archetypes, the modern world's psychic wealth has been vastly increased. The message is one that goes beyond the rational or the literal, and carries us into the dreamscape of our metaphoric mind.

The view of the ancient world has been recast to include idyllic visions of a time of harmony and peace. It is as if our cultural psyche is revealing itself out of the depths of our past, and a collective dreaming is taking place, a reclaiming of ways of being that have been lost. The synchronicity of this moment is not lost on those who are striving for a better life and a future that could bring us back into harmony with life and all that is holy.

Since 1859, when Darwin published *On the Origin of Species*, science has established humanity as part of Nature. At the same time, humanists have declared that we can transcend this genetic heritage, as if a leaf of a tree can live without its branches and roots. With all that science has given us, we are now quite capable of understanding our embeddedness in Nature, and how desolate and destructive our collective lives can be with no sense of the sacred. We are now conscious enough and intellectually sophisticated to a sufficient degree that we can, with our free will, choose the path to walk. We need not fall into harmful superstitious patterns nor blindly follow the dictates of any form of fundamentalism.

Buddhism believes that all life is suffering and it is through the nectar of wisdom and compassion that our hearts can break open to embrace the world, with all of its horror and all of its beauty. We would be wise to bring a compassionate view towards ourselves, the environment, science, fundamentalism, and our long-standing Western traditions. Cultivating compassion towards others allows us to see the similarities rather than the differences; it also allows us to feel the depths of pain and suffering of others and become as one beating heart.

·3·

THE ONCE AND FUTURE SHAMAN

> He who understands has wings. We know that among many peoples the
> soul is conceived of as a bird. Magical flight assumes the value of an
> "escape from the body"—that is, it translates ecstasy, the liberation of the
> soul, into plastic terms. But while the majority of human beings are
> changed into birds only at the moment of death, when they forsake their
> bodies and fly into the air, shamans, sorcerers, and ecstatics of all kinds
> realize "emergence from the body" in this world and as often as they wish.
> This myth of the bird-soul contains in germ a whole metaphysics of man's
> spiritual autonomy and freedom.—MIRCEA ELIADE

OUR ANCIENT PAST

From the beginning, humanity has set aside special times and places to commune with the divine. For tens of thousands of years our sense of the sacred recognized humanity as being kin with the animals and the plants, and that the cycles of Nature were mirrored in the body of women.

Shamanism is as ancient as human consciousness itself, and from Paleolithic times the magic of the shaman involved the cycles of Nature, the spirits of plants and animals, and especially the hunt. In the cave of Les Trois Freres, there is a bird-headed male figure dressed as a bison who is dancing and playing a hunting bow; this image has been named the Sorcerer. The shaman's capacity to transform into an animal and read the signs and omens of Nature to find game is a phenomenon found throughout the world. Shamans become the "Bringer of the Beasts." From ancient times we find repeated motifs of bird-headed shamans, animal familiars, and animal costumes of bears, lions, stag, and bull.

The amulets and talismans of the Upper Paleolithic are essentially identical to the medicine bundle of a shaman living today. Thirty thousand years later, remnants of this ancient way can be found in almost every indigenous culture still existing today, whether it be amongst the Kung bushmen of Africa, the Australian aborigines, the Mongolians, or the native Indians of the Americas. This body of shamanistic information passed from generation to generation is a basic survival guide to planet Earth. It speaks of true sustainability in terms of hunting patterns, the collecting and growing of plants, the medicinal uses of plants, the construction of shelters, and the rules for living together, including the taboos of kinship and mating patterns. It is no wonder that it has been said that every time an old shaman dies it is the equivalent of a great library burning down.

TECHNICIANS OF THE SACRED

Mircea Eliade tells us that shamanism is a religious phenomenon of Central Asia and Siberia, and that the original word comes from the Tungusic word *saman*. Eliade defines shamanism as a "technique of ecstasy." The shaman is an ecstatic visionary who comes into power in a number of ways. Among the people of Siberia, shamanic power is passed through the mother's line as part of a person's inheritance. In other cultures, the calling to Shamanism comes through divine intercession, dreams, vision-producing plants, the appearance of totemic clan animals, or illness.

Regardless of the path taken, the making of a shaman is the process of soul-making. The shaman is capable of traveling into the depths of the underworld, or taking flight and soaring into the sky realm. This shamanic journeying enables the shaman to come to grips with the mystery of life and death and to return to ordinary reality as a transfigured being. The shaman thus becomes an intermediary between the subterranean world of the unconscious and the rarefied world of the superconscious.

The task of the shaman is to make this spirit-journey for their people, to find the source of an illness, to understand what spirits have been offended, to locate a lost soul, to find game, or to make amends between the spirit world and the community. To perform these sacred duties, the shaman may also shape shift into animal forms. The shaman is thus a master traveler who knows how to transform consciousness and reality at will.

The appeasing of Gods in the lower world of the dead and upper worlds of the Spirit is the shaman's primary task, but none attempt this great work on their own. A shaman spends years cultivating relationships with a number of spirit-helpers or guides. These spirit-allies are of tremendous value to the shaman, both as protection and as a source of insight into a particular problem. The spirit-helpers often appear as animals who can perform tasks for the shaman and offer protection and guidance.

The recognition of totemic animals is an ancient wisdom. In native cultures, clans and secret societies are often named according to their guiding animal spirit. Remnants of this animal kinship can be found in contemporary culture with families who carry such names as Wolf, Lark, Salmon, Robin, and Eaglehart, and with civic groups such as the Elks or the Moose Lodge.

Today, it has become quite popular in the human potential network for people to participate in shamanic journeys to find one's "Medicine Animal." The Medicine Animal is way to connect on a soul level with a particular species. Often the connection is the result of real life interactions with wild animals. In traditional cultures if you are bitten by a rattlesnake and survive, you would be recognized as having "snake medicine." Sometimes a Medicine Animal appears at an auspicious moment—perhaps during a vision quest—and encounters with bears, eagles, snakes, or lions are not viewed as accidental. Animals who appear in dreams are seen as divine intercessions from the animal world. And strange or seemingly magical encounters with a wild animal are viewed as the animal offering itself to the person as a spirit guide and as a source of protection. This source of protection and power does not come from an individual creature, although it might manifest through a special relationship with a particular animal. The power of the Medicine Animal comes from the collective spirit, or morphogenetic field of the species. It is the spirit of the individual animal and its entire line of ancestral beings who comes as the Medicine Animal.

TEACHER PLANTS

Spirit guides are not limited to the animal kingdom, however, for there are also plant spirits that guide and direct. Among American Indians they are simply called "teacher plants." Consciousness-expanding plants, such as hallucinogenic mushrooms, peyote, and ayahuasca, have a long history in the development of human consciousness. Anthropologists and ethnobotanists can trace the use of mind-altering plants from the Paleolithic to advanced civilizations, and the role of these plants in the development of society is now thought to be far greater than has generally been imagined.

From Africa to Australia, North and South America, to Europe and Asia the ingestion of these teacher plants continues. Mushroom cults have been traced back to early cultures in Greece, the Middle East, Scandinavia, India, Asia, Russia, Siberia, and Meso America. Homer's *Odyssey* speaks of plants used to alter consciousness, and the Vedic hymns of India refer repeatedly to Soma as the "food of the Gods."

In the New World, mushrooms have played a part in religious ceremonies in the Aztec and Mayan cultures, as well as with tribes in the Amazon. Peyote, a New World cactus with hallucinogenic properties, is found throughout Mexico and the Southwest United States and is still used as a sacrament in the Native American Church, the largest growing native church in the United States.

Amazonian shamans brew a drink from *ayahuasca,* also known as the "Vine of the Gods." The drink and accompanying ceremony is primarily used for healing and locating game. The active ingredient in the plant mixture was originally named "telepathine" by biochemists, because the experience of ingesting the drink in a ceremonial setting often produces a collective mind phenomenon. One group of Indians reportedly took it with an anthropologist and decided that they wanted to visit the homeland of the academic. During their ceremony they saw tall stone houses and people sitting inside of metal boxes that were traveling quite fast. They had never seen a modern city or an automobile, yet they accurately described an urban environment. When a group of urban westerners were administered the substance, they had shared visions of the jungle: huge snakes, jaguars, and dark-skinned people.

In Africa, in an area near Zaire, the Fang people ingest the hallucinogenic plant *iboga.* The plant was originally used to help men sit still as they hunted. Today a movement toward the sacramental use of iboga in Africa is similar to that of the Native American Church of the Americas' use of peyote, in that it is part of the attempt of native peoples to hold on to their old ways. Interestingly, modern medicine is now exploring the use of iboga as a way to break alcohol, cocaine, and heroin addictions. Studies indicate that one session with iboga appears to reroute the neural pathways that carry addiction, and people are apparently permanently cured. The clinical use of iboga is officially sanctioned in Holland.

Each of these substances is known to have its own, and very particular guiding spirit, and it is recognized among indigenous cultures that in order to have a safe journey with these plants, a proper and respectful relationship must be cultivated and maintained. The shaman must obviously keep his or her psychic economy in order, or risk being called to task by the spirit of the plant. Assuming the shaman is in proper relationship with the plant, the spirit-helper will be of the utmost service to the shaman, providing the required information needed to heal the patient and/or appease the offended spirits.

The critical element involved in the ingesting of such powerful substances is that of ceremony. Native peoples do not have a problem with members of their community abusing these substances. The community-sanctioned use of such healing substances is for the benefit of all and is conducted under the guidance of the shaman. The nature of the experience does not call an individual to desire to repeat it again and again, for the power of the dreams, visions, and insights must be digested in the weeks that follow. Because the plants are taken in a sacred way, with community approval and participation, they do not carry the problems of other mind-altering substances. "Recreational" drugs, such as heroin or cocaine, are usually taken as a simple escape from reality; rather than expanding awareness the intent is most often to annihilate consciousness as frequently as possible.

Today, in spite of the war on drugs, plants like ayahuasca, peyote, and iboga are finding a niche again. They create social cohesion among people, and do in fact seem to curb alcoholism and other drug addictions. The Native American Church, and its sacramental peyote, is a legitimate church in the United States with a membership of over 250,000 people. It has been a boon to American Indians in helping them reclaim their culture. It allows people from a variety of tribes to sit down together and speak a common spirit language. In South America, the use of ayahuasca has also achieved the status of a recognized faith. The Santa Daime religion and the União do Vegetal are two religious organizations that have combined the sacrament of ayahuasca and Christianity with the traditional wisdom of the Amazonian tribes.

Animism and Shamanism

In addition to the spirits of the plants and animals, the shaman will
also establish relations with forces of Nature such as the River Spirit, Stone
People, or Rain Gods. This world view of every aspect of life being imbued
with spirit is a cross-cultural phenomena linking shamanism to animism.
By maintaining relationships with the Gods who inhabit the world of
Nature, the shaman ensures the survival of the people. Finally, the shaman
will also have contact with the ancestral spirits of the tribe, clan, or family.
These particular beings are very important because of the collective spirit
they embody, especially if they include powerful shamans from the past.

It is obvious that the shaman is working in a variety of realms: the
mineral kingdom with its crystals, gold, silver, and precious stones and
gems, the plant and animal kingdoms, the forces of Nature, the Earth, the
sky, the cosmos, and the spirits of ancestors. All of these helpers are enlist-
ed by the shaman at one time or another, and these relationships must be,
and are, well cultivated. It is also obvious that the world of the shaman
leaves little ground for the skeptic. Instead, shamanism plunges you into a
polytheistic world of animism and pantheism. A living, breathing, world of
interpenetrating kinship. It is what scholars have referred to as "participation mystique" and what Martin Buber meant when he spoke of the "I-and-
thou" relationship. The shaman, like the early Greek Thales, sees the
world as "being full of Gods."

Animistic cultures struggle for their existence in the modern world.
Their capacity to live simply on the Earth is fatefully out of step with consumer society and most are going the way of the elephant and the tiger.
The tropical island of Bali is one of the last places that can truly be called
an Earthly paradise. In spite of a large population, over 2.5 million people
on an island of 2,000 square miles, Bali continues to thrive against all odds.
Almost all of the population lives rurally and the Balinese define themselves as Hindu/animists. They live on a volcanic island with a chain of
mountains that regularly lets the people know that the Earth is alive. The
island has been home to its inhabitants for the last 5,000 years. The
Balinese themselves are a distinctive Malay race with roots in Southeast
Asia and southern China. The sheer beauty of Bali and its people is heartbreaking to the sensibilities of most tourists. It's as if visiting Bali provokes

an ancient memory of a life well lived, a time of innocence before the Fall, and a deep longing for kinship.

Unlike most indigenous cultures, Bali has never been missionized and the Balinese have never starved. At the end of the twentieth century, traveling in Bali is a rare treat. Balinese ceremonies are acts of beauty and joy. In any given year Balinese villages host over 35,000 ceremonies. Offerings of flowers, fruit, and art create a continual atmosphere of beauty. Daily offerings are made by each family to their own ancestors and the spirits of their family compound.

I once had the pleasure of being in Bali in the early spring when the island-wide New Year ceremony *Nepi* was being celebrated. It is a special ceremony to drive all the evil demons off the island for the coming year. For months, each village creates elaborate demons in the form of large floats. As evening falls the young men carry the demons through the village to the crossroads. For the rest of the night, up until midnight, the demons are burned with much revelry, drumming, gamelon, and general glee. At midnight everything abruptly stops. No speaking, no laughter, no music, motorcycles, or automobiles. For the next thirty-six hours, all mechanical devices cease. Tourists arriving by jet discover there are no taxis. The Balinese stay at home without electric lights, sitting quietly, for any loud noise or machinery is thought to attract the demons. If any one attempts to drive their motor bike, they are attacked and stopped. During the following day, people eat food they have prepared in advance, no one works, and families stay inside their compound. In the early evening they may begin visiting with neighbors and talking quietly. That night people retire early and near dawn once again the sound of motor bikes calls one back to the modern world.

I found this ceremony very beautiful and powerful. Every Westerner who has ever experienced it wishes it was a world-wide event. For one day out of the year, everything stops, and the modern world is suspended. Perhaps we instinctively need this one day to drive our demons off the Earth and for the sounds of Nature to be heard.

SHAMANIC THEATER

There are other motifs that occur cross-culturally in shamanism, such as the use of masks, drums, songs, and ceremonial activity. Together these form a vehicle in which the shaman recreates the world. Shamans are often very skilled actors and stage magicians, and anthropologists have often dismissed the work of the shaman as theatrics. Nothing could be further from the truth, for shamans use drama as a way of deepening their connection with the spirit world. When a shaman dons a mask and mimics the sound of birds or animals, they are not play acting. The shaman has become that animal spirit, and the shaman's journey carries the tribe into the crack between the worlds. Everyone present is transported as the line between the real and the unreal world disappears.

When anthropologists or outside observers see what they believe to be sleight of hand used by the shaman in healing, they often protest, saying it is deceit on the part of the healer. What they often ignore is the fact that actual healing has taken place. Eco-philosopher David Abram, who is himself a sleight-of-hand magician, once confronted a shaman about his use of sleight-of-hand. David recounted to me that during a healing ceremony, he had watched the shaman palm the entail of an animal and then make it appear as if he had pulled the object out of the body of a sick person. After the ceremony, when David was alone with the shaman, he asked him how he could resort to such trickery. Rather surprised by the accusation, the healer declared that he was not trying to fool any of the people present but rather the malignant spirit who was attacking the patient. The shaman knew that by passing the disgusting entail in front of the ailing person, the spirit would be attracted to the smell of blood and decay and enter the entail, thus leaving the person to mend and heal.

This difference of perspective and acceptance of a world inhabited by living spirits, some of which may be malign, is contrary to Western rationality. We prefer to call these malignant spirits 'germs' and when questioned on how it is that one person gets the flu and another does not, we resort to an explanation of 'blind chance' and administer antibiotics.

In contrast the shaman seeks to place an illness into the larger context of the person's life, often questioning them about their behavior and how they might have caused offense to the surrounding community or spirits. When healing occurs under such unorthodox conditions, the scientific mind labels it as the "placebo effect;" an ineffectual remedy was administered, the person got better anyway, so the illness must have been all in the person's mind. The error is that the rational mind focuses on the placebo and not on the fact that healing has taken place. Not to mention that the deeply profound relationship of the mind and body is ignored.

In Somalia, if someone is experiencing physical, mental, or spiritual distress they can call together a *bahilowi*. They invite friends and relatives to come at night to a place away from human habitation. There the people gather in a circle around the afflicted person. The ailing one then begins to chant his or her suffering and symptoms as a question to the group. The group, in turn, responds by chanting back what they perceive to be causing the illness. In this case the community performs as shaman, and a sick person has wholeness restored by seeking the wisdom of the community and its traditions.

THE HEALING SOUND

Besides plants and animals and sleight of hand, the use of the drum, rattle, and song is of the utmost importance to the shaman. The drum and rattle are often referred to as a "horse" that the shaman can mount and ride into the lower or upper worlds. The drum in particular serves as a link between the worlds. Made out of a tree and covered with the skin of an animal, it is the center of the world from which the shaman goes out and returns again. The beating and galloping rhythms of the drum carries the shaman and his people into trance and into direct contact with the spirit world. The drum holds energy together, while the rattle breaks energy up; the rattle opens up the road and the drum keeps everyone moving up or down that road.

Shamans are always singers, and they carry the oral tradition of their people's songs, blessings, and stories. They also contribute to their tradition with their own songs. As Isaac Tens, an American Indian reports:

> I began to sing. A chant was coming out of me without my being
> able to do anything to stop it....The songs force themselves out com-
> plete, without any attempt to compose them. But I learned and
> memorized these songs by repeating them.

It is this ability to surrender to the spirit that allows the shaman to let songs come forth spontaneously and completely. The shamans I have met have all used chanting and song as an integral part of their ceremonial and healing activities.

A few years ago I had the pleasure of meeting Rueben Snake (now deceased). At the time he was leader of the Native American Church. Rueben was perhaps the most open-hearted medicine man I had ever met. He and his family came to dinner. This meant his wife, children, and grand-children—we totaled around twenty people. After dinner we gathered in the living room, and he and his family sang for us in the style of the Native American Church. The songs were sung deep inside the chest with a par-ticular resonance that only American Indians seem capable of producing. The words were a combination of a spirit dialect and English words that spoke about "Jesus being the light of the world." I was very touched by Rueben and his family, and especially by his willingness to answer questions about his Church. He was, at the time, researching the history of peyote use in the Americas and had just returned from Mexico, where he had partici-pated in a Huichol Indian peyote ceremonial. He had been profoundly moved by the Huichols and the pure, ancient form of their ceremony.

I found myself discussing the plight of contemporary people, our search for the sacred, and how we might develop ceremonies that would really work for us. I explained that sometimes our attempts to create cere-mony seemed a bit corny. At which point he laughed and said a little corn wasn't too bad. I asked him what we could do to bring more power into our ceremonies. He responded by saying the first thing we must do is get our songs together. We should learn to drum and rattle and let the Spirit bring us our prayers in the form of songs. I then took the risk of singing him a couple of songs from contemporary ceremonies that were prayers about the Earth. When I finished he said, "Yes, those songs were gifts from the Spirit. If you open up to the Great Spirit he will give you songs and the cere-monies to go with them." Drumming and singing is perhaps the most read-ily available channel we have to the sacred. It is one of our great cultural losses, that so many traditional religions have all but eliminated chanting and singing from their services. I can think of nothing that creates a greater sense of community than singing together.

WOUNDED HEALERS?

One popular idea about shamans is that they are "wounded healers." That is, they are people who have experienced a crisis so severe, be it phys-ical, mental, or spiritual, that it propelled them into altered states of consciousness. They have experienced a process of psychic dismemberment, from which they emerged strong and whole and with a vision. Another school of thought maintains that the shaman is a supernormal member of society, who has never been sick or psychotic and is a pillar of strength for the community. Anthropological literature validates both ideas about the shaman and also indicates that healthy cultures produce supernormal shamans, while cultures that are sick or faltering produce shamans who go through major illnesses, heal themselves, and in turn attempt to heal the members of their society.

This attraction to the concept of wounded healer is an obvious statement about the world in which we live, although it becomes potentially dangerous when people interpret their own breakdowns or illnesses as part of a shamanic initiation. I don't want to invalidate the power and courage that comes to any one after defeating a major illness of mind, body, or spirit, nor to deny that people who have healed themselves from a particular affliction often have a gift in helping others overcome the same affliction. The question is: are these people now shamans? In most cases, the answer would be no.

A few years ago the word *shaman* was unknown to the average Westerner. Today almost everyone has some idea of what shamans do. When questioned most people would say that a shaman is a healer, a medicine man or woman, a sorcerer or a magician. Some people speak of psychotherapists as contemporary shamans, and the New Age movement has a number of self-ordained shamans. I have met people who after attending a workshop or two on the subject have decided that they are shamans. The reality is that most people living in the Western world will probably never meet a real shaman, let alone become a shaman themselves.

But where does all of this leave us as modern day people? It is obvious that world of the shaman is a highly deified reality and one in which the shaman cares little about validating one reality over another. Most people, holding a rational view of a singular reality, are either delighted, amazed, or terrified when they actually have something paranormal happen to them that does not fit into the accepted world view. Some people spend years seeking out unusual experiences; when "it" happens, they spend years trying to figure "it" out and make it conform to what they know as "reality."

Many people have come into contact with the spirit world completely unprepared for its actuality. This is where psychosis and paranoia can creep in, and why a support group or tribe is essential to the shamanic quest. One aspect of the shamanic world that is rarely talked about is the danger that lurks about when one is dealing with spirits. You either take them seriously, believe in them, invoke them, make friends with them, propitiate them in appropriate ways, and maintain a healthy autonomy, or you take them half-seriously and run the risk of offense and misfortune.

CONTEMPORARY SHAMANISM

Today there is a growing interest in shamanism. Although traditional shamanism is disappearing, there are now international conferences on shamanism being held. Is it just a passing fad, or is it something brought about by an ancient longing for wisdom grounded in the Earth, in plants, animals, forests, rivers, and the seasonal cycles?

The popularity of shamanism in today's modern world reveals a psychic need for a world that is alive and connected. I suspect that the veneer of civilized rationality, detachment, and denial that most people profess towards matters of the spirit is actually quite thin. A living world, seen as Gaia, is attractive to our deepest sensibilities. It encourages us as to see ourselves as part of Nature and thus to correct our arrogant and deadly moves to control and manipulate life.

This growing interest in shamanism does have its downright irritating side. People who attend workshops held by dubious shamans and, after a couple of these experiences decide that they are shamans themselves have trivialized deep realities. Granted, most of these people will abandon shamanism when the next esoteric wave rolls through, but in spite of the superficiality of this interest I still think it points a finger to a deeper longing. And I do not want to dismiss all interested parties as shallow and insincere. There are a few, just like in any indigenous culture, who have the skill, the genes, and the capacity to become highly skilled shamans.

Those steeped in ancient tradition and wisdom acknowledge this time we are living in as a critical moment. Native peoples everywhere are faced with their greatest challenge: ultimate survival in a truly hostile world, ruled by people who are ignorant of life's mystery. Most modern people do not want to be reminded of what lies in the wake of the push for progress, and yet we can not remain numb with denial. The horror stories of a hundred years ago of active genocide continues at this very moment in the Americas, India, Southeast Asia, Tibet, Polynesia, Australia, and Africa. The destruction of Nature in the name of progress, and the number of species of plants and animals that are destroyed daily is mind boggling. In Geneva, Switzerland, a tally of species going extinct daily is kept: the loose-leaf volumes can no longer be lifted by a single individual. What is good and kind in each of us naturally finds this type of information painful, but it is through acknowledgment, not denial, that the heart can break open into compassion. By being engaged with all aspects of the world we can be inspired to create a world of beauty for future generations.

STOP STEALING OUR RELIGION!

Recently there has been much controversy in the United States and Europe between American Indians and the modern shamanic movement. The Indians justly accuse Europeans of taking everything from them: their land, their culture, and now even their spirituality. It is easy to sympathize with the native people's dilemma of what to do with their wealth of sacred knowledge. The old shamanic world view can only be preserved by encouraging the young of native cultures to pick up the old ways of their people, and by protecting these people, their ways, and their habitat. This failing, many shamans find themselves facing death, unable to pass on their sacred information, and some would prefer to take their knowledge to their graves than pass it to an outsider.

The dominant culture responds by saying that shamanism is a worldwide phenomenon, and that they have legitimate links into the shaman's world, be it through Celtic-Druidic, Nordic, or Mediterranean ancestry. Did not Moses and Christ both seek visions on the tops of mountains?

But the question remains, should we be dressing like Indians, praying like them, and teaching courses on esoteric tribal symbolism? It is, of course, one alternative, but is it our best choice? And what does it mean in terms of who we are as a people?

Because Western culture voraciously consumes indigenous cultures, particularly if they taste of mysticism, North American Natives may find the only alternative open to them is to begin to open up their traditions to sincere, dedicated outsiders, as the Tibetans and Huichol Indians of Mexico have done. These people in turn will pass the wisdom of life on to future generations as part of a lineage, for part of that wisdom is the fact that we are really one people living on a bountiful planet that has no national boundaries or borders other than those existing in the minds of humanity. But I do not sense that this is the answer, either for American Indians or non-Indians, nor do I believe that it ultimately will serve either's best interest.

One alternative to "becoming Indians" is to steep ourselves in Old World magics. We can become white witches and warlocks or tap into our Celtic-Druidic roots. We can make pilgrimages to ancient Goddess sites and attempt to recreate the Eleusinian mysteries of Greece. If none of these are appealing, we can abandon the shamanic world view and become Buddhists, Hindus, or Sufis. If this does not suffice, we can simply try to revitalize Christianity or Judaism.

Somehow, none of these possible solutions really addresses this urge, this hunger towards a ceremonial life rooted in the Earth and with an animistic world view at its core. We must address the question of who we are and where we are.

We can begin by asking the question: who are we? Most of us were born in North America, as were our parents and grandparents. I am always struck by my encounters with American Indians and one particular conversation that I found myself engaged in again and again:

"Where do you come from?"

"I live in California."

"But where do you come from?"

"Oh, you mean where was I born? I was raised in Pennsylvania."

"No, I mean where do you come from?"

"You mean where do my ancestors come from? They come from Europe...."

This conversation haunted me for years. I am after all a native-born American. I had never been to Europe until well into my adulthood. My parents had never been to Europe until they were adults, and my grandparents had never been to Europe at all. When I thought about this conversation I realized that it made me feel displaced, adrift in the world without roots. I am of European descent but I am not European, I am a native of the United States, but I am not a Native American. It made me deeply question who I am and where my place is. I got my first answers to these questions from the field of botany.

Field biologists have long recognized that if an exotic species is introduced into a foreign environment it either adapts or dies. Those species that adapt usually do so to such an extreme that after a number of generations they may no longer even look like the original species, and if taken back to their host country will need to readapt to the original environment.

My sense is that Americans are going through a similar process. After a number of generations of being an exotic species of colonizers we are indeed in the process of "going native" on North American soil. In fact, this is more than a simple metaphor. During World War I medical officials noticed that soldiers who were second generation Americans had in one generation lost what appeared to be their native ethnic characteristics and had acquired an American physique and skull structure. It could not be attributed to a change in diet, and I can only think it came from the land itself.

In this light, "going native" begins to take on an entirely new dimension. We are sinking our roots deep into the soil and are acquiring a sense of place. If I had to place the source of contemporary interest in American Indian cultures I would position it in the back-to-the-land movement that began in the 1960s. Publications like *The Whole Earth Catalog* taught a generation how to move towards self-sufficiency, and Heyemeyohst Storm's book *Seven Arrows* provided a spiritual context for living close to the land.

One thing that happens when people return to the land and set up agrarian communities is that they began to notice the seasonal cycles, full moons, equinoxes, and solstices. It was only natural that the back-to-the-land people looked for ways to begin to honor and celebrate these changes. In the United States, the only knowledgeable people around were often American Indians, and many people picked up the spirituality of the Indians. Running parallel to this course was the use of psychedelic drugs. Those who considered psychedelics a sacrament found validation for this idea amongst indigenous cultures who were engaged in shamanism with the ingestion of such plants as mushrooms amongst Meso-American Indians, peyote with the Huichols and Native American Church, and ayahuasca throughout the tribes of the Amazon region.

This was not a conscious attempt to steal or pervert American Indian spirituality; people were simply seeking elders who could guide them back to Nature. I don't believe that anyone understood how the human-potential movement would impact the blossoming interest in shamanism. Books like Carlos Castenada's *The Teachings of Don Juan* and

Joan Halifax's *Shamanic Voices* opened the way for shamanism to join the workshop circuit, and by the end of the 1980s Shamanic Counseling had become a registered trademark. The entrepreneurial spirit saw a ready market for smudge sticks, medicine pouches, and workshop solstice events.

As is usually the way, no one stopped to question how American Indians felt about all of this.

The reality of the situation is that modern Americans are attracted to Indian spirituality because when they have the chance to be in a *real* sweat lodge, smoke the sacred pipe with a *real* pipe carrier, or attend a *real* Sun dance or peyote meeting they often have a genuine and profound experience with the spirit world. These people are not just simply interested in ceremony; they are interested in the Spirit of ceremonial animism, because when they are with natives of North or South America or Africa or Australia they have direct experiences of a living animistic world in all of its glory, terror, and true awesomeness.

But the question still remains as to what to do about all of this. It brings us back to the fact that we must indeed go native, but in our own way. To do this, we must ask where a ceremonial life or culture comes from. It is clear that the underlying skeletal form of ceremony has a universal quality. Indigenous people everywhere conduct initiations and rites of passage and participate in seasonal celebrations. What differs from culture to culture is the content of how these ceremonies manifest themselves. Ceremonies of initiation that come out of the rain forests of the Pacific Northwest are quite different from those of the Desert Southwest, and yet they both are examples of proper initiation. Simply stated, ceremonies are shaped by the environment and the Spirits of the Place.

When a people are rooted in their land, the land and all of its creatures—mineral, plant, animal—and all the ancestors human and otherwise become available as teachers. This is what ceremony and animism is about. The native tribes of this continent have been here for tens of thousands of years, they know who they are as spiritual beings, and they have well-cultivated relationships with the Spirits of their place. We are but babes in the woods so to speak, but we should not let this discourage us in our desire to have a shamanic ceremonial life.

As a people transplanted to this continent, we owe it to ourselves and to future generations to fully honor our unusual position. Given the state of the global environment we can no longer afford to feel displaced and disconnected from our homeland. We are not tourists passing through and should not act as such. We must claim our place as home with all of our hearts and souls and treat it with the respect it deserves. If we feel the longing to have proper initiations and to do ceremony on the land, we must begin by listening to the land and the spirit of the place in which we inhabit. This is a long process that will reveal itself through time and through future generations.

We are really in a quite novel position as a colonizing species going native. The old ways of other people and places cannot possibly work for us. The ceremonies of Native Americans belong to them: They received the visions, they cultivated their connection to the Spirit, and they clearly know their taboos. We, on the other hand, have broken our connection to our motherland. Given our predicament we should not be embarrassed by our attempts to create American ceremony. We must learn to trust in the authenticity of our own visionary experience. This means that sometimes when we create a ceremony the spirit is undeniably present and other times, well—its just plain hokey. So what? We should not let this discourage us; we do not have to get it right in one generation.

A STATE OF GRACE

I have found that there is a period of grace that comes with trying to create ceremony. It's almost as if the Spirits of the Place are so intrigued (or perhaps amazed) by our attempts to communicate with them that they honor us as the children we are. I mention this because I have met a number of people who were interested in shamanism and ceremony, and they were told by Indians—and often not very trustworthy Indians—that they were doing it wrong. That they were in fact putting themselves in "mortal danger." This deadly danger could be anything from finding an owl feather to praying at an ancient sacred site. Inevitably their response is to take up with an Indian teacher (who is usually selling his or her wisdom) and become the "wanna be" that the Indian world is now so vocally against.

One of the weaknesses of self-generated ceremony is its lack of tradition, but this is also a gift, making anything possible. When people first begin to create a ceremony there is a childlike innocence to the event. These newly developed ceremonies sometimes emerge as pageant plays, psychological dramatizations, or corny ritual theater. It is a stage every ceremony and every people passes through. We should not become discouraged; it takes time to cultivate and develop a relationship with the Spirits of our Place.

Begin by taking the spirit world seriously, be respectful and courteous, make offerings, and make pilgrimages to local places where you feel the Spirit. Trust in the Spirit and know that there is a period of Grace where the spirit world embraces you as a mother does a lost child. Do not let other people tell you that you are doing it wrong, but be open to guidance along the path. One people's taboo is another people's medicine. We must learn to trust in the authenticity of our own experience.

Remember that the grace period does come to an end. As we become more adept at listening, we also must become more responsible; we must not simply play with such matters as invocations, offerings, or initiations. We need to take our role as modern day rite-makers seriously.

In the end, I still maintain that most of us will never meet a real shaman, let alone become one. But this should not discourage us from shamanizing to our hearts' content. By shamanizing we can enter into the process that initiates contact with the world of the sacred. The use of the drum and rattle, chanting, the understanding of the ceremonial function, and the seeking of vision through ordeals such as the vision quest, all activate the shamanic temperament, and no one culture holds the patent on these activities. But we must do it in our own way and in our true voices.

The immediate sense of alienation that permeates most modern people is contradicted by the message of the shaman who tells us "we are not alone, there are Spirits everywhere." I suspect that it is this deeply held open secret that attracts many people to things of a shamanic nature, for most people do feel there is more going on with the nature of reality than meets the eye, so to speak.

If shamanizing turns out to be more than just a passing fad, we may begin to see the emergence of true shamans in our culture. These will be people who are willing to dedicate their lives to cultivating a connection with the Spirit of Nature and to offering themselves and possibly their children to that world. We could in the next generation recapture the shamanic thread and weave it back into society in a new and exciting vision of reality. Then we might begin to have proper celebrations and initiations for our children and our own life passages. Wouldn't it be wonderful to find ourselves in the twenty-first century living in harmony and balance with the rest of creation?

·4·

DANCING THE DANCE OF THE GHOST

Between the mounds of mother breasts I lie comforted. But what shall I do when she is gone? Who shall comfort me?—EUGENE MONICK, Betwixt and Between

Anthropologists have long noted that whenever a culture reaches the breaking point, a movement frequently rises up out of the chaos, putting forth a vision of survival and renewal. These human attempts at warding off cultural extinction are known as *revitalization movements*. It was James Mooney's late-nineteenth-century governmental field monograph on American Indians, and the Ghost Dance of 1890, that brought the role of revitalization movements into a broader consciousness.

Near the end of the last century, as the last free Indians were being destroyed, a Piute Indian named Wavoka had a vision of a "ghost dance" in which the Indians would dance themselves back into power, bring back to life the spirit of their ancestors, and recreate the huge herds of buffalo. It quickly spread from tribe to tribe, renewing the hope and self-esteem of the Indian people. This revitalized energy of the Indians did not go unnoticed by the U.S. government, who realized they had to put a stop to it before they had a full scale uprising on their hands. The Ghost Dance came to a violent and heartbreaking end with the massacre of hundreds of men, women, and children by U.S. soldiers at Wounded Knee. It devastated the indigenous mind of North America, making total surrender the only possibility for survival. As a revitalization movement, the Ghost Dance was a complete failure.

The insights gained from Mooney's study of the Ghost Dance can be applied to our own history. Our ever changing relationship to the sacred exemplifies how culture has historically revitalized itself during perilous times. When the Romans destroyed the Temple and razed Jerusalem, it caused the Diaspora of the Jewish people. At the same time, the destruction of Jerusalem, and the collapsing Roman Empire set the stage for a very successful revitalization movement known as Christianity.

In the past, revitalization movements have occurred as the result of a vision given to a charismatic leader, who would then inspire the people to reformulate themselves into a broader vision, ensuring the continuation of the culture. Today, we are unlikely to see the arrival of such a visionary, or to have a single vision sweep among the people, gathering power as it spreads. Thankfully the world culture of today is too diverse and too large to follow one charismatic leader's vision of the future. Contemporary revitalization movements reflect an honoring of diversity and a respect for the complexity of the world by not wishing to homogenize all that is different into a monoculture. The revitalization of the modern world is happening through a number of different movements that spread by word of mouth, from state to state, and country to country. These movements rarely have a single leader or spokesperson and tend to be egalitarian in structure. Separately, none of them rank as a major revitalization movement, but together there is the possibility for synergy.

We no longer live in small, separate villages, but we do, however, acknowledge the global village. The technology of the Information Age, coupled with a worldwide media, provides access to the news of the day, whether you live in the middle of the Amazon or the streets of New York. It is through the media and medium of the Global Village that we gain access to the grass-roots movements that eventually shape international mores. The revitalization movements of the day take many shapes, and we do not have a shortage of movements trying to revitalize our lives. Some of them are sociopolitical, others are environmental or spiritual but they all dovetail together in their desire to create a compassionate and sustainable way of living on the Earth.

KWANZAA AND BLACK AMERICA

A large part of the challenge of creating a meaningful ceremonial life is how to actually go about establishing a new tradition. For the last thirty years, a new tradition has been born inside the American black community, one that is attempting to link the past and the present with a relevant vision of the future. *Kwanzaa* was conceived by Maulana Karenga, director of the African American Cultural Center at California State University, Long Beach. It is a nonreligious, seven-day ceremony that focuses on hearth, home, and heart. It is celebrated between December 26 and the first of January, and each family and community is encouraged to make the ceremony their own. The word *kwanzaa* comes from a Swahili word for "the first fruits of the harvest."

There are an estimated 18 million people of African origin who make up a worldwide Kwanzaa community. From Europe, to Asia, to the Americas, and Africa, the black community is finding a way to connect with their cultural roots. According to a Hallmark cards representative, an estimated 10 million people in the United States celebrate Kwanzaa, twice as many as in 1992.

According to Kwanzaa there are seven principles that make up the basic guidelines by which one should strive to live. The principles are called *Nguzo Saba*, and are as follows: *umoja* (unity), *kujichagulia* (self-determination), *ujima* (collective work and responsibility), *ujamma* (cooperative economics), *nia* (purpose), *kuumba* (creativity), *imani* (faith). The seven days of Kwanzaa is a time to reflect upon those principles and how each person is living life in accordance with them. It is also a time when restless spirits are brought into harmony with the principles and the community. The altar that is established in each home contains a cup or chalice that represents unity, seven candles for the seven days of the ceremony, ears of corn representing the children, fruit symbolizing the harvest, and gifts such as books and statues reflecting black culture.

The seven-day ceremony is a way for black families to affirm their African heritage and, for some, stress the need for black pride. Self-respect and respect for others is also stressed as a way of establishing a deeper understanding of cultural values. But the real strength of Kwanzaa has to do with cultivating collective and community values. As a revitalization movement Kwanzaa fits into the contemporary model of how cultures can be reinvigorated. It is not dogmatic; there is a symbolic framework that everyone can share, and within the framework there is a certain degree of freedom to adapt and modify the ceremony to one's particular needs. It does not have a single leader, and yet Kwanzaa has spread into a worldwide movement. The focus on hearth, home, and heart in context of the greater community also carries a way to collectively create a sustainable vision of the future.

THE JEWISH RENEWAL MOVEMENT

Inside traditional religions movements are afoot to make the ancient holy traditions speak more directly to the needs and hearts of contemporary people. In Arizona, Rabbi Ayla Grafstein and her *Ruach Hamidbar*—Spirit of the Desert—congregation have found a way to combine the old and the new. It is all part of a fast-growing and ultraliberal Jewish Renewal Movement.

Although many rabbis are hesitant to modify traditions that are thousands of years old, others feel that in order to keep pace with a rapidly changing world, the ancient traditions must find ways to make their essence relevant to the needs of modern day people. In the past, the Jewish God was known as God; in the Ruach Hamidbar congregation many different names might be called, including names of the Goddess and other feminine aspects of the divine. In preparation for Rosh Hashana and Yom Kippur, Grafstein has established a "Shofar Line." A telephone call allows people to hear a recorded daily meditation, followed by a blast from the ram's horn known as the Shofar. Members say that it helps them reflect daily on the deeds and misdeeds done through out the year. The holy days of Rosh Hashana mark a time of repentance. Yom Kippur is a solemn day that follows the ten days of repentance; it is a time of forgiveness and absolution from mistakes and folly.

This new ceremonial direction in Jewish practice is going beyond the written word into a more personal spirituality connecting people more deeply with all things held as holy in the Jewish tradition. The emphasis is on family issues and how to build and renew stronger ties in the community at large.

In traditional synagogues, during the High Holy Days rabbis change the mantle color on the altar to white as a symbol of purity. Grafstein and her congregation work with color, and colored cards represent the four cardinal directions blue, red, white and green. These colors also symbolize the individual, family and friends, other people, and the many life forms of the Earth. Members are asked to write upon the cards any misdeeds they may have committed during the last year against any of the groups. At sundown on Yom Kippur the cards are set on fire as a burnt offering to God, eliminating the misdeeds of the people and acquiring God's forgiveness. Grafstein incorporates into her ceremonies singing, dancing, drumming, and meditation. She feels that by actively participating together people experience their higher selves and have the opportunity to receive messages from God.

FEMININE SPIRITUALITY

Beginning in the 1960s the women's movement became the voice of women worldwide, demanding equal rights, equal pay for equal work, sexual freedom, educational reform, and legal and economic equality. It was not long before women activists realized the issues went much deeper than political reform; women themselves would have to reform their own concepts of who they were. This reformation began as small grass-roots circles of women getting together in order to raise consciousness and support one another in freeing themselves from thousands of years of enculturation. As women began to speak their truth to one another, a fire was lit in the soul of the Feminine, a fire that had been all but extinguished over the past few thousand years. Women began to reclaim their sense of inner power, and a new story began to emerge in terms of who we have been historically.

As a young woman who came of age during the sixties, I was swept up into the women's liberation movement. My involvement was not so much as a radical activist, but as a young woman from a small town who recognized oppression when she encountered it and supported equality, democracy, and freedom because it made good common sense. I remember my roommate in college being driven out of the veterinary program because, as her professor told her, "Find another major, we don't graduate women in this program." Experiences like this are radicalizing moments. We had both been raised to believe that we could accomplish anything we wanted in life. Education was the key and our innate capacity to succeed was the doorway. I was shocked by this professor and his lack of fairness, but back then there was no affirmative action, no one to file a complaint with, no due recourse of law, no Women's Studies. I had understood and supported the civil rights movement, but until then I did not understand my own minority standing, or the possibility of being discriminated against because I was born a woman.

In the seventies, I was in graduate school, and like many women from my era, I began to wonder how it was I was acquiring an education that seemed to ignore the role of women historically. I began to suspect that I was only being told half of the story of who we are as a people. Through archetypal psychology I discovered a pantheon of ancient Goddesses and a combination of history and myth indicating that women in the ancient world had status, power, wisdom, and ties to an even more ancient lineage known as matriarchy.

In graduate school, something possessed me, demanding that I begin to actively cultivate a relationship with some aspect of the Goddess. I had been aware of such books as Jane Harrison's *Prologomena to the Study of Greek Religion*; J. Bachhofen and his *Mothers, Myth, Religion and Mother Rite*; Robert Graves' *White Goddess*; and Erich Neumann's *The Great Mother*, and I began to view these works in a new light. They were no longer fairy tales or elegant scholarly works; they seemed to hold an important message for me personally.

I began a deep inner work to cultivate a living relationship with the Spirit of the Feminine. It felt crucial to my well-being to activate a positive self image in relationship to the Feminine. I sought out information concerning the Goddesses of past civilizations, as well as the many historical women who had contributed to the well-being of the world. I was elated by the wealth of information I found, and the power and contributions of a multitude of women, and at the same time I despaired my education for not teaching me any of this. I remember asking my faculty chairman in psychology: "Where are all the women?"

Like many women, I thought I was alone in my quest to find the women of our past. I gathered together with women friends and we shared the fruits of our research, had heady discussions, and imagined what a Goddess oriented culture would be like. We made maps of the different archetypes such as: Maiden, Mother, and Crone, and adopted patronesses as our guiding Goddess. We wanted to know which Goddess we were currently living out. We were amazed to see how each one of us appeared to be a distinct manifestation of some aspect of the Great Goddess. We explored what it was like to really live out aspects of the Goddesses such as Artemis (the young maiden), Aphrodite (goddess of love), Hera (goddess of hearth and home), Demeter (the Earth Mother), and Hecate or Kali (the dark aspect of the Feminine as the destroyer). We discovered hundreds of names for the Goddess in every culture and found ourselves spiritually connected to a divine Feminine principle.

In 1976 Merlin Stone published *When God Was A Woman*. This ground-breaking book made public what many women had already discovered: the Goddess and women had been revered in our past, and the art and artifacts of the world substantiated the reign and demise of the Goddess in culture after culture. Over the last twenty years many books have been written by women scholars like Maria Gimbutas, Phyllis Chesler, Starhawk, Charlene Spretnak, and Mary Daly. *The Dinner Party*, created by Judy Chicago was a transformational experience for everyone who passed by its table of offerings. Chicago's art piece was a series of plate settings laid out on three tiled tables which formed a triangle. Every place setting was unique: the place mats were embroidered, the dinner plates one of a kind—each representing a mythical or historical woman. Arranged in chronological order, *The Dinner Party* was a visual history of the Feminine from around the world. It nourished women deep into our souls.

The spiritual lives of women and the men who love them was and continues to be forever altered by the reintroduction of the feminine as sacred. Over the last twenty years, the Goddess has gone mainstream, while feminism has diminished in popularity. Feminine Spirituality is about wholeness, compassion, love, healthy sexuality, and the Earth. It encourages a balanced integration between mind, body, and spirit. The healing arts and ceremony are crucial elements in feminine spirituality. Women of all ages, in all parts of this country and Europe, now have working knowledge of the Goddess. Goddess pendants and earrings are now sold in mainstream catalogs as gift items, while modern reproductions of ancient Goddess figures continue to be a thriving business.

As for feminism, discounting its impact would be foolish. Many young women have reaped the benefits of feminist initiative and perhaps take for granted the hard-won rights and freedoms of the Women's Liberation Movement. Feminists recognize how the media has trivialized women's rights, and blame the long arm of the patriarchy for making feminism a dirty word. The reality is that feminism has changed the face of the world. I don't think it really matters if the next generation refuses to label themselves as feminists. What does matter is that women, young and old, are choosing to live their lives consciously, awake to the wonders and the horrors of the world, and with power and dignity. The momentum of women helping one another stay strong and free is more widespread and pervasive than ever before, even though fundamentalist regimes of every type continue to oppress and deny women basic human rights. The internal battle between spirituality and politics in the feminist community should be declared complete. Many women who have come round to a feminist viewpoint have done so as a result of their interest in the Goddess and ceremony. They may not identify themselves as feminist, but they think like feminists; they support one another in being whole, strong, and free; and when they vote, they vote like a feminist.

THE NEW AGE COMMUNITY

Utopian visions were not the invention of 1967 San Francisco's "Summer of Love" but have been the hope of mystics for centuries. Luminaries such as Meister Eckhart, Jacob Boehme, Emanuel Swedenborg, Hildegard von Bingen, and Julian of Norwich all strove to remind us of the true self in everything. Their common theme was one of radical transformation, with humanity achieving its highest potential. Thomas Mores' Renaissance work *Utopia* more than hinted at the possibility of an "earthly paradise," while centuries later George Bernard Shaw, the wittiest liberal of his time, funded a journal whose focus was on the development of a social utopia. The journal appeared in 1906 in London and was called *The New Age*. It was the success of the Enlightenment, the Industrial Revolution, and Darwin's theory of evolution that sparked a slow revolution in the visionary minds of such people as Henry Thoreau, Ralph Waldo Emerson, Margaret Fuller, Emily Dickinson, John Muir, G.I. Gurdjieff, Alice Bailey, Annie Besant, and Madame Blavatsky. They all sensed a terrible, soul-numbing, and life-threatening impulse emerging out of the rational, mechanistic, intellectualism of the day.

Theosophist Annie Besant had a vision: In the 1930s, she foresaw that by the early 1970s there would be a movement back to the land, a need for collective living, new styles of education, and practical ideas of self sufficiency. She purchased a large tract of land in the Ojai valley of California and made provisions for that land to be available when the time came. In the late 1970s, Besant's land became the home for the Ojai Foundation, a nonprofit organization committed to educational reform, eco-psychology, shamanism, and a meeting ground for spiritual teachers.

At the same time, theosophist Alice Bailey, in her *Treatise on White Magic*, predicted the "dawning of the age of Aquarius," while Mme.

Blavatsky, founder of the Theosophical Society, had a vision of the "cere-monial Purple Ray." In Blavatsky's vision, the children of the west coast of America would become the "new Seventh Root Race who would guide humanity into the light." But it was Aldous Huxley, author of *Brave New World*, *Doors of Perception*, and *Island* who played the most pivotal role in inspiring those young seekers, baby boomers, forever after known as the "Sixties generation."

Huxley was a man well ahead of his time. He was a conscientious objector to both world wars and was part of an international network of artists, scientists, and intellectuals who had caught a glimmer of the hope and despair that surrounded humanity. His interests and pursuits included decentralization of government, consciousness research, ecology, paranor-mal studies, alternative healing, and altered states of awareness, including those induced by psychedelic substances. Huxley turned a generation on with his books, while at the same time he cautioned Timothy Leary to act slowly in promoting LSD. He advised Leary to first administer it to the intelligentsia and artists of the day, and then allow it to trickle down towards the masses.

Perhaps Huxley's most radical moment came at his death. While lying on his death bed, he asked his wife Laura to administer LSD (a then legal substance that had widespread therapeutic use) to him. A few hours later he asked for more LSD and died as she read the *Tibetan Book of the Dead* to him. The date was November 22, 1963. As Huxley died, so ended "Camelot," for president John F. Kennedy had just been assassinated.

For the next ten years, the Viet Nam war dominated the news, civil rights and the free speech movements spread across the land, and a world-wide environmental movement was launched by Rachel Carson's book *Silent Spring*. The arrival of the birth control pill and women's liberation heralded a time of sexual freedom, and in 1967 the Summer of Love flow-ered in San Francisco. The children conceived out of World War II, dis-covering that everything they knew was wrong, began to restructure their lives, their relationships, and their politics. They experienced America at the end of the police club and tear gas canister, and saw Richard Nixon leave office in disgrace.

For the next twenty-five years the Baby Boom generation worked their way back into the mainstream. They returned to college, cut their hair, married, raised children, and entered middle age. Even so, many managed to hold onto a vision of a better world. The idealism sparked in the sixties would not die easily. As the Summer of Love came and went, it is clear that the "revolution" did not happen, at least not as anticipated—but as time goes on, the values, tastes, and psychic needs of the '60s have permeated the culture at large.

What began as alternative thinking and living became mainstream. Humanistic psychology, the Esalen Institute, biofeedback, Eastern mysticism, yoga, and consciousness raising became major businesses. It was Blavatsky who first introduced Buddhism to the West, and Besant and Bailey who were Krishnamurti's "spiritual mothers." Therapies like EST, scientology, gestalt, rolfing, and support groups flourished across America. Massage therapies and holistic healing techniques from acupuncture to crystals also found a ready market. The old arts of astrology, tarot, and psychic readings went through a major revival. People also turned to more refined eating styles requiring organic food, vitamins, and vegetarianism; health food is a multimillion dollar industry. The human growth industry, "how-to books," and tapes promoting consciousness of all kinds are also big business and best sellers. The economics alone of what was spawned in the sixties should be enough to illustrate the success of the New Age.

As a revitalization movement, the New Age has the potential for great power. It has also cultivated extreme narcissism. Beaten by the political machinery of the Old Guard, many people from the sixties have avoided the political arena. It is as if personal human growth became a pacifier, a means to avoid the larger issues of human survival. The New Age movement could be accused of being guilty of practicing transcendental self-importance and of placing too much importance in past lives and not enough importance on the well-being of future generations.

As a revitalizing force it cannot be discounted, despite bad press. The fundamental impulse of the New Age still beats strong, and the manner in which it has unintentionally infiltrated religion, education, the health industry, diet, agriculture, and our relationship to the natural world speaks to a force that flows strong.

CREATION SPIRITUALITY

Creation Spirituality has been popularized in North America by Matthew Fox. A Dominican priest, theologian, and educator, Fox was silenced for a year in 1988 by pressure from the Vatican. Here we see the potential for a charismatic, visionary leader to create a successful revitalization movement. But in keeping with the times, Fox is not interested in becoming a new Messiah. Instead he empowers others to honor their own mystical nature. He guides us back again and again to our own innate creativity in celebrating life and joining Christian mysticism with contemporary struggles for social justice, ecology, and a feminine integration of the divine.

Fox states in his book of the same title that Creation Spirituality is both old and new. It is an ancient tradition handed down to us from our ancestors in the communion of mystical saints. It is new, in that it makes the old traditions come alive through awakening a sense of moral outrage at the state of our relationship to all of life. It has gained widespread popularity among all people who are touched by the suffering and exploitation of other people or other life forms, including political activists, ecumenists, native peoples, feminists, and scientists.

Fox believes that it is important to name the four paths of creation spirituality, for they tell us what really matters. It also allows people to share a common language and avoid getting stuck in any one path.

Path One, the *Via Positiva*, encourages the awe and wonder that a child has for the world. As adults, maintaining our sense of delight with the natural world keeps us in touch with "all of our relations." It means maintaining a constant flow of love with all creation.

Path Two, the *Via Negativa*, takes us into the depths. Letting go and letting be are part of our sacred journey into ourselves. It means getting in touch with those things that drive us to addictions and despair. The "dark night of the soul" is the realm of the shadow, the information that we do not want to know about, the place where knowledge can cause us pain and anger. It goes beyond numbing out to the unsavory sides of life and death, politics and oppression. The *Via Negativa* requires that we acknowledge our grief over the suffering of the world.

The third path, the *Via Creativa*, urges us to give birth to beauty. It is through placing our imagination and creativity in the service of compassion that we make real contributions to the world. He quotes Ernsto Cardenal, the former cultural minister of Nicaragua as saying "people do not consume culture, they create it." Fox goes on to say that "A culture is

an environment where creativity is honored as a great value, where it happens around and through people." Part of our obligation towards life is to
share in its creation through acts of love.

The fourth path, the *Via Transformativa*, is about cultivating compassion on a broad scale. To experience our widespread connectedness, to see
our long history, our relationship to the ancestors and all of creation,
requires us to become fully mature. It means that all of our actions and the
fruit of our lives should be in harmony with our state of mutual interdependence. It is the place where we can take on a prophetic role. The nature of
the prophet interferes with the status quo and with events that seem
inevitable or beyond our individual control. It is not about self-righteous-
ness, but about coming into equilibrium with one another, the Earth, and
the universal life force. It is getting in step with the great cosmic dance.

In his *Creation Spirituality*, Fox distinguishes liberation theology as
not a liberation *from*, but a liberation *to*. He gives many examples such as
liberation from the secular into the sacred, from waste into conservation
and recycling, from fear into trust, from institutionalized religion into a living mysticism, from dead ritual to living ceremony. He invites people to
leave behind all those things that are oppressing them and drink deeply of
true freedom.

Creation spirituality, or liberation theology, as it is known in South
America, has gained widespread acceptance by thinking Christians. It connects the Christian world with its true roots. It encourages people to live
out of their own mystical experiences. Fox reminds us that thinking about
God is not the same as experiencing God. People participate in the company of saints through themselves, not through sterile forms. Religion can
be revitalized once the Spirit is allowed to flow free. If we give ourselves
permission to liberate the mystic within, and gather together with other
unashamed mystics to worship, sing praises, and give thanks through joyful
ceremony, our creative acts of compassion could bring about a living transformational Christianity.

DOWN TO EARTH ECOLOGICAL MOVEMENTS

All of the revitalization movements described so far have been primarily of a spiritual nature. The recent emergence of worldwide environ-

mental movements elicit from people a caring for other life forms and a desire to maintain and sustain a rich natural environment. Once again, animals play a particularly important role—both literally and symbolically—in soliciting people's attention. The World Wildlife Fund was, after all, the premier environmental organization. The plight of the elephant, rhinoceros, tiger, and gorilla were the first animals to touch the world with the great loss of what extinction means.

Decades later, Greenpeace would astonish the world as members placed themselves between Russian whaling ships and whales. The response of the world's people to the plight of whales and dolphins has resulted in their protection and also in their recognition as fellow sentient creatures. The destruction of the Amazon and the redwoods of California has rallied those who care about our planet. The average person who finds themselves supporting Greenpeace, the Sierra Club, or the World Wildlife Fund may or may not consider themselves to be an environmentalist, but they are apparently touched by the beauty and sacredness of creation. A recent worldwide Gallup poll asked people if they would accept a reduction in lifestyle in order to save their environment. The overwhelming response was yes, even in impoverished countries like India and China. The global impulse to protect and connect with Nature, whether through spirituality or environmental activism should not be overlooked as a revitalizing force.

Permaculture is a practical system for creating sustainable human environments. The founder of Permaculture is Tasmanian-born Bill Mollison. Mollison grew up living and working in nature and is one the few real natural historians of our time. After working as a fisherman, hunter, and logger, he began to notice a massive deterioration of the natural world. He had not realized until then that he had developed a love of Nature, and wished to dedicate his life to creating a system that would focus on sustainability rather than extinction. In 1974 he coined the term Permaculture. It began with designing sustainable agricultural systems based on multi-crop, species-rich environments, and then grew into including legal and financial strategies for land conservation, business structures, and regional banking systems. It is a whole system encompassing the human and natural world, causing people to realize that we too are part of the natural world. It is a philosophy of working with Nature rather than against Nature.

Mollison states: "I think harmony with Nature is possible only if we abandon the idea of superiority over the natural world. Levi Strauss said that our profound error is that we have always looked upon ourselves as 'masters of creation,' in the sense of being above it. We are not superior to other life-forms; all living things are an expression of Life. If we could see that truth, we would see that everything we do to other life-forms we also do to ourselves."

Permaculture is a hands-on system for restoring the natural balance of the world. It can be done in our homes, our backyards, our community and our country, and is currently practiced in over seventy countries throughout the world. It is a quiet revolution, coming out of the needs and necessities of our time. As a system, it has by-passed governmental agencies; in fact, Mollison says, "Don't bother taking over governments, take over the function of government, make yourself and your community self-reliant."

Mollison sees ethics as moral beliefs and actions that impact our survival on planet Earth. The ethics of permaculture are care of the Earth, and care for all living and nonliving things. It implies right livelihood. Care of the Earth means care of people and the meeting of their basic needs. When our basic needs are met then we can share time and resources with others, helping them to achieve comfort in meeting their basic needs. The basic life ethic of Permaculture recognizes the intrinsic worth of every living thing. Everything has value in and of itself. Cooperation, not competition, is the key.

In the two-week design course that certifies people to teach Permaculture, Mollison and his 15,000 graduates teach people how to pattern think, how to see the relationship of one thing to another, and how to design whole systems that model themselves on Nature. It is brilliant, simple, and effective. After completing the certification course one is left with the feeling of being extremely stupid for not having thought of it one's self, it makes such good common sense. Mollison has been most diligent in avoiding setting himself up as a guru, and in making sure that Permaculture not be turned into a bureaucratic organization. He has patented the name Permaculture, and then gives it away to every graduate. The success of Permaculture is in the living example it presents to the community at large. When neighbors see a piece of land transformed from a wasteland into a thriving beautiful garden, they naturally become curious.

Part of the focus of Permaculture is how to live together in villages or communities. In terms of the social structure, Mollison again goes for diversity, diversity in crops, diversity in thinking, and diversity among people. Only then does life become really rich. Interestingly enough, he does not believe in consensus decision making. He feels this gives too much power to the nay sayer, and that uncooperative people can control and block an otherwise healthy community. He follows indigenous peoples' one rule for living: Never do anything that will endanger the life of the tribe. In other words do not foul your water, or poison your land, or injure, or molest your friends, family, or neighbors. The punishment is banishment from the community.

Permaculture requires a knowledgeable and sane sense of place. It asks us to think about the long-term consequences of our actions. In terms of the natural world it emphasizes sustainable small-scale, energy-efficient practices. It uses Nature as a model and from there goes about restoring damaged environments including families, villages, the landscape, and the economy. Permaculture encourages polycultural diversity in relationship to the environment and the social system and establishes concrete ways for people to become self-reliant while promoting community responsibility. I cannot begin to present Permaculture in its complexity, but encourage anyone who has an interest in the environment, healthy life styles, or a desire for supportive community to seek it out. It goes far beyond abstract idealism, into a practical, hands-on creation of a sustainable world.

REVITALIZING OUR LIVES

When we look closely at these attempts at revitalizing our world, it becomes obvious that all of them share many ideas and concerns in common. The person involved in any one movement is likely to be interested or involved in a number of others. Care for the family, the community, and the Earth is a common theme. The spiritual, psychological, and political dimensions of these movements cause us to move beyond the personal and become actively engaged with the problems facing the world. A woman who becomes interested in the Goddess eventually becomes interested in Gaia and the environment. Ceremonies that connect us into the spirit of our ancestors or the well-being of future generations causes us to question living only for the moment. If we care about our health, we prefer organic food, and we probably make some attempt at recycling. If we recycle, we become aware of finite resources and, becoming aware of resources, we question the destruction of Amazonia.

The anthropology of the moment must take into account the developments of the last one hundred years, especially the archeological studies that have brought forth new visions of our past such as the discovery of the Paleolithic caves, the reemergence of Goddess culture, and the thousand-year reign of peace in ancient Crete. All these are part of the synchronicity of the moment. The revisioning of peaceful cultures, the role of Jungian psychology in awakening us to mythology, and the current interest in all things of a shamanistic nature indicates we are in the process of reforming our imaginations. All of these things cause us to revise who we have been and who we might become.

Underlying all of this is a sense of some spiritual quality working through all of these diverse groups and trains of thought. This respiriting force is calling us to something within the ever-present, ever-new, and ever-ancient, in order to bring it forth into the outer world. This new paradigm is actually the oldest of paradigms, known as the Perennial Philosophy, which sees the world as alive, and comes as light, sound, form, and a resonant field. The new paradigm is an appearance, a reforming of the imagination, in response to a world that has become too concrete. All of the current movements towards revitalization are leading to a revelation that has not yet occurred.

The difficulty with the scientific paradigm is not about knowledge, but about seeing things in disparate parts. Science is an indirect knowing that knows only through breaking things down into separate pieces. As ordinary people we "know" certain truths with our whole being, we know in ourselves; it is innate, not outside ourselves. These new forms of revitalization movements are a way to "know together."

Likewise, fundamentalism differs radically from revitalization movements. Fundamentalists of all persuasions, Christian, Jewish, Islamic, and scientific, rely upon the literal truth of the written word of their holy texts or technical journals. Unlike revitalization movements, which look toward the future, fundamentalism looks toward the past.

What has happened in the last twenty-five years goes beyond mere consciousness raising. It has not been linear, and it has not been a case of the follow-the-leader. The grass-roots networking that has been taking place is beginning to bear fruit. Where people thought they were alone in their concerns and efforts to live more meaningful lives, they now find they stand in the company of many others. There is great power in this type of movement, and a great challenge to stave off the cynicism of those who say nothing can be done to save the world. The strength of this confluence of awareness is that no one is in charge, except each and every one of us.

When the Berlin Wall fell and Communist Europe collapsed, not a single statesman could have predicted it a week before it happened. Undeniably, a radical moment of change took place, yet no one heroic person was in charge. Perturbations in the field of consciousness are like pebbles being dropped into a still pond—the circles eventually reach the entire shore.

·5·

AWAKENING THE SACRED WITHIN

> *Creative mythology springs not, like theology, from the dicta of authority,*
> *but from the insights, sentiments, thoughts, and visions of an adequate indi-*
> *vidual loyal to his own experience of value.*—JOSEPH CAMPBELL,
> Myths We Live By

The very heart of this book is embedded in the sacred, what it is, how its loss has affected us, and how we might recapture it through ceremonial practice. This chapter will guide us into the sacred by looking at how a ceremony is structured and what tools are useful for its creation. It is essential for us to understand that the creation of ceremonies, rites of passages, and seasonal events are more than thera-peutic moments.

IN WHOSE LIGHT?

Awakening the sacred requires us to look inward into the core of our spiritual nature. Twelve years ago I was fortunate enough to be part of a month-long retreat focusing on shamanistic practices from around the world. It was a truly international gathering. Teachers included a Korean Zen master, a Tibetan Rimpoche priest, an African witch doctor, Native Americans, an Aboriginal elder, and a number of Western intellectuals who recognized the value of shamanistic work. These included radical psy-chiatrist R.D. Laing, British anthropologist Francis Huxley, scientist Rupert Sheldrake, mind explorer Terrence McKenna, rune expert Ralph Blum, and chaos mathematician Ralph Abraham.

All together, with participants and teachers, we were 100 strong.

Very soon the event seem to collapse into a chaos that thrilled some and terrified others. Early on, Francis Huxley began asking various members of the faculty an important question. "In whose light do you do what you do?" The responses surprisingly varied in the fact that everyone on the faculty, was in a sense, viewed as a spiritual teacher. For some the question provoked silence as they considered their life in this context. Others replied, "Well, my own." More heart warming were the number of people who answered: Christ, the Earth Mother, Kuan Yin, Sarasvati, Buddha, my grandmother, all of my ancestors, or the beings of the future.

It is an important question that each one of us should answer before we attempt to guide others into the sacred. This question confronts the level of comfort or discomfort each of us might feel in regard to our own spirituality, for in entering into a ceremony it is essential that we be clear about who we are serving.

The question also provokes us to see our lives in a larger context, one in which the spirit is a living presence. Immediately we see that the spirit is a guiding and protecting light. Our relationship with this light-spirit is something that requires cultivation in the way that any friendship requires time, acknowledgment, and conversation. So if you have not already asked yourself this question please do so. Like many of the people who have answered this question over the years you may be very clear about who you serve. Others may need to think long and hard about this question, and then seek out a guiding light in which to operate.

In answering this question each of us sets the stage of our life to be acted out in conjunction with the divine. As a person interested in ceremony, you should let this question guide you into creating a ceremony for yourself and your guiding spirit. If you have a clear image of whose light you live under perhaps you already have an altar, photograph, artifact, statue, or symbol of your guiding light. If not take the time to create such a space and to consciously connect to this God-force in your life. Choose a time when you will have privacy. You may want to begin by setting up a special place in your room to erect an altar. Make it beautiful! A special piece of hand-woven fabric is a good beginning. Your altar will be a gathering place for objects that are precious to you, objects such as photographs of loved ones, a statue of a particular deity, candles, feathers, seashells, crystals, plants, or simply small bowls that contain earth and water to connect you to nature.

Let your altar creation be your first ceremony, one with a beginning, a middle, and an end. Light a candle and burn some incense. Seat yourself in front of your altar, take a few minutes to center yourself by closing your eyes, and breathe deeply and regularly. Reflect upon what you are doing as you invite the sacred into your life. This is an opportunity to formally place yourself in the service of the greater good. You may want to dance, sing, move, and speak your thoughts out loud. Be on notice though, the conscious act of doing this will change your life. The honoring of your spiritual nature is the first step towards becoming a rite-builder.

In my travels as I teach, it is always refreshing to discover the depth of people's spiritual nature and their hunger for the spiritual. What surprises me, though, is how alone people often feel in acknowledging this connection. It's as if the modern world has made us feel embarrassed by our experiences of the Spirit. To create ceremonies in our lives, family, and community, there is simply no room for this embarrassment. We need to feel at ease with our spiritual nature and how we may wish to share that with others. I know this from my own experience, for I was unwillingly led to ceremony.

In the mid-1970s I was in graduate school in California studying cognitive psychology and working as a teaching assistant—teaching statistics, computer applications, research and design methodology, and personality theory. Early one morning I was startled awake by a dream. In the dream I found myself entering a cave where I found an old crone who pointed her gnarled finger at me and commanded, "Teach ritual!" I could not believe this. I did not *want* to believe it. It was too embarrassing! I could not teach ritual, I did not even know anything about it, it was too corny, and just plain weird. What about my credibility?

At least I knew enough to go to my faculty advisor and tell him the dream. He immediately said, "You must do this." As the saying goes you always teach what you need to know. The very next semester I was winging my way through a graduate level course entitled "Ritual and the Imaginal Process," and my entire life changed. I repeat this story because it was such a pivotal moment in my life. I chose to follow the dictate of my dream rather than continue on my course into academia. But before that semester began I found myself leading my first ceremony in earnest.

The telephone rang and it was the police asking me if I could come identify a body. My best friend and roommate, Kim, had died. Her car had skidded out of control and crashed into a redwood tree. She died instantly of a broken neck. Ironically, Kim had always wanted to be buried under a redwood tree. I found myself holding a vigil over her body until her grief-stricken family arrived three days later. Not knowing what to do, I thought about a class on Buddhism Kim and I had recently completed. Kim had loved that class, so a mutual friend and I visited her each day at the morgue and read the Tibetan *Book of the Dead* to her. Later I realized how devastated her family was, for they had her cremated and asked me if I would take her ashes and do something with them—after they were gone. I can now see that I was being initiated into ceremonial life, and I was to take my role seriously.

Kim and I had met while majoring in environmental studies. She was a brilliant and beautiful redhead who cared deeply for Nature. Together we worked on two wonderful projects, one in which we studied the predation of coyotes on the local sheep population of Sonoma County, and another in which we wrote an environmental impact report on the relationship of erosion and wild Russian boars in a nearby state park. The coyote study revealed that about eighty percent of sheep kills in the county were from dogs and that the county had $3,000 worth of sheep kills a year yet spent $15,000 on baiting and killing coyotes, resulting in a $12,000 overkill. In the state park forest officials had considered killing the boars because of the erosion damage caused by their rooting. To our amusement this study showed that the Park Service actually caused more damage and erosion problems by cutting roads improperly than the boars, and that it would be more advantageous for the park to eliminate the Park Service than the boars. Memories of being in Nature with Kim, and the absurd truths of our conclusions came flooding back.

The first day she was dead, as I stood over her, I felt her confusion and her natural good humor as she discovered that she could no longer return to her body. The second day, as we read the *Book of the Dead*, her acceptance of her state was tangible in the room. On the third day my friend and I both experienced her returning from somewhere else to be present for the reading. And then there was the cardboard box that contained Kim's remains.

The ceremony I created was simple. On a glorious sunny morning, friends gathered and we hiked into the redwood forest to one of her favorite places. It was a trail many of us had hiked with Kim. The silent walk was beautiful, with shafts of light beaming down and the pungent aroma of the warm forest floor greeting our senses. We hiked along a stream, past a waterfall, and up a canyon to a pristine meadow blooming with wildflowers. There we lit incense, formed a circle and held a moment of silence, while a friend dug a hole under a redwood tree. I passed a ball of yarn around the circle and we each tied the yarn to our wrist as we passed the ball on until we had a circle of yarn. This was our connection to Kim. Each person then took turns telling a story about Kim, the mood changing from laughter to tears and back again. When all had spoken we placed her ashes in the hole and, untangling ourselves from the yarn, we placed it on top of the ashes to represent our connection and our gift of letting her go. I said a spontaneous and simple prayer for the joy she brought us and the time we shared and wished her God speed on her journey. We took turns replacing the dirt and when we were finished we drummed, rattled, chanted and sang. Later we sat in the meadow, feasted, and told "Kim stories."

In the sixteen years since Kim's death many changes have appeared, and many people across the land have taken part in self-generated ceremonies that honor life passages. We are learning how to overcome our awkwardness and how to speak from our hearts without shame about our spiritual nature. As we move toward initiating ceremony into our lives it becomes clear that ceremony, rites of passage, and true initiations are more than simple symbolic acts designed to further some psychotherapeutic process. They are a gateway into the deep connection of universal kinship with the Spirit.

WHERE DO WE BEGIN?

People's interest in ceremony varies from the academic to the magical. For some it is difficult to imagine ever wanting to lead one, though they may enjoy participating. Others, like educators or therapists, would like to know how to work a bit of ceremony into their jobs, or some would like to introduce it into their families or circle of friends; a few receive it as a calling and devote their life to it. All of these ways are wonderful for it implies that meaningful ceremony is once again finding its way into our lives. Small bookstores often become central headquarters for local ceremonial events. They now sell smudge sticks (bundles of sage or cedar) and other ceremonial items such as drums, rattles, and feathers. The Western world is waking up to the need for true rites of passage and reclaiming the ancient heritage that is ours as people of the Earth. But where do we begin? We begin by understanding what the cross-culture skeletal components of ceremony are and by clarifying our intention. The answer to the question "In whose light?" serves as the ground from which a sacred way of being grows.

My own understanding of the structural form of ceremony was clarified after meeting social anthropologist Virginia Hine through my work at Rites of Passage, a non-profit organization specializing in vision questing. In the last years of her life Virginia was working on a manuscript about "self-generated ceremony," as she called it. Much of what follows in this chapter comes from her work and research. Her mapping of this territory is concise and to the point, and once grasped, the elements of creating ceremony will come together easily for those wanting to become ceremonialists.

Obviously ceremonies were being created by people, for people, long before scholars provided their technical expertise. For those who have an interest in the cross-cultural view of ceremony I suggest you read the works of such people as Mircea Eliade, Arnold Van Gennep, Victor Turner, Joseph Campbell, and Franz Boas. Here we will explore what has been distilled from the works of these scholars.

There are three basic types of ceremony. Those that mark or facilitate a major life transition such as birth, puberty, marriage, divorce, or death. These are known as rites of passage.

Ceremonies are also performed for the primary purpose of healing. This healing can be for an individual, a family, or an entire community, and it can be physical, mental, emotional, or spiritual.

Then there are ceremonies whose primary purpose is to reinforce social cohesion. These include solstice, equinox, full moon celebrations, and the traditional holy days. Virginia Hine has called these events "rites of intensification," for they increase group harmony and aid in resolving conflicts among people.

Ceremonies are always done with a purpose in mind. Here are some useful questions and ideas that should be explored by anyone planning a ceremony.

1.   *What is the intention of this ceremony?* Be specific. Is it a rite of passage, a healing ceremony, or a community celebration? Who will it serve? What do we wish to achieve? How can we hold the focus of the intention?

2. *How do we create a beginning, middle, and end to the ceremony?* These elements are crucial to any powerful ceremonial event. It is important to consider what kind of energy we might be releasing as we go along. If it is celebratory, how do we keep it from dissolving into a party with no closure and people drifting off into the night? If it is healing, how do we know when to stop? Will one person be leading the entire event, or will different people take charge of the various movements? If a number of people will be leading the ceremony let the participants know who is who so they are not surprised by someone suddenly coming forth. I have found it useful when planning a ceremony to imagine the entire event as a well-choreographed piece of music. Does it begin with a bang and then ease itself down into a meditative state or start off slow and quiet and crescendo in the middle? Plan for a definite ending. Remember closure is the most important aspect of any ceremony.

3. *How do we bring the symbolic into the event?* Joseph Campbell believed that the power of symbol "lies not in what meets the eye, but in what dilates the heart." Human beings are unique in their capacity to symbolize. Certain shapes, colors, numbers, and forms work deep within the psyche. But a symbol is more than an object that represents something else. Virginia Hine said: "Symbols connect the definable with the indefinable, the manifest with the unmanifest, the microcosm with the macrocosm. They point beyond what they represent." The symbolic can be introduced into ceremony in a number of ways. The colors red, white, black, and yellow are found throughout the world as symbolizing the four directions, the four races, and are also the most commonly found clays and ocher paints. Circles, triangles, sun and moon shapes, and the cross are also universal symbols used by all peoples. Incorporating the four elements of fire, earth, air, and water is a common theme. Participants can be also be asked to bring an object that symbolizes themselves at this moment. This is a wonderful way to introduce symbol, because most people take this task quite seriously.

In setting up the space for the ceremony, a threshold can be made that people pass through upon entering or leaving, or an altar constructed with objects that are evocative of the intention of the ceremony. In the end what is most important is how the symbolic items presented affect those participating in the ceremony, whether or not they have ancient historical significance. For those interested in understanding the interpretation of symbols, refer to J.E. Cirlot's *A Dictionary of Symbols.*

4. *Form or free form?* Once you have an idea of what the general flow of the event will be—say starting off in silence, processing into the space (be it a room or meadow), a time for individual sharing, and an ending with singing and dancing—it is important to figure out how much formality or informality there will be.

    Total spontaneity is rarely effective, although spontaneous acts add life to ceremony. It is important to try and blend these two ingredients—the formal and the spontaneous—into the ceremonial recipe you are creating. If it is a group of people who are creating the ceremony, agree ahead of time on who will say what and when, know what your cues will be. Make use of drums, bells, or chimes to mark the transitional moments from one mood to another. The way these acts are ordered is symbolic in itself. Avoid having the participants feeling confused about what they should be doing next by keeping things flowing. Don't be embarrassed to speak out and say "At this time we invite people to speak or move... "

5. *How do we choose the time and space to hold the ceremony?* In ancient cultures the timing of major ceremonies was largely determined by tradition, which encompassed seasonal cycles and social requirements. Even today important events like a marriage are often timed to coincide with a full moon, solstice, or holiday. It seems very natural that people try to enhance important moments in their lives by choosing auspicious dates. Choose your time thoughtfully. Solstice ceremonies should be held on the solstice, not on the weekend before, even if it is more convenient.

    Choosing the space is equally important. Should it be outside or indoors? Can the space accommodate everything and everyone? Not all ceremonies are large public events. Quite often they are intimate moments between a family or a couple, perhaps a blending of a family or puberty rite for a shy teenager. Choose carefully an appropriate time and who will be present. If it is to be in the living room or in the garden find a way to transform the space so it is no longer ordinary. Light candles, move furniture so people can sit in a circle, burn incense, drape fabrics about, and invite people to dress up. Make it beautiful so people know immediately that something extraordinary is about to happen.

THE STRUCTURE OF CEREMONY

Once the five preceding questions have been addressed and a general feeling for the ceremony has been formulated, it is time to look more deeply into the structure of the ceremony. The most powerful ceremonies move beyond pageantry into transformation. Historically a true rite of passage confers a change in status upon the individual. A child enters the ceremony, a young woman or man emerges. The remaining chapters will provide numerous examples of how people have found their way through the challenges of life by relying on ceremony. For the moment, however, let us look more closely at what historically has held ceremony together.

Traditionally, ceremony has three internal aspects to it. This threefold pattern has been called: severance, transition, and incorporation. The severance phase is the moment when the past is left behind; it is a separation or turning away from life as it has been known—a mini-death. This part of the ceremony can be either real or symbolic. In a marriage ceremony for instance, the couple generally leaves their parental homes to begin a new life of their own. The bride enters the church on the arm of her father and leaves on the arm of her husband. The severance phase can also be purely symbolic in ceremonies where people process from one area to another, perhaps passing through an arbor or gateway that marks the entrance into the ceremonial space.

The transition phase is the liminal or threshold experience, where transformation, change, renewal, and shift in status takes place. This is generally the main body of the ceremony. In the case of a marriage, this is the exchanging of vows, the public enactment, the change of status from being single to being married. This phase contains the opportunity for a death and rebirth, renewed spiritual connection, and a guiding vision of the future.

The final phase is the incorporation, or re-incorporation, for it is the reunion, the turning back into ordinary life. It is the recrossing of the gateway, and it is the most important phase of any rite of passage. In this phase the initiate returns to the world and to the community but with a new status and awareness. As the Lakota Indian Black Elk stated, one's vision must be performed on Earth for the people to see in order for it to have real power. The initiate must now live his or her life with new responsibilities and new relationships. This is true of a marriage and also in all puberty rites. In fact, in order for puberty rites to be effective, the community of family and friends must really recognize the change in status and welcome the young man or woman into the circle of adults. What makes puberty rites so powerful in indigenous cultures is that they are real. The young person emerges as an adult with all of the freedoms and responsibilities that adulthood carries. If the community refuses to acknowledge this change in status the rite is meaningless. There will be more on this topic in the chapter that concerns itself with puberty rites.

When planning a ceremony it is not an imperative that every ceremony clearly have the three phases of severance, transition, and incorporation consciously built into it. Some rites of passage naturally focus on one aspect or another, puberty rites mark transitions, marriages emphasize incorporation, and death is an exercise in severance. The cyclic nature of life, like ceremony, has a beginning, middle, and an end. Birth, transformation, death, and the idea of the eternal return is part of the human psyche, just as the seasonal cycles are part of life on Earth. In our own lives we know these rhythms, rebirths, awakenings, mini-deaths, and chaos that often appear as we approach an ending and a new beginning. We can trust in the archetypal nature of reality that this threefold process will find its way into our rite building.

CEREMONIAL TOOLS

The following ceremonial elements are meant to inspire and encourage you to be creative. Some ceremonies might use a number of these components, others only one or two. Although this is a comprehensive list you are invited to come up with additional tools of your own.

Invocation
The calling in of a source of energy, spirit, or particular deity is a way of acknowledging "In whose light do we do what we do?" It focuses the awareness of the group on a common source of power. For some it may be in the name of the Father, Son, and the Holy Ghost. Others may call in the

various names of the Goddess, the four directions, the Sky Father, and Earth Mother. The invocation can also be in the name of a deceased loved one, a grandmother or grandfather, or simply in the name of the family who has gathered together.

Incense

Ceremony should draw in as many of the senses as possible. The sense of smell is our most powerful source of remembering. The burning of traditional incense resins or plants such as frankincense, sage, cedar, myrrh, copal, and sweet grass alerts the mind that we are crossing a threshold into ceremonial space. The lighting, burning, and smoke coming from incense or fire is in itself a rite of purification. Many cultures believe that the smoke cleanses those present and carries their hopes and dreams skyward to the Great Mystery. The burning of a particular resin at the beginning or end of a ceremony is a signal to everyone present and is especially powerful if used at every gathering.

Praying and Sharing

Prayer is common to every tradition and is a beautiful element in any ceremony. Vocalized prayer is a way of focusing intention. Sometimes people write their own prayers or bring in poetry or lyrics to songs that are shared as a prayer. Often a ceremony has a planned time in which people can pray spontaneously, speaking from the heart if they are moved to do so.

Sharing around the circle is a common occurrence at many events. Often an object is passed around the circle. This can be many things: a rock, feather, crystal, statue, or photograph. It is passed and held while speaking and then passed on to the next person. In sharing circles it is not necessary to speak when the object comes around and sometimes just sitting in silence is a relief. A word of caution about this form: If you are planning on having a sharing circle as part of a ceremony please be aware of how many people will be present. If there are fifteen people and each person speaks for five minutes, that will be one hour and fifteen minutes. I have been in ceremonies such as these where the sharing has gone on for two or three hours, and I must say I always find it cruel and inconsiderate of the organizers. You can feel the energy seeping out of the room as people get restless and bored. Asking people to keep it brief does not seem to work either, for everyone wants their chance. An alternative in groups with over fifteen people is to ask everyone around the circle to share a word or simple phrase that encapsulates where they are at the moment or how they feel about what has taken place. This can be done in few minutes, is enjoyable, and can easily be repeated a second time.

Offerings

Offerings have traditionally been a way in which human beings acknowledge their connection with the divine. The pouring of libations—wine, water, milk, and honey—or the offering of the first fruits of the harvest are still enacted around the planet. In today's ceremonies many people incorporate offerings as a form of renunciation or the sacrificing of something for a higher good. I have seen people write on paper those things of which they would like to be free and then burn that paper in a ceremonial fire. Participants in divorce ceremonies may offer up their wedding rings, bridal gowns, or photographs to the fire or ocean or bury them in the ground. In renewal ceremonies people may plant seeds or trees. Placentas from home births may be buried with trees planted on top of them. Crystals and other semi-precious stones may be planted in the ground at sacred sites and places viewed as power spots. Women may offer their menstrual blood back to the Earth.

Music

From the cathedral organ to drums, sticks, and rattles, music has always been a part of the sacred and all ceremonial life. Modern ceremonies can use taped music of any variety from Gregorian chant to Aboriginal *didjiredoos*. During the last few years drumming has gone mainstream. A recent headline in *The New York Times* heralded: "Drum fever rolls across the country." The article says, "People have discovered the physical, psychological, and spiritual rewards of drumming." From nuns to nursing homes to corporations like Hewlett-Packard, Motorola, and Apple Computer, team spirit is built through drumming. Because so many people now have their own drums, drumming is one of the easiest and most powerful ways to bring music into a ceremony.

Singing and Chanting

Along with music and percussion, song is also an essential ingredient to ceremony. Do not be too concerned with vocal expertise; like drumming, chanting and singing is finding its way into the mainstream. In 1979 a group of ceremonial friends and I recorded the first chant tape of contemporary Euro-American sacred songs, entitled *In Search of Native Roots*. As unprofessional as this tape was, the songs went around the world and have been rerecorded by people here and in Europe for the last sixteen years. Simple chants for the Earth, Great Spirit, and the reclaiming of many traditional songs from every faith have become common. If words fail, there is always simple toning, in which a vowel sound is held. The act of singing or toning together creates a resonant field that aligns the energies of a group.

Ceremonial Silence

Silence can be a very powerful element if it is understood by everyone present. Let people know if it is two or twenty minutes that they are expected to sit in silence. Give some guidance about what they should be focusing on during that time. Is it a meditation for peace? Self-contemplation? A healing for a loved one? Or a tuning into the group energy?

Movement and Gesture

Contemporary ceremony is breaking away from what Virginia Hine called the "Victorian stiffness of the sit-stand-kneel pattern of religious ritual." People will naturally start to move, sway, and shuffle if they are holding hands. Dancing around a fire must be one the most ancient of communal activities. Simple dances are best, especially with a group. I have seen a number of people try to teach complicated dances to large groups only to have it end in chaos. Plus, if an instructive dance is anywhere but at the beginning of the event it breaks the energy of what has happened before. Suddenly, people are required to follow directions and then demonstrate that they understood the instructions. At the end of a ceremony where everyone is lingering, holding hands, perhaps chanting, it is sometimes quite effective to lead the group in a snake dance or simple circle dance, where everyone has the chance to look into the faces of those present.

Gesture is a more formalized way of moving the body. It can be as simple as a bow, the sign of the cross, the palms pressed together as in the Buddhist tradition, or a gesture that means something only to those present.

Vigils

Vigils are a very powerful way of acknowledging the sacred. People who have the insight to stay with the body of a deceased loved one for at least a few hours find enormous strength and comfort through their mourning process. Sometimes vigils are more spontaneous events. After the murder of John Lennon people with candles gathered outside of his apartment building. Here in Santa Fe, we recently had a violent crime in which a man raped a woman and murdered the good Samaritan who heard her screams and went to help. The crime scene became a vigil site where people brought flowers, lit votive candles, and left prayers. Keeping a candle burning is another way of holding a vigil for someone who is ill, giving birth, having surgery, or recently passed over. Many people hold all-night prayer circles on full moons or solstices. Sitting up through the night and watching the dawn come in is an ancient rite in itself.

Mana and Power Objects

Mana is a sacred blessing. Many traditions believe a blessing can be conferred by touching a sacred object. Statues of saints from every tradition often show signs of enormous wear from pilgrims touching and rubbing them. Many people hang everything from crosses to feathers in their automobiles, presumably for protection. Touch is another simple and beautiful way that blessing is transmitted, such as holding hands or the laying on of hands for healing. The Christian "kiss of peace" is a wonderful example of healing and goodwill in the liturgy. In a ceremony, objects can become sacred through their repeated use in a sacramental way. Many people now make sacred bundles for themselves that consist of objects that are precious to them, perhaps a feather that was found or a rock from a special place. Objects are placed in pretty piece of cloth or leather and then wrapped up and tied. At certain times the bundle is opened up, perhaps to renew vows or recall memories. Chapter eight gives a beautiful example of how families have found ways to make bundles that represent the family and then use this bundle as a center for family meetings.

Taboo

Abstaining from normal activities as part of a ceremony is a powerful act. Fasting or the elimination of certain foods like meat, pork, or alcohol are common to many traditions. Sexual abstinence is another common taboo. These acts are generally part of a rite of purification that prepares the body for the ceremony proper. The honoring of the taboo focuses the attention of the participant upon the ceremony and increases awareness.

The Trial by Fire

The use of ordeal or trial by fire has always been a part of ceremony and proper initiation. The psychological effect of the ordeal pushes the mind, body, and spirit into new states of awareness. In my opinion the most successful rites of passage always contain some sort of ordeal. The death and rebirth that is required in a rite of passage has to be more than just a metaphorical story. The use of hunger, fatigue, thirst, hallucination, solitude, sensory deprivation, and wilderness experiences serve to push the mind forward into spiritual insight.

These time-honored ordeals prepare the individual for a true shift in status. Vision fasting has a long history throughout every culture in the world. In the Christian tradition, Jesus endured forty days and forty nights of fasting on the mountain as he was being initiated into his public life.

The element of ordeal must be taken seriously. In many cultures puberty rites literally leave a number of participants dead. I suggest that people seek out trained ceremonial professionals if they wish to experience ordeal as a rite of passage. Vision fasting should not be attempted without an experienced guide. Details of this kind of experience follow in chapter eleven.

Altered States of Consciousness

All ceremony alters consciousness, which is why people enjoy it. Altered states have traditionally been induced through prayer, drumming, singing, dancing, fasting, meditation, ingesting psychoactive plants, sensory deprivation, trance, and hypnosis. It is up to rite-builders to decide how much and how long they wish to be in an altered state—a few moments through meditation, several hours accompanied by drumming and dancing, or several days of fasting in the wilderness.

Vows

The speaking of vows in front of witnesses can take many forms. The witnessing of vows by family and friends serves to reinforce one's commitment, as in a marriage ceremony. Vows of renunciation can be taken concerning a certain behavior or addiction. When vows are formalized through ceremony there is usually a symbolic binding together or dissolution as with a wedding ring or through the burning or burying of some symbol of addiction, old pattern, or relationship.

Celebratory Feasting

The tried and true perfect ending to any ceremony is the sharing of food and drink. Be it a naming ceremony for a newborn, a wedding, or a funeral, the gathering together to feast, share stories, and reaffirm connection is essential. Some events call for a real catered feast, others for a potluck dinner. Still other occasions are complete with the simple breaking of bread and drink. It is important to stay mindful of the various ethnic groups that may be participating and to honor their heritages or taboos in the food that is served.

A CEREMONIAL FUTURE

You now have the necessary tools to begin creating ceremonies that suit our lives and needs. We know that the world is changing more rapidly than ever before. The sense of a new age dawning, a paradigm shift happening, or even the end of the world occurring is a whisper in all our ears. We know that in order to survive, the internal sociocultural changes must keep pace with the technological advances or life will be rendered meaningless and empty. People are starving for spiritual nutrition. The current myth we are living by is the scientific paradigm, and although it satisfies and contributes to the rapid acceleration we all experience in our lives concerning "objective reality" it contributes nothing at all to our spiritual or psychic necessities. The result of this split between science and spirit is at the root of the dysfunctional being. As we approach the end of the millennium this hunger is driving many people into reviving traditional religions and disciplines. Christianity, Buddhism, Hinduism, Judaism, Islam, and the more ancient shamanistic traditions are being approached in new ways as women become ministers, gay couples seek marriage, and people in general assume more involved roles in breathing life back into ceremonies that lack meaning.

Other people have completely abandoned these traditional systems and yet still recognize their relationship with the Spirit. Whether individuals are inside or outside of a tradition, meaningful ceremony and real rites of passage offer a ray of hope in reweaving into the fabric of our lives a sacred way of living. Embedded in this process of making sacred is the way in which ceremony becomes traditional, and with that we can expect a whole new era of myth-making to emerge.

·6·

EXTENDING THE CIRCLE OF SELF—
A PRAYERFUL COMMUNION

| *"Only Connect!"*—E. M. FORSTER, Howards End |

ARE YOU YOUR BROTHER'S KEEPER?

Q: So what are you responsible for?

A: I'm responsible for my acts and for what I do.

Q: Does that mean you're responsible for others too?

A: No.

Q: Are you your sister's keeper?

A: No.

Q: Your brother's keeper?

A: No.

Q: Are you responsible for you husband?

A: I'm not. He makes his own decisions. He is his own person. He acts his own acts. I can agree with them or I can disagree with them. If I ever find them nauseous enough, I have responsibility to leave and not deal with it anymore.

Q: What about your children?

A: I…I would say I have a legal responsibility for them, but in a sense I think they in turn are responsible for their own acts.

There is a lot of fuzzy thinking going around these days. Like the woman above who was interviewed by Robert Bellah and his colleagues in *Habits of the Heart*. She is certain she is not responsible for her husband, but hesitantly states that she may be at least legally responsible for her children. Part of this confusion comes from the human-growth industry, where many well-developed ideas are diluted into psychobabble or New Age euphemisms. People naively speak of "creating their own reality," and often disavow any responsibility towards others or society. This is contrary to how humans function together as social beings.

When I was age five I was not allowed to go to the local park unless accompanied by an adult. At the far end of the park, near the river, lived an old cowboy who had a small stable of ponies and horses. Once I discovered the ponies, I longed to go there every single day, and one day I went there by myself. Old Charlie was quite friendly to me, and to my delight he invited me into the stable to help feed the ponies. Once inside, he asked if I would give him a nice hug. I openly obliged. Old Charlie hugged me tight, pressing me into his crotch. I remember being mystified as to how it was that Old Charlie suddenly seemed to have three arms—there were the two arms pressing me into his body, and then there was the third arm that seemed to materialize between me and Charlie. At that moment a woman's voice called out to Charlie from outside. It was Mrs. Decroo wanting a pony ride for her daughter. Charlie and I came out of the stable, and I ran home.

That afternoon Mrs. Decroo paid a visit to my mother. She told my mother that she had seen me down at the stable with Charlie, and looking at me, she said that this could be very dangerous for me without an adult. I remember feeling angry at Mrs. Decroo for being a "tattle tale" and feeling like she was a real "busy body." But I also knew that what she said was true—there was something dangerous about going alone to visit Charlie. In fact, I lost all interest in ever visiting Charlie and his ponies again.

Mrs. Decroo was a neighbor; she lived on the next street over and down a block. I knew who she was, she knew who I was, and we knew where one another lived. She obviously suspected Old Charlie of being up to no good. When I think back on this experience, I thank my guardian angel in the name of Mrs. Decroo. If she had not arrived when she did who knows what would have happened to me. As a neighbor, Mrs. Decroo was willing to be my keeper. Thank you, Mrs. Decroo.

As recently as the 1950s, when I was growing up, there was still a sense of a neighborhood. I had never spoken with Mrs. Decroo, but we knew one another by name. She felt a responsibility to inform my mother and chastise me in front of her. My mother had the grace not to be offended and the good sense to talk to me later about not repeating my adventure.

Today, we live with a sense of disconnection, inner emptiness, vague anxieties, and depressions that contradict both poverty and success. All of these feelings are symptomatic of a psycho-spiritual crisis. Educated, well-meaning people often cannot imagine the world beyond their own immediate needs. Even the words "love" and "meaning," according to cultural critic Christopher Lasch, have been defined by therapists as being primarily concerned with an individual's personal fulfillment. Any submission of one's personal needs, interests, or desires to someone or something outside of oneself is now thought to be a form of co-dependence, while "mental health" is all too frequently interpreted as the capacity to gratify every desire and never feel guilty.

People are encouraged to feel responsible only for themselves, rather than feel the deep thread of connection that links us all. To put others' needs first or give one's self over to a cause for the betterment of society has become almost offensive to current common sense concerning our personal well-being. A common phrase among those deeply immersed in therapy is: "The best thing I can do for the world is work on myself."

This is symptomatic of some illness much larger than personal anxiety and depression. The reality of the present moment has become so overwhelming that the therapy room has become a refuge for the sensitive. In the past, it may have been true that the individual had work to do, that the sickness did in fact abide inside our individual psyches, but that is no longer the case. As we approach the end of the millennium, the pathology that afflicts us all abides in the culture at large. Spending twenty years working on what our parents did to us as children no longer addresses the real issue of where that feeling of inner emptiness comes from. It may be more simple to confront our childhood traumas via the therapist than to confront the current, desperate state of the world. If enough people look away, only work on themselves, and continue to believe that they and they alone create their reality, what kind of world will we leave for the next generation?

WHAT IS A FAMILY?

There is much talk in America about the state of the family, family values, and how to save the family. The importance placed upon the family should not be confused with some ideal of what constitutes a family in

America today. We must expand our vision of what a family is. According to a recent report published by the Population Reference Bureau, the idea of the "traditional family" leaves out a lot of people. For instance, 42 percent of the population is made up of couples without children. Some of these couples are young and have not yet had children, some are older couples who have grown children, and other couples are childless by choice. A growing number of families with children, 36 percent, are blended stepfamilies. Nearly one in eight families is headed by a single parent, usually a woman. One quarter of all the children in the United States, 16 million of them, live with only one parent. Between 1960 and 1991, the number of people living alone or living with unrelated people doubled from 15 percent to 30 percent of the population, and this particular group has certainly increased even more over the last five years.

In today's modern world most of us no longer live in a village or near the other members of our families. From our own experiences, we know that family members often live in numerous places around the globe. Parents live in one state, grandparents in another, a brother in Europe, a sister somewhere across the country. Many children live with one parent, while the other parent lives hundreds or thousands of miles away. The effort required to keep up family connections now includes long-distance telephone calls and sometimes large travel expenses to visit family members.

Families are frequently uprooted by the demands of a job. It is not uncommon for children to be enrolled in twelve different schools in as many years. (I had one friend who had been to thirty-nine different countries by the age of seventeen.) The end result of this mobile life is that people find themselves involved in serial social relationships or, sadly, with no real family or community at all. This trend is not new; in America it is safe to say that for the last three generations families have moved further and further away from one another, and lifelong friends have become a thing of the past.

With this type of mobility comes greater freedom and perhaps higher economic gain, but it also produces a greater sense of alienation. There is less of a support system for the young family to stay together, more single parent families and latchkey children, and more homes where the television becomes a surrogate baby-sitter. Many American families only share an average of one meal a week with one another, and that meal is often taken in front of the television with little or no conversation between family members.

Growing up in this environment is devastating to the development of a socially integrated individual. The end product is someone who is fearful of intimate relations and who exhibits a genuine absence of social skills, such as good manners or the art of simple conversation. Instead we end up running the risk of becoming a nation of hyper-individualized, insensitive boors. As Oscar Wilde wittily noted almost a hundred years ago: "America is the only nation in the history of the world to go from barbarism to decadence without the usual intervening stage of civilization."

In fact, many college graduates now enroll in "finishing school" courses, where they are taught how to hold a fork and knife, not talk with their mouths full, and role play how to mingle at social events—skills that in the past were taught at home around the dinner table.

WHEN HELP BECOMES A HINDRANCE

A few years ago James Hillman published a book entitled *We've Had a Hundred Years of Psychotherapy and the World's Getting Worse*. Hillman is considered by many to be one of the most influential psychotherapists of the last half of the twentieth century. This book shocked the therapeutic community. A well-respected leader had broken ranks and denounced the benefits of therapy. In essence, what Hillman is saying is that too much therapeutic processing can be damaging, and in the end this processing can become another form of repression. He questions the human-potential movement's focus on "growing" and suggests that unlimited growth can be detrimental to our soul, just as it is detrimental to our cities and our environment.

Andrew Feldmar, a well-known Canadian therapist, recently spent a week teaching at a human potential institute and told me that he met a lot of "wrinkled fetuses" in the shape of grown adults who wanted to grow forever. This desire to grow, fix, or transform everything into something useful is just another form of consumerism, mining the psyche of its richness and ultimately creating a large body of clients who have been homogenized into a boring sameness, like boxes of processed cheese.

Hillman believes that life is about devotion to the Gods. He quotes Marcus Aurelius: "What I do I do always with the community in mind. What happens to me, what befalls me, comes from the Gods." Hillman goes on to say that the "self is the interiorization of the community" and that the community is more than just other people: It is a psychic field, a locale both ecological and animistic that includes people, animals, plants, and even buildings. This is the very essence of what it means to live in a sacred way. To partake and participate in this psychic field of mutuality is the act of being in true relationship with the Divine.

IT TAKES A COMMUNITY

In my work with people, and especially my work with women, I have witnessed the emphasis placed upon the "R" word—"relationship:"

"If I only had a relationship...."

"I am working on my relationship...."

"We need to decide if we are having a relationship...."

"By my next birthday I am going to have a relationship...."

In all of these circumstances "relationship" has been defined so narrowly that the entire arena of human interaction is reduced to one special and private individual. A relationship is viewed as if the connection two people feel can either be spoken into or out of existence. Witness the woman who was a lover with a man for over six months, yet was desperate to know from him whether or not they were "having a relationship."

Therapy, as it is often practiced, is designed to get people in touch with their own desires, needs, and wants. Therapists who treat only the individual create and shape people who think of themselves as being isolated from the world and society. They actually believe that they are in control of a private destiny, forgetting any connection to their ancestors, children, or contemporaries. It's as if they spontaneously appeared on the screen of life and just as spontaneously will disappear, without any connections, responsibilities, or repercussions. Finding one's self is not something one can do alone, or even with a therapist. Hillary Clinton is correct when she says it takes a village.

The one-sided relationship of the therapy room cannot be translated into real life, especially if the therapeutic room is the only place that the client finds human intimacy.

Likewise, Twelve Step programs, as helpful as they are in assisting people to overcome addictions, were never meant to be a substitute for a real social life or a network of family and friends. Human beings must enjoy diversity and the richness of differences that other people bring to this party called Life. (One of the more restrictive support groups I came across required "unpartnered, non-smoking, lesbian women who are mothers of sons....")

These contractual relationships, whether with a therapist, in a Twelve Step program, or in a marriage contract, cannot engender real intimacy. They all too often unintentionally turn love and human connection into a medium of exchange, where people come to expect a return on their investments. And if they don't get a proper return, they simply find a new therapist, go to a new support group, get a divorce, or contract for a new relationship.

COMMON GOOD, COMMON CAUSE

Today there is much talk of ecology. The word used to be limited to the physical environment, but now many people speak of eco-psychology, eco-philosophy, social ecology, moral ecology, and even spiritual ecology. I believe that this is a hopeful trend in our use of language. It indicates that we are beginning once again to envision ourselves and our lives in the context of the surrounding environment, be it physical, social, or spiritual. When we experience our life sharing a common cause with others for a common good, we experience a moral and ethical understanding. Our lives begin to take on meaning, the sense of alienation begins to slip away, and we realize that how we treat one another matters. We also realize that our individual lives matter. We have a shared responsibility towards everyone we know to be a better person.

Historically, healthy communities of families and friends have always held to a standard of common good. A member should be able to count on the community to provide the highest form of loving, honest feedback. To be willing, in a family or a group of friends, to abide by a sense of the common good can be both perilous and challenging. Communication is the key and caring the foundation. Otherwise, if someone is becoming a criminal or an addict, or simply behaving in a way that is unethical, there is no possibility for family or friends to intervene without horrible repercussions. Likewise, anyone who simply gets by as a flatterer by telling someone what they want to hear and failing to tell then the truth can never be a true friend. They do a disservice to the person they are flattering and ultimately do not properly serve themselves. Deep and lifelong relationships cannot take root in this type of environment; both parties end up having an ongoing sense of distrust. If you do not trust me enough to be honest with me, how can I trust you?

BRINGING THE SACRED HOME

Given all the variables that go into creating our modern lives, it is not surprising that we feel so alienated. Even the reactionary impulse to hold onto the concept of a traditional family is understandable. We have seen, however, that the trends of contemporary family life do not support a return to conventional lifestyles. As a culture we have said farewell to Ozzie and Harriet and to Ward and June Cleaver. The American family no longer resembles the family of the 1950s, with its 2.2 children, a working father, and a mother who stays at home to raise the children. In my work and travels I meet many kinds of people who, more often than not, are searching for better ways to raise their children, make their work meaningful, or find the skills to improve all of their relationships. People are anxious to find a way to deeply nourish themselves in a time of spiritual drought.

Couples, families, and friends can deepen relationships by allowing a sense of the spirit to come into the ordinary moments of our daily existence. Simple ceremonial form can transform our communication process from the profane towards the sacred, from repetitious ritualized actions to meaningful ceremonial connection. When we place ourselves in the context of a greater good or a greater light, we invite those present to bear witness to our words and actions under the auspices of something larger than our individual selves or our individual needs and wants. We can create a sense of the common good, and out of that naturally arises a sense of meaning.

The first step in the ceremonial process requires someone willing to suggest to their partner, family, or community the idea of creating a sacred way to be together. Sometimes this can happen most graciously around the idea of celebrating the summer solstice or full moon. A sacred way can also be introduced into our more intimate connections so that lines of communication go beyond the therapeutic or simply symbolic ritualizations into something deeper and more soulful. Our intimate relationships can become part of our spiritual practice.

The previous chapter on the structure of ceremony is like a well-stocked kitchen. The spices, seasonings, ingredients, and utensils are there.

Each of us, no matter what our spiritual background, can find a way to bring our own ethnicity and authenticity of soul into our lives. The ceremonial examples in the following chapters are not meant to be a new form of dogmatism. They are instead meant to jog the creative spiritual impulse in each one of us. These are ways in which ordinary people have taken particular moments in their lives and introduced an element of the sacred. Take them, add your own spices, and make a delectable feast for yourself and those you love. This is soul food.

DARE I PRAY?

People are coming out of the closet and admitting that they pray. This is a very hopeful sign. The United States has always had strong religious roots, but we have passed through a dark night of the soul concerning our spirituality. The modern rational world challenges our capacity to be honest about our personal relationship with the Spirit. Skeptical scientists tell us repeatedly how nonsensical and superstitious prayer is; God has been declared dead.

Scientists prefer to project onto our DNA the attributes that were previously God's, but science isn't the only culprit against prayer. Many people find the world of money-seeking television ministers and far-right fundamentalists to be a powerful antidote to religion and spirituality. Still, there are those of us who quietly hold to the belief in a Godhead and continue to find moments in which to pray. In fact, one third of the adult population in the United States admits to praying regularly, and more than half the population admits to praying in time of urgent need. According to a *Newsweek* poll, 33 percent of all adults report having had a mystical experience.

When I give a workshop around ceremony one of the first things I do is give people permission to express their spiritual nature. The entire room sighs in relief. People often express a feeling of shyness or embarrassment around publicly sharing that they believe in something other than themselves. The question: "In whose light do you do what you do?" is another way of asking who do you pray to, or at whose altar do you worship? Some people have very specific deities—Jesus, Isis, Shiva, Jehova, Sakti, Aphrodite, Allah, the Virgin Mary, Pan—others have entire pantheons beginning with the four directions: North, South, East, and West; the four elements: Fire, Water, Earth, and Air; and medicine animals in the form of eagles, coyotes, bears, dolphins, buffaloes, or other creatures. Some people pray to their ancestors, Nature, the Goddess, the Saints, and Gaia. Others simply communicate through their dreams with "archetypes."

Sadly, there are those people who no longer believe in God but still practice idolatry. A few years ago the then president of the World Bank was being questioned about the ethics of a large dam-building project in India. The dam would relocate over three million people from their tribal lands. He was asked how he felt about the ethics of such a project and unabashedly stated that he "worshipped at the altar of economic pragmatism." In our desacralized world the old god Mammon, god of material riches, often dominates our judgments. When we worship at the altar of economic pragmatism we no longer consider the common good; instead, we only acknowledge what will benefit few and jeopardize many.

But what is a prayer? A prayer is a form of spiritual communion that uses words and is made more powerful if the words are expressed out loud. Prayer is more than a visualization or a conscious act of positive thinking. Prayer indicates by its nature a relationship with the Other. As such, repeated prayer is a way to cultivate and deepen our connection to whomever or whatever we conceive the nature of the divine to be. Prayer can be simply the act of giving thanks out loud or saying grace before a meal, or it can sing the praises of life itself. Prayer can ask for blessings, healing, peace, forgiveness, or release from suffering for oneself, one's loved ones, or even strangers.

PRAYER'S HEALING POWER

"We are wired for God," says Dr. Herbert Benson, author of *Timeless Healing: the Power and Biology of Belief.* "We have a tremendous healing capacity if we can tap into what I call the 'faith factor.'" Serious illness is often a motivating factor in bringing an individual or family member around to prayer. Many of us have experienced the power of prayer. One woman's account of a childhood illness attests to both the power of prayer and the power of motherly love:

> As a child I was prone to sudden and life-threatening fevers
> and deliriums that would often last for days. I remember being very

delirious one night and in that twilight world being aware of several robed figures who were approaching me. My terrified reaction was to fight them off, because I felt as if they were going to take me away with them. The experience was a repeating nightmare. It was both strenuous and exhausting. In the middle of the night I awoke and saw that my mother was at my bedside with a lit candle and a statue of the Virgin Mary and was praying over me. She wiped my brow and told me she would stay with me. An immediate sense of relief washed over me. I did not have to battle anymore; she would do it for me. In the early hours of dawn my fever broke as I slept peacefully. I remember having such a sense of gratitude towards my mother and a real feeling of her powerful motherly love, coupled with that of the Virgin Mary. I have always felt as if I came close to dying that night, and that without my mother and her prayers I very well might have.

Today, many doctors are examining the relationship between prayer, spirituality, and healing. Almost every doctor has experienced patients who get well with no scientific or medical explanation. The American public's relationship with traditional medicine is based on a paradox. Scientific advances are supported and embraced, while at the same time people, when confronted with a serious and life-threatening illness, still seek alternative help in the form of cleansing diets, homeopathy, acupuncture, or herbal medicine. Many choose to seek out healers who practice laying on of hands or indigenous shamanic healing rites that may include attending sweat lodges, ingesting psychoactive substances, or doing soul-retrieval work to discover the psycho-spiritual component of the disease.

Recently, the medical establishment has been seriously considering the relationship of spirituality and physical well-being. In 1995 Harvard Medical School hosted a three-day course to discuss the relationship between healing and spirituality. Nearly one thousand doctors, theologians, psychologists, and sociologist debated the issues. Many doctors are now openly discussing the roles of faith and prayer with their patients—after all, four out of five Americans believe prayer can help people recover from an illness. Dr. Dale Matthews, of Georgetown University, reviewed over 200 studies, some dating from the 1950s, and discovered about 75 percent of them indicated that people with "religious commitments" appear to receive health benefits from their spirituality.

Doctors Larry Dossey and Tony Rippo, founders of the Santa Fe Institute for Medicine and Prayer, are eager to educate health care professionals about the possibilities of prayer. The Institute offers nondenominational prayer-based therapy to the sick and dying. Dossey, in his 1993 book, *Healing Words: The Power of Prayer and the Practice of Medicine*, documented 130 scientific studies where prayer influenced the healing process. The most dramatic study was done in 1987 at the University of California San Francisco, where a group of coronary care patients who were prayed for by Christian volunteers required less antibiotics, diuretics, and assistance over a ten-month period than patients who were not prayed for.

The power of prayer is effective for more than just the healing personal illnesses. During the 1980s when the cold war between the United States and the Soviet Union was threatening to erupt once again into the possibility of a nuclear war, a worldwide effort of praying for peace occurred. A global prayer community emerged on both sides of the Iron Curtain. I participated in two groups as part of the peace effort. One was called Praying for Peace in Particular Places and focused on potential hot spots along the Iron Curtain—the same cities that rose up overnight and tore down the Berlin Wall. The other was a Full Moon Meditation for Peace. Both of these prayer groups involved people praying together at specific times and places around the world. Tens of thousands of people participated regularly in these activities. People believed that the conscious focusing of their awareness in a sacred way, even if they were praying to different aspects of the Divine, would be effective in promoting peace. The experience for many people was akin to being on-line, only without the technological interface of the World Wide Web. We simply did it with our minds in coordinated efforts.

·7·

CEREMONIAL CONNECTIONS

> *The real true self—the real pure heart—we can come together.*
> —FRANKLIN KAHN, *Navajo Elder*

MAKING A CONNECTION BUNDLE

People meet, connect, enjoy, and fall in love with one another. We usually think of this experience in context of a couple who ultimately share sexual intimacy, but this experience also holds true for all who become our friends. Relationships come in all forms, from our blood family, our best friends both male and female, to our roommates, neighbors, and co-workers, and even the sales clerks we come to know. One way that people have been consciously acknowledging their connections and their responsibilities to one another is through the creation of a Connection Bundle, also called a Marriage Bundle or Marriage Basket. The general form of this ceremony is used among people who are working on a project together, among a group of friends or roommates, and between two people who wish to partner. The Bundle serves as a resource to return to in times of difficulty or when there is a breakdown in communication. People always benefit by remembering what their connection means.

In the past family, community, and shared values helped keep couples together. Today, every couple is a pioneer and must find their own formula for building a healthy relationship. To stay together, the deep structure of a relationship must by mutually satisfying. Relationships based on partnership rather than domination make living and loving a transformative journey, while recognizing that creatively dealing with gender-based divisions is essential in today's modern world. Here is how one young couple deepened their connection to one another.

John and Christine had been living together for over a year. They both felt that they were not prepared for marriage and the concomitant public event it might entail. Nonetheless, they did have a sense of long-term commitment toward one another. When they heard of the idea of the Connection Bundle they both saw it as a way to create a private ceremony that would fit their needs.

Each agreed to gather together a number of symbolic objects that would represent an aspect of themselves, embody what they each had to offer the other, express who they were as a couple, and stand for what they needed to keep as their own. Christine agreed to bring a beautiful piece of fabric to use as the bundle itself.

They decided to put together the ceremonial bundle out in Nature, since they both enjoyed hiking. They also felt that choosing a particular day would be helpful. The full moon would be around in about two and half weeks, and they felt they needed at least that much time to gather their respective objects. Here is Christine's account of the ceremony:

I felt a nervous anxiety around doing this ceremony with John. Neither of us are very religious, but I do feel as if we have some sense of a spiritual life. I am attracted to what little I have read about the early Goddess religions, and John has a deep love of Nature. It was kind of surprising how anticipating this thing worked on me. I thought about it a lot and both of us put a lot of care into the objects we brought.

A few nights before the full moon I had a dream in which I saw John as an old man in the middle of a large gathering. It seemed as if it was his birthday or some special event. A very large watermelon was brought in and John was given the honor of cutting it open. As soon as the knife touched the melon, it burst open. We all yelled, "Surprise!" Suddenly John became a young man again and I was by his side. The other guests were smiling and congratulating us. I took this dream as a good sign and continued my preparations....

We decided to hike to the top of our favorite mountain and create our Bundle there. The hike up the mountain was a bit serious; I think we were both feeling a little awkward. When we arrived at the summit, we wanted to take some time alone and really feel what our intention was, so we separated and agreed to come together in about half an hour. During that time I was able to get my thoughts straight and relax a bit.

When we came back together, we sat down on the ground and I lit some incense and suggested that we might both make some sort of a prayer. At first, this felt a bit embarrassing since we had never done anything like this together before. John said I had to go first since I thought of it. We both laughed at this, and the laughter seemed to allow us to be more natural with one another.

Not being religious by nature, I had to figure out who or what I was praying to. In the end I decided to ask all of the women in my family line to come and witness this moment. I really got into it. I called in my sisters, my mother, and then my grandmothers. I experienced this realization, more like a revelation, that a lot of people did something right in order for me to be alive. I had the image of generation after generation going backwards in time. Each generation had to pass through the body of a woman, each generation had to survive long enough to give birth and care for the next generation. This meant surviving wars, droughts, famine, disease, and simple bad luck. In the end I was overwhelmed with gratitude.

John was obviously moved by my prayer, and when it was his turn I was surprised by the emotion that welled up in him. He began by saying that he did not know who to pray to, but he could ask for help from Nature. Glancing around he began. He asked the birds that sing to bring him a melody for his life. He also asked the ground beneath his feet for the support that he might need to really become a man. From the forest he asked for the wisdom to keep his life straight and strong upon its course. As a breeze stirred, he invited the Holy Spirit into his life, that he might speak the truth kindly and gently.

Silently we sat and looked into one another's eyes, knowing that something larger than we anticipated was whirling around us. I then brought out an old embroidered piece of cloth that had belonged to my grandmother and offered it to John. Together we spread it open before us. We had already decided that the ceremony would address four different aspects of who we are.

The first part of the ceremony had to do with who we are individually.

John began by holding up a small lacquered Russian box. It was a family treasure that he felt represented his heritage. The beauty of the craftsmanship was to remind him of his creativity and capacity to make his way in the world. He removed the lid and showed me that it was empty and yet held the possibility of being full, just as his life held a promised of a well-crafted future. He then placed it in the bundle to represent his life being on track.

I then presented my object, which was a rosy quartz crystal. I chose this object to represent the part of myself that is feminine and of the Earth. I offered it into our bundle with a promise to remain clear and willing to bring my clarity and honesty into our relationship via the feminine.

I began the second round by addressing what I had to offer to our relationship.

I placed a spool of red silk thread on the cloth. The silk thread I gave to him as a way to be connected. It is both strong and yet beautiful. I felt it was important that our connection not be like an overwhelming chain, but something soft, yet secure. I asked that our connection continue and that it always have an element of silkiness to it, that it never bind, suffocate, or restrict our ability to change. I chose the color red intentionally to represent our sexual connection. I hoped that we would continue to enjoy open and honest love-making with one another, and that all the things that might bind us together be soft and sensual and filled with love.

John then placed a package of mixed vegetable seeds on the bundle. He offered me the hope of a future together, and that over time the seeds might all be planted and that he would tend and nurture their development. He said he was confident in his ability to create a field for our relationship and that he was willing to be a responsible partner to me. That his early roots with his own family were strong and he was not entering into the creation of this bundle lightly. In the end he offered himself as someone who is trustworthy.

The third round of objects symbolized how we saw ourselves as a couple.

John surprised me by placing a forked stick on the cloth. He said that this stick signified how we could be united as a couple and yet remain distinctly different from one another. He felt it was essential that each one of us keep our autonomy like the forked branches and yet could be of one branch together.

I then presented a small handmade kaleidoscope to our bundle. I told John that it symbolized our combined many facets. That by turning it one way an image appeared and by turning it another the colors changed, and so did the pattern. I wanted us to also be aware of the sense of magic and delight that we shared, and that change need not be a bad thing. That if our lives ever became so black and white or drab, we might remember to bring back the color and the magic.

The final round of the ceremony addressed what we desired to keep as our own and still be in the relationship.

John had brought a roll of film. His hobby is nature photography, and he really relishes his time in Nature and the dark room. He expressed a desire to not feel pressured into spending every spare minute together. He wanted me to know that his time alone was a source of renewal for him. He spoke about his last girlfriend and how she had felt jealous and insecure about him going out in Nature by himself. She had also teased him about spending too much time in the dark room. In the end he simply stated that he would have more to offer me if he had time to pursue his creativity.

I brought an old charm bracelet to represent my connection to my sisters and good girlfriends. We have a small group of friends who are quite close, and we enjoy getting together for lunch, dinners, and a night out. I did not want to feel as if I had to ask permission to spend time with my friends, or that I was slighting John by going out with them. We both realized that our time apart was as important as our time together.

After I placed the bracelet on the cloth, we sat in silence and looked at the things we had gathered together. I took up the corners and tied the cloth with a piece of braided cord and gave the Bundle to John. He would be its caretaker. We both agreed that if things got really difficult for us that we would unwrap the Bundle and remind ourselves of what each of the objects meant. Afterwards we talked in detail about what we had revealed to one another concerning our hopes, fears, and expectations in the relationship. This ceremony helped us drop into a new level of trust and love with one another. It made clear our desires and we really heard one another.

We had never done anything "spiritual" together before and it was like breaking through a barrier in terms of reaching a new level

of comfort with one another. I feel that the act of calling in something larger than ourselves to bear witness was very powerful. It's as if
our relationship now stands in the light of something greater.

Christine's account of the Connection Bundle exemplifies what can
happen when a sense of the spirit is invited into a situation. Overcoming
the initial embarrassment of exposing an aspect of their spiritual nature
brought them into deeper contact. It transcended the therapeutic model of
play-acting with symbols and laid a foundation for soulful intimacy in their
relationship.

STAYING CONSCIOUS OF FAMILY CONNECTIONS

We can stay conscious inside the structure of the family. The most
important activity a family can generate together is honest, heartfelt communication. This is always done in families who value their relationships.
Perhaps one of the simplest ways to bond with children is through the bedtime ritual. Children love having a sense of rhythm in their lives: the
nightly bath, a regular bedtime, the tucking in, reading of stories, and saying of prayers used to be common in most homes.

One couple I know have a live-in nanny, but in the evening the parents take over. First there is supper and then the two boys, now ages three
and five, sit with their father at the piano as the children pick out favorite
songs to sing. Visitors always participate in the sing-along and it is a very
merry experience. Then it's off to the bath tub, then bed for storytime. The
children now refuse to be read to, and require a new and made-up story
every night. They tell you who the characters are—wizards, witches, dragons—and give them names; you are expected to create a story for them. I
must admit I was a little intimidated by my task when I last visited them,
but it worked wonderfully. They wanted a story about a good witch and
provided me with a girl and a boy who were off on an adventure, and of
course, if I got stuck, all I needed to do was ask them what they thought
happened next!

As children grow older it becomes more challenging to keep the
lines of communication open. There are so many problems that plague the
modern family, and the simple formality of ceremony can ease the pain.

The darker realities of the modern world can be dealt with in creative and healing ways. A crisis like divorce can be an opportunity for a couple to remain aware that their relationship exists in the larger context of family and friends, and that they have a duty to create a safe space for the children involved. Likewise blended families can ease the pain and the confusion of step-siblings through rites of incorporation. The following ceremony is an example of how one blended family found a meaningful way to speak from the heart using an elegant variation of the Circle Process, a form in which a safe place is constructed to allow genuine, loving communication to be expressed.

A Rite of Incorporation for the Blended Family

Carl and Nancy's marriage provided them with already made families. Carl brought his children, Alysa and Robert, ages eight and ten respectively, and Nancy brought her daughter, Samantha, age twelve, into the relationship.

Carl and Nancy told me that they did not think that they were going to magically turn into the Brady Bunch, but they did want to give themselves the opportunity to have a happy new life as a family. A few days after the couple and children had officially moved in together, the family created a ceremony which they have returned to again and again.

The ceremony began in a candlelit room with Carl and Nancy explaining to the children that they wanted to live and work together as a family. Carl had a beautiful box and inside the box was an even more beautiful crystal geode. He told the family that he would like this rock to be the family Heart-Stone that would mirror back to them their connection.

Carl went on to explain how the Heart-Stone would be used. In times of need or joy anyone could call a family circle and share the Heart-Stone with one or more members of the family. It would be kept in a special place accessible to everyone. The only rule was that when you held the Heart-Stone you must speak honestly from the heart, no one was to interrupt or pass judgment, and whoever was present must agree to stay in the circle until everyone felt complete.

With that Carl passed the Heart-Stone to his new wife. Nancy began by expressing her hopes and fears about embarking on a new family life.

She acknowledged her daughter Samantha as being born from her womb and therefore special. She asked Samantha for her permission to love Alysa and Robert and to be a second mother to them. She then expressed to Alysa and Robert her desire to be accepted by them, recognizing and honoring that they too had a mother out of whose womb they came, and that they would always have a special relation with her.

From that point on the ceremony unfolded quite naturally as the Stone went round and round. The children, at first awkward, opened up and were able to express their fears concerning new rivals, the sharing of toys, space, and, of course, parents. Everyone agreed that they were scared but willing to try to be a family together. Tears and laughter flowed freely, and the sense of mutual vulnerability was reinforced with love.

The ceremony did not instantly turn them into a cohesive family unit, but everyone agreed they wanted to do it again. Five years later the family had used the Heart-Stone many different times. The bond of respect that grew out of simply having a safe form in which to talk has proved invaluable.

This simple ceremony shows how the power of form and symbol can work to create a safe space. The passing of the object from hand to hand gives people a chance to focus, and because they can speak their truth unimpeded by discussion, they feel safe to express themselves and to be heard. Designating it as the Family Heart-Stone empowered everyone in the family to use it to call a meeting together whenever desired. Because family members honored the form, its use over the years grew in power and when normal communication broke down the Heart-Stone became a way to mend the pain, anger, or grief that people were experiencing.

THE TALKING STICK AND THE CIRCLE COUNCIL

The act of coming together around issues, whether it be with one's family, friends, neighbors, or co-workers, can be facilitated without bringing in experts. One form that is gaining popularity around the country is the Circle Council. This is essentially what Carl and Nancy introduced into their family with the Heart-Stone. This form is very effective in a number of diverse situations, including schools, intentional communities, and the business world, and I encourage its use.

The use of a Talking Stick or other "talking objects" serves two practical functions. It helps to focus each person as they speak, and when we pass it on to the next person it is clear that we have finished speaking and that it is now someone else's turn. Carl and Nancy used a geode, other people have used a feather, a crystal, or a figurine of some sort. Sometimes it's as simple as picking up an object in Nature such as a rock, flower, or shell. It feels good to pass the object from hand to hand, to hold it while focusing one's thoughts.

Making an actual Talking Stick can be a ceremony in itself. Schoolchildren have made them to use in the classroom, as have family and friends. They are even being used in the boardroom by innovative consultants. The stick itself is usually about three feet high and can be a natural stick from Nature or a favorite tree, or a piece of worked and polished wood. If it is being made by a group everyone can bring a special small object to hang from the stick. Generally people will wrap part of the stick with cloth, yarn, or leather, and then decorate the stick with feathers, beads, pieces of jewelry, or seashells. The only limitation is whether or not you can actually get an article attached to the stick.

I work with a Talking Stick and prefer it to other types of talking objects. The Stick must be held upright with one end resting on the ground. If someone gets the stick and becomes flustered, ending up waving the stick around, ask them to keep the end of the stick on the ground to help contain their energy. My experience is that it helps people to feel grounded—they can lean on it. The other aspect of the Talking Stick is twofold: There is a beauty to it and a dignity. Smaller objects often cannot be seen when held inside the hand. A Talking Stick is by its nature fairly large and beautifully decorated; it is in fact a magic talisman. As it is passed around it often requires that people change their posture to hold it. Looking around a circle as each person speaks while holding the staff, I am often delighted by how dignified the people look as they sit upright with the stick in their hand, speaking from the heart and their inner authority.

To sit in a circle with a group of people is a most ancient custom. As human beings we have circled around the fire for eons and are naturally comfortable there. A circle is a great equalizer. No one is above another, no one is at the head of the table, and everyone has an opportunity to speak. The most common structure has people seated in a circle, either on the ground or in chairs, so that everyone is visible to everyone else. In the center there can be a fire or candle or even an altar set up to focus energy. Usually there is a topic or issue up for discussion. The basic rules are as follows:

1. Everyone has an equal say and responsibility.
2. All must attend to the person who is speaking.
3. When it is your turn, speak from the heart.
4. Use a sacred object, like a Talking Stick, to pass around the circle.
5. Only speak or comment if you are holding the object.
6. The person calling the circle must join in as an equal.
7. It is permissible to be silent and/or pass on your turn.

To sit in council with a group of people requires that we agree to participate and to listen. For the individual, it means giving up the impulse to manipulate the group. For the group, it means not giving up its power to a dominant voice and to not make a decision until everyone has spoken. In other words, everyone has the opportunity to change their mind about an issue. We become like a many spoked wheel, with each person carrying an important and critical point on the wheel.

A Circle Council usually begins with some sort of invocation or intention, which may be something as simple as naming a topic or issue, saying an actual prayer, or sitting together in silent meditation. Often the first round will be a check-in, an opportunity for each person to state what's going on with them or how they are feeling. This informs the group of each individual's current state of mind.

Being attentive is a real challenge. As the Talking Stick is passed around, it is all too easy to begin anticipating your turn. I call this Pre-Talking Stick Anxiety. It usually happens when the Stick is two or three people away. The mind takes over; we are no longer listening to the person speaking, we are busy inside ourselves creating our speech for the group. Every time this happens stop, breathe, and remind your mind to stay attentive to the person talking. When it does become your turn, take a few seconds to ground yourself, breathe, go inside, and speak from the heart to the topic under discussion. When you have passed the Talking Stick on, remind yourself to stay attentive once again. The tendency is to go into Post-Talking Stick Analysis—rather than being attentive to the people who follow, we are busy either congratulating ourselves on what a profound job we did or criticizing ourselves for making a fool of ourselves. The end result is the same: We are no longer attentive and we have missed what the people on either side of us have had to say.

The Circle Council builds trust and that trust needs to be respected. Each council needs to create guidelines for establishing and maintaining confidentiality. It is important that outsiders not be told about who said what. If it is an ongoing group, guidelines should be set up to determine if it is acceptable for group members to discuss what transpired outside of the Circle.

There are also variations in how the Council may be structured. Usually the staff is passed from person to person, clockwise around the Council, but sometimes the Talking Stick is placed in the center and each person chooses it from the center when they wish to speak. With larger groups or particular themes or issues, four or more people might go into the center while the rest of the circle bears witness to their progress.

The Circle Council should never be used to scapegoat someone; it is a place of safety and heartfulness. That does not mean, however, that it is restricted to only love and light. Real pain, grief, and all aspects of the Shadow should be welcome inside the Council. We should also never forget the discipline of humor, for all too often sacred is equated with serious, and this can be soul-numbing.

·8·

CEREMONIAL WEAVING AND MENDING

Other people can rape and damage my body. Only I can damage my soul.
—AMERICAN INDIAN WOMAN ELDER

SHATTERED TRUST

Inside coupled relationships there is often a need to heal shattered trust and broken promises. Ceremonial space can hold the powerful contradictions of love and hate, anger and sorrow, connection and alienation. Couples who find themselves dealing with broken trust, such as an affair by one of the partners, can hold on to the pain until they virtually kill off the relationship. But if willing, they can create a healing ceremony that allows them to create a new way of dealing with the situation. The act of creating a ceremony together for the expressed purpose of healing can in itself be healing, as it shifts the tone of communication from guilt and blame to one where a sense of empathy and even humor might emerge. Together they might remember what they stood for as a couple. In this situation a ceremony that contains powerful symbolic acts or imagery such as burying the past or burning painful memories can engender healing.

One couple I knew had suffered for years over an affair. Reaching the end of their tether, they finally acknowledged what the affair had done to their relationship and decided to act out its "freezing" effect. They literally put various items into the deep freeze. These included their wedding album, wedding rings, sexy lingerie, and photos of the children. During the next month they agreed not to speak about it or make apologies, but simply feel the deadening effect of the "big chill." A month later, on the full moon, they removed the objects and let them thaw out in front of the fireplace. For the first time they were able to speak about the matter in a way that did not inflame old hurts. In looking through their wedding album they sensed the love and support they had from family and friends, and remembered the love they felt for one another. They were able to re-exchange wedding rings, and make new vows of love and commitment; in essence, they were finally able to forgive.

THE UNFORGIVABLE

There are times when forgiveness seems impossible, at least not without a lot of time and distance. Violent acts of battering, rape, murder, and sexual molestation are shattering to family and friends. Calling upon the law, seeking the help of social workers, getting a divorce, and moving to another state may be the first step in reclaiming one's dignity, but then the healing must begin.

When there is little hope of ever resolving a hurt with another human being, it is possible to ceremonially work with the trauma and find peace within one's self. One client of mine had been horribly sexually abused as a child and the perpetrators were now dead. Allison was a forty-two-year-old professional woman who felt as if she would never be able to come to a point of resolution with them, even after years of therapy. They would always dominate her. Furthermore she worried that she would always live in the shadow of deep fear and humiliation.

She chose to confront her fears in the wilderness as part of a Vision Quest. Her task would be to spend three days and nights alone and fasting in Death Valley. She was part of a group of ten people, including myself and another wilderness guide. (Details of Vision Quest work will be further explained in chapter twelve.)

After a month of preparation time we headed off into Death Valley. After several days of continued instruction, including how to create self-generated ceremony, the day arrived for the group to go out for their time alone. Allison was terrified to go off on her own, and in the morning I had to walk with her to the place that she had chosen to spend her time. I seriously wondered if she would make it through the three days and nights. She did.

On the fourth morning, when she returned to base camp, she was radiant and strong. She described how terrified she was at first to be alone and how safe she felt in the end. She said it was perhaps the safest she had ever felt in her life. She was very surprised by her experience in Nature. She was a city dweller and had never camped in her life. She spent the first two days and nights making herself comfortable and feeling her own strength. On the third day she began her ceremony in earnest. At sunrise she began to gather stones to create a sacred circle of safety. At sunset she entered her circle, and called on her ancestors to witness her process. She also invoked the powers of the four directions to protect her. That night she would not sleep; she would confront the darkness. Allison described her experience as follows:

> As the sun set and I found myself alone with the darkness, I knew that I would confront both my fear and my power. I had never expressed to either my uncle or my mother my rage and hurt around my abuse. When I left home, that was basically it. I had superficial contact with my family, but we never spoke about my sexual abuse. In my twenties, both of them died and although I had grief I mostly felt relief. Buried underneath the relief was a lot of pain and unexpressed feelings. I decided that what I would do would be to call both of them to the outside edge of my circle and finally say out loud all of the things that I had suffered for so many years.
>
> First, I called my uncle in and then I waited until I felt his presence. Then I exploded with uncontrollable rage. I read him the riot act. I asked him to remember how he had threatened me, how he had taken advantage of an innocent little girl, how he had muffled my tears, and the terrible physical pain he had given me. I let my hatred flow. I actually felt him cower in my presence and for the first time I was the powerful one and he had to submit to my will. I relished the moment.
>
> I told him to stand by as I called my mother to the circle. I sobbed my heart out over her and how it was that she could have allowed me to be so abused. She should have protected me and she didn't. I have not had children and probably won't. I feel as though I both want to stop this line of people and fear that I might somehow be incapable of being a good mother myself. I needed her to hear how terrible the consequences of my childhood have been for me.
>
> At a certain point I felt as if I was in the presence of a many-

tentacled octopus, and it was terrifying. The tentacles were attached to different parts of me. Some of them went into my body and some of them went into my soul. I knew that it was critical that I remove each and every one of them. One of them was wrapped around my uterus and was the source of physical pain. It was also the root of my sexual dysfunction. I imagined myself with a light sword, like in the movie, and began to slash away at it. I did not want to be a victim any longer. I refused to have my uncle destroy my life from beyond the grave. When I felt the tentacle release, I moved on to the one entwined around my heart. This one took my breath away, the hurt was so large. My inability to be intimate with anyone was knotted up there. It extended back to my mother and I knew I had to sever the connection. She had failed to keep me safe. I will never understand how that could happen. Each tentacle brought up an aspect of my woundedness. As I continued on I went through enormous anger, then tears, as I expressed to them my horror. With every tentacle I would first cut it, and then go back and clean the wound.

The final tentacle seemed to attach down inside my core. It was big and black and as I followed it, I realized that it was the most powerful. To cut it and remove it would mean cutting and removing a large part of my identity. It was the place where I had hid behind my suffering. In order to let go of it I would have to let go of my rage, my anger, and my fear. I heard a voice ask: "Who are you, if you are not a victim of sexual abuse?" My immediate thought was "but I am a victim sexual abuse." Then I realized that I am also much more. I saw my life, and I saw myself living through it as a cripple. I understood that I was a victim to my victimhood. Then I experienced true pain as I acknowledged the trap that I had been living in. My primary identity was built around my sexual abuse. All of my other accomplishments meant nothing in comparison to my feelings of being victimized by my mother and uncle.

I suddenly got very calm and present to the darkness—I might even say comfortable with the darkness. The path became clear. I must release both my uncle and my mother. Yes, they had done something terrible, but I had spent most of my life maintaining and feeding their power over me. Even though they were both dead, they were still controlling and destroying my life. I could choose to no longer be at the effect of the past. I could move on to a healthier and more beneficial identity. I saw how I had exhausted friends and lovers with my ongoing story of pain and abuse. Now was the moment for me to forgive myself, now was the moment for real healing to take place. I declared out loud: "I choose life over story."

When I was finished with disconnecting all the tentacles, I used the image of a big psychic vacuum cleaner coming along and cleaning up the debris. I did not want any of this garbage around. In the end there was still my mother and uncle.

Forgiveness is a big word. I know that I discharged a lot of my anger and hurt, and that felt really good. I felt clean for the first time. I couldn't honestly say the words, "I forgive you," but I was able to put them to rest. I asked that the spirits of my ancestors, the ones who really love, guide, and protect me, that they might help my mother and uncle in finding peace. I took a solemn vow to be more conscious about not continually invoking them into my thoughts or my life. I sent them away with the words, "Peace be with you." As the first rays of sun crested the ridge, I stripped off all my clothes and poured the remains of my water over me, clean at last.

The ceremony Allison created for herself was very powerful. Her invocation of the ancestors, the creation of a sacred circle, speaking out loud her feelings, are classic elements of shamanic traditions. Her experience in the months to come reinforced that she had indeed turned a corner. She recognized that she would always carry the scars of her childhood horror, but she need not let it control life or her desire for fulfillment. Her mother and uncle had taken not only her innocence but also her life up to that time. She was determined not to give them one minute more.

DEALING WITH GRIEF

Situations of unimaginable horror such as sexual abuse or murder are shocking to our civilized sensibilities, yet not a day goes by without news of an atrocity somewhere. Women are stalked and murdered. A man with a gun opens fire at a restaurant or in school; the workplace is invaded by a disgruntled worker who shoots his co-workers; a building is bombed, killing innocent people. Sometimes the disaster is not caused by a person but by an act of Nature, such as a fire, flood, or hurricane.

In all of these situations the grief and trauma counselors arrive to ease the survivors' pain. Ministers, priests, and rabbis work with the people from their particular congregations. All of these nightmares-come-true may also be soothed by a calling in of the Spirit. Personal grief counseling is useful, but a public ceremony where the community gathers is critical. A skilled ceremonialist or minister who is sensitive to the inter-denominational aspects of the community may be of use in lifting the healing process out of the psychological dimension into the spiritual.

When TWA flight 800 exploded off of Long Island, nearly one thousand mourners gathered for a memorial service at the beach front closest to the crash. Media wire services reported: "Some walked into the Atlantic Ocean as if they never wanted to come back....One woman stood at the water's edge, her shoes off, crying as the water rushed across her feet. Grieving family members looked to the sea for a measure of comfort that has eluded them since 230 loved ones perished in the Atlantic Ocean....They sat in white folding chairs facing the ocean.... Some clutched red, yellow, and pink roses in memory of the victims. They listened as the New York Boys Choir sang 'The Wind Beneath My Wings,' and a minister, a rabbi, and priest offered prayers in English, Hebrew, and French.

"At the close of the ceremony bagpipes sounded and family members walked slowly to the water's edge. Many stood silently in clutches, holding and stroking each other. Some, pant legs rolled up and skirts lifted, waded knee-high into the surf, tossing roses into the waves. Several stuck roses in the sand, where they remained as silent sentinels to grief."

The horror and tragedy of an airplane crash, and the sudden death of loved ones is unimaginable to anyone who has not suffered such a loss. The impact of this simple and elegant ceremony is obvious. For friends and family to visit the scene of the disaster together, publicly grieve, and to begin the process of saying farewell is essential for healing. The offering of prayers from religious leaders in three different languages helps us to recognize what universally binds us together; family, friends, community, love, and Spirit.

A few years ago there was a devastating fire in the Berkeley Hills of California. One ceremonialist gathered together the children whose homes had burned and took the children on a Walk of Remembrance through the remains. Already there were signs of renewal—the grass was growing, the deer were returning. The children remembered old playing places, pets who were lost, homes and neighbors that were gone forever. The children were introduced to the four elements—Earth, Air, Fire, and Water—as part of the Spirit of Nature and given the opportunity to address what the elements meant to them. They were then given wildflower seeds to scatter for the rebirth of their neighborhoods. Simple and sacred acts remind us all that our connections run deep and that no matter how horrible a situation is, there is still a larger and greater reality in which we are all embedded.

SANCTIFYING DIVORCE

There are many reasons why marriages fail—broken trust, substance abuse, financial pressure, diverging career paths, and mental health problems. Whatever the issue, it can become an insurmountable problem. The only reason to stay together in any relationship is that it continues to be richly satisfying to all involved.

Without the support of extended family and friends, it is easy to call it quits. Today most nuclear families live isolated lives. Lacking a larger support system, couples often expect to have all of their needs met by their partner and it is difficult to satisfy inflated levels of expectation. This is a tremendous burden to place upon another. Sometimes divorce is the only sane response to a home filled with ill will. Divorce can be an act of kindness toward the children, especially if the dissolution is amiable. But when a divorce becomes a battle ground, the children suffer the most, especially when used as pawns in the negotiations, kidnapped by one parent, or deprived of contact with a mother, father, grandparents, or other relatives.

Organized religion must recognize divorce as a rite of passage. Rather than maintaining a judgmental view toward divorce, ministers and rabbis must begin to assist divorcing couples. This requires acceptance of the fact that a couple has reached the end of the road. Most pastors end up feeling helpless as they counsel a couple ultimately headed for a divorce, and for the couple, the church can no longer be a source of refuge but becomes a source of judgment and shame.

Robert Elliot, a United Methodist Church minister, pastoral counselor, and professor of theology at Southern Methodist University, has an innovative approach. Frustrated by what he perceived as the church's incapacity to minister to the needs of those whose marriages had fallen irrevocably apart, he created a divorce ceremony. He calls the ceremony "a service of ending and beginning." Elliot believes that the church should help in the healing process of a divorce, rather than remain silent or actively critical.

A divorce ceremony obviously is not for everyone, but Elliot feels that couples who took their marriage vows seriously may need an equivalent service to say "good-bye," to forgive, and to release their partner and themselves. This ceremony can be especially important when children are involved.

He performed such a ceremony with a couple whom he had married thirteen years earlier. Eight months after their divorce, he and the couple collaborated in creating the divorce ceremony.

The couple stood before the minister. The couple's three children, family, and friends stood behind them. The minister began with the well-know passage from Ecclesiastes:

> To everything there is a season...a time to kill, and a time to heal...
> a time to weep, and a time to laugh...a time to keep, and a time to
> cast away...

He then addressed the couple and reminded them that they had stood in good faith in church before and made marriage vows of commitment to one another. He acknowledged them in their struggle to keep those vows and recognized that sometimes a marriage cannot endure. A difficult decision had been made, and it was time once again to stand before God and declare a release from the marriage vows.

The couple then took turns releasing one another, affirming love and respect, apologizing for hurts, offering forgiveness, and praying for each other's good life to come.

The minister then released them from the bonds of marriage, but reaffirmed their commitment to parent their three children.

Each parent declared their intention to care, protect, and guide their children. They then apologized to their children for the pain the divorce caused them, letting them know that they were not the cause of the divorce. They ended by asking their friends and family to remember them in their prayers and to bless their new lives. The service ended with the Lord's Prayer.

This type of ceremony allows for an elevated type of closure on a relationship, and one in which the children are held sacred. It does not need to be done as publicly as this service. I have known other couples who have undone the connection bundles that they have made, and families who have used their heart-stone or talking stick to hold a council in which similar releasing and reaffirming has taken place. They all did it in a prayerful way and with love. It is not confusing to leave someone feeling love. To leave someone you have loved feeling hatred and anger *is* confusing. The emotions aroused through hatred or anger have a very long half-life. They give birth to depressions of all sorts, obsession, paranoia, revenge, sometimes even murder.

To be able to end a relationship consciously, especially one that involves children, can be done most easily if one asks "In whose light am I doing this?" It then becomes possible for the individual to say good-bye and forgive and release both their partner and themselves.

ONE-SIDED ENDINGS

All of us have experienced a relationship ending. It may be a relationship with a spouse or partner, a family member, or a friend. Other times the ending has to do with a job or a move to a new location. Sometimes it is a sudden and unexpected loss of life. A number of unresolved issues may be present in these dissolutions, especially if one person feels angry and simply refuses to have any further contact with the other person. This may leave a person feeling incomplete with the relationship, and incomplete with themselves.

Whenever we feel incomplete with another individual, it returns to haunt us. We wake up in the middle of the night with them on our mind. Or we find ourselves thinking about them at inappropriate times during the day. They may become an obsession where we replay old conversations or arguments, and reactivate all the emotions that come with reliving the drama. Often what we are experiencing is pain and grief over the loss of the relationship. Every time we experience a broken connection in our lives it is like going through a death. There is always a mourning period when we lose someone in our life. A ceremony of completion can be healing, even to the person who cannot or refuses to participate.

It is important to honor the mourning period, to feel the loss, anger, or pain. The ceremony should not take place prematurely. As the initial wave of emotion subsides and we are left with grief concerning the loss, we can then begin to think about coming to completion through a ceremonial act.

The healing work of ceremony in this situation is to cleanse the psyche or soul of the painful debris left behind by the loss and to help us come to terms with our role in the drama. Broken connections are rarely a one-sided affair. Both parties have a story to tell, which they experience as true. There may be a larger pattern at work; perhaps it is not the first time that someone has rejected another or been rejected, or it may be that others have criticized a particular aspect of our personality. We must pay attention to this kind of patterning or feedback.

Estranged relationships provide us with an opportunity for growth, a chance to untie a pattern or knot of behavior inside ourselves. When we only look to blame the other person, we do not take responsibility for our lives. We allow ourselves to become victims. What usually happens is we find ourselves attracted to the same type of person as before, and go through an almost identical experience all over again. How many times have we witnessed ourselves or our friends repeating the same relationship pattern over and over? It's as if we did not learn a thing from our past experience.

I frequently hear this type of pattern being blamed on "karma," as if it is this person's destiny to have one bad experience after another with the people in their life. These patterns or karmic configurations are actually lessons. If a person repeatedly attracts people who abuse and hurt them, there is a lesson to be learned there. When we do not learn the lesson, the pattern or karma returns in the form of a new person, but with the same old story and the same unhappy ending. Once we understand the lesson that this type of person has to teach us, we can move on to attracting healthier people into our lives. We can then take full responsibility for how we might have been setting ourselves up for a lifetime of hurt. Whenever we break an old pattern or psychic program we are then free to experience a new level of relationship, and a new level of teaching that will spur us on to further challenges.

After a broken marriage or love affair, or any broken connection in which the people involved are estranged from one another, it is possible to find resolution. I always suggest that people go through the appropriate period of mourning and self-reflection before attempting a ceremony.

Begin by choosing a time and place to conduct a ceremony of release.

Part of the preparation is to think about what binds you to that person. As part of the ceremony bring objects that remind you of the person and the relationship. These may include photos, pieces of art, journal writings, articles of clothing, and gifts received. Set up an altar in response to the question "In whose light?" Light candles, incense, and find your center. Sometimes it is useful to invite a special friend to bear witness to your process. Call in the Spirit to help and guide you. Speaking out loud, invite the person who is estranged to your circle, and do it with love, if at all possible. Explain to them what it is you are doing, stating this is a ceremony for release and healing.

The ceremony itself is defined by your creative imagination. People have taken various objects, told the story behind them, and then proceeded to burn or break them in order to find release. Others have buried objects or thrown them in the ocean. People have taken objects that they wished to keep and buried them for a month, from full moon to full moon, as a way of cleansing them of past connections. With each item it is important to be clear about the intention, and with each conflict explore a way to claim your responsibility and, ultimately, your power in the situation. Be guided by the Spirit to find the place of forgiveness in your heart for the other person and also for yourself. Remember to release the person at the end of the ceremony and to ask for peace.

This type of ceremony is very powerful, and many people have reported that often within days of the ceremony they either bump into the person or receive a telephone call from them offering peace. Part of the power of prayer is that it can affect people at a distance.

I had one client who told me she had been sick for the past six months and could not figure out what was happening to her. As we talked she told me that her lover had left her, and she had been heartbroken. He had been quite sudden and definite in his ending of the relationship and she was still shocked by his leaving. At a certain moment she decided to take a bracelet that he had given her and bury it. One part of her thought this would be a way for her to release him, the other part was still conspiring how she might get him back. I asked where she had buried the bracelet and she sheepishly said that she had taken it out to his land. She then confessed she had buried it there with the intention that somehow he would remember her and return his affections to her. My next question was how long ago did she bury the bracelet. Her answer was six months ago. I suggested that she return to the land, dig up the bracelet, and if she still desired to get rid of it, do it completely. Within a week of digging up and giving away the bracelet, her illness vanished as quickly as it arrived.

The explanations for this occurrence are not very nice. Ceremony must be taken seriously. Her ceremony of supposed release was actually a ceremony to bind her ex-lover to her. Voodoo is never very appealing and interfering with another's will, even at a distance, will only bounce back with unforeseen ramifications. She had tried to use love magic to win back her lover, but more importantly she saw how easily she was tempted into playing with magic. For her, the period of grace had ended and in the future she would approach such matters with a serious view toward the light.

·9·

THE BLESSINGS OF CHILDREN

We can know the future only in the laughter of healthy children.
—ANN WILSON SCAEF

A RITE OF CONSCIOUS CONCEPTION

There is perhaps nothing more wonderful than two peoples' desire to have a child together. Today many couples carefully plan their pregnancy and eagerly anticipate the birth of their child. The forethought that comes with conscious conception yields many benefits. For the couple, the pregnancy does not come as a surprise, allowing them to plan their careers and finances around the coming birth. The woman is confident in her partner and his desire to have a baby with her. The lack of ambiguity toward the unborn baby means the baby, from his or her conception, exists in a completely secure environment.

One study of teenage suicides indicates that the early response of the mother toward the *in utero* baby has lasting effects. A book entitled *The Psychological Aspects of Abortion*, contained "The Embryology of Consciousness," an essay by psychotherapist Andrew Feldmar. Feldmar had been seeing a number of teenagers who had all made repeated attempts at suicide. He noted their depressions and subsequent suicidal tendencies occurred with a seasonal regularity. He then interviewed the mothers asking them questions about their pregnancies. Each of the women admitted to unsuccessfully attempting to abort her child during the first trimester. Counting backward from the birth date of the child, Feldmar noted there was a correlation between the mother's desire to abort the baby and the suicide. If the mother attempted abortion, say in the month of March of her pregnancy, it was during this time period that the teenager would become depressed or attempt suicide. In other words the teenage suicides corresponded to the seasonal cycle in which they felt acutely unwanted. Furthermore, the style of the suicide mirrored the style of the abortion attempt. If the mother used a mechanical means, so did the child; if the mother used a chemical, the child tried an overdose.

Feldmar then invited the mother to tell the child about her pregnancy and the abortion attempt. The mothers may have never before confessed to anyone her abortion attempt, least of all to her child. Once the child absorbed this information, he or she no longer felt compelled to complete the abortion through suicide. None of the children attempted suicide again, although they might still become seasonally depressed.

Couples who choose conscious conception enjoy a peace of mind, for they know they have done everything right. On the practical level they have probably stopped smoking, abusing drugs, and drinking irresponsibly. They have been anticipating the time in which they will make love to create a child. Many people report feeling the presence of the unborn spirit in the room; they often know if it is a boy or girl child that has been conceived.

The couples I have known who have chosen conscious conception have worked with a number of elements to create a sacred vessel in which they make love. For most couples this takes place in the comfort of their own bedroom, but I have known couples who have chosen to travel to traditional pilgrimage sites in the world, such as Jerusalem, Egypt, or Glastonbury to conceive. Others have gone to special places in Nature. Everyone I have encountered who has successfully conceived has set the tone with prayers and verbally called in the spirit of the child. Often they call upon the spirits of the ancestors, and especially if they are risking passing on a genetic disease, they ask for special blessings form the Divine and the ancestors. Prayers frequently include asking for a healthy pregnancy and a normal birth. Couples who have longed for the child to be of a particular sex, perhaps after a number of children of one sex, have been successful by following and honoring some of the "old wive's tales" that address how to sex a child. These include observing lunar cycles, using special positions for making love, and altering the body's pH level by either increasing or decreasing alkalinity or acidity through diet or douching.

The joy of conceiving consciously carries a couple through the pregnancy. Children who were wanted even before they were conceived are unique and special. And their parents are also unique, in that they are determined to be loving and aware parents.

BIRTHING WAY CEREMONY FOR THE EXPECTANT MOTHER

The Birthing Way ceremony is a very good example of how working with the Spirit can transform the social occasion of the "baby shower" into a sacred event. Traditionally the Birthing Way is a time for women to gather around the expectant mother and support her in her birth vision. This ceremony is performed in a number of ways. Sometimes it is for women only, sometimes men and women meet separately and then come together later in the day, or sometimes men and women participate together from the beginning. All of these considerations should be taken into account when creating such a ceremony. The following ceremony was held with both men and women present from the beginning, including the pregnant woman's midwife, father, and teenage son.

Patricia and Douglas were expecting their first child as a couple. Both already had adolescent boys from previous marriages, and both of the boys had almost died at birth from unforeseen complications. The couple was determined to be conscious throughout the conception, pregnancy, and birth of this much desired child.

Near the end of Patricia's pregnancy, she was given a Birthing Way ceremony—what most people would think of as a baby shower.

On a Sunday afternoon people arrived bringing food, flowers, and gifts. We invited everyone to come into a special room where we had pillows arranged on the floor and an altar in the center containing a statue of mother and child, lit candles, and flowers.

Once everyone was settled I spoke to the group expressing our intention to honor Patricia and her desire for a natural home birth, free of complications. We began by passing the Talking Stick around the circle, with each person speaking her best wishes for Patricia and the baby. Many women told stories of the birth of their children, and spoke of how they wished they might have had such a ceremony. Patricia's father said he had never seen Patricia look so beautiful as with this pregnancy; her face was full and radiant. He then recounted what he could remember of her own birth. Carol, Patricia's longtime friend, spoke of being present at the birth of Patricia's first son, how he had almost died in her arms, what a nightmare it was, and how different she envisioned this birth to be.

At the end of the circle the midwife brushed Patricia's hair and wove flowers into it, while I washed her feet in a bowl of water in which flower petals had been scattered, then dried them in corn meal, symbolizing a long life, a strong birth, and much fertility. The nature of the ceremony is to nourish the pregnant woman and make her feel beautiful and special. Patricia and Douglas then took turns expressing their vision of what the perfect birth would be, reaffirming their love for one another and for the coming child. They spoke of a successful home birth, no complications, and a healthy and happy child. The people present then came up to Patricia, and if they felt so moved, touched her pregnant belly, spoke their blessing, and gave Patricia their gifts. Some gifts were practical, like a stroller from her father, and some were magical to aid her in the birth itself. I gave her a special carved box from Bali that traditionally holds the umbilical cord. I suggested that she should be the keeper of the cord until the baby grew old enough to leave home; perhaps that would be a good time to really cut the cord between mother and child by returning the cord to the grown child.

After more well-wishing we blew out the candles and went into the dining room to feast and make merry. About five weeks later, Patricia gave easy birth, at home, to a healthy baby boy.

As with any of these ceremonies, the personality of the people involved should be of primary consideration. As a friend or family member, it will be in your hands to create a rite that is in keeping with the person. It should be enjoyable not embarrassing, and sacred but still light-hearted wherever possible. The creation of any of these ceremonies is limited only by our imaginations. I have been at Birthing Way ceremonies where hard boiled eggs have been passed around and those present have decorated the eggs and left them for the mother-to-be. Other ceremonies have incorporated a Buddhist tradition of tying a piece of red string around the neck or wrist of everyone present as a way of keeping vigil for the birth, a daily reminder to hold the woman in our prayers as she approaches the moment of motherhood.

Rites for a Lost Child

There is perhaps nothing so wounding to our soul than the loss of a child. Miscarriages, death due to illness, child abuse, accident, suicide, and even murder are unfortunately part of our daily reality. Abortion, although a choice, is not an easy decision to live with and often leaves lasting scars for the woman. All of these moments call out for a sacred acknowledgment. It is impossible to suffer through this type of loss alone. We need the support of loved ones and a way to connect with the eternal divine.

When a woman loses a baby through miscarriage, stillbirth, or sudden infant death syndrome (SIDS), the loss can be tremendous. Often she and her partner have been preparing for the birth, creating a room for the baby, and buying the many objects that are required to welcome an infant into the world. In addition to dealing with their grief, the parents are then faced with the heartbreaking and delicate task of undoing all of their preparations.

I have heard from many women who have miscarried how devastating the experience was and how abandoned they felt in their grief. They report that many friends and relatives ignore their loss or find it very difficult to address. A mourning ceremony can be of tremendous comfort after the initial shock and grief. A family member or good friend should suggest that a ceremony be held for both the parents and the child. It is important that the person initiating the ceremony be willing to coordinate the affair. The couple, however, should choose who they would like to have in attendance and approve the general flow of the ceremony. This begins their process toward healing as they come to realize what it is they need to do or would like to have said as part of the rite of mourning.

One woman I know had tremendous grief over a miscarriage that occurred early in the second trimester of the pregnancy. Afterward she realized that she did not ever have the pleasure of holding that child in her arms, nor the completion of burying the body. She asked her minister to help her in finding a path to healing. The minister and the couple worked together to create a mourning ceremony. They invited a few close friends and family members to come to their home, in order to bear witness to their grief and loss. The minister began by addressing the sadness of the occasion and the importance of acknowledging grief. He used traditional prayers and conducted himself as he would at a funeral. The couple then took turns speaking from their hearts about their hopes and dreams for this child. They also spoke of their feelings of guilt concerning the loss of the baby. The father felt that he had not been attentive enough to his wife, expressed guilt concerning the fact that she was still working although pregnant, and how inadequate it made him feel. The mother felt that somehow she was responsible, that she could have taken better physical care of herself. She also felt guilt around her fears about giving birth and that perhaps she secretly did not want to be a mother. Later, both parents expressed how cleansing it was to speak about their own self doubts and guilt concerning the miscarriage, and how those doubts were beginning to interfere in their relationship.

When they were finished the other people in attendance took turns speaking. Some addressed their own experiences of loss, others offered encouragement and affirmation to the couple as potential parents. People were very sensitive to the moment, no one told the couple that they could have another child, although everyone secretly wished for a healthy baby for the couple.

The parents then took a beautiful box in which they had placed the baby's receiving blanket, a dress, and a small stuffed bunny, and buried it in the yard. They then planted a peach tree over the spot in remembrance of the unborn but still loved child. When they were finished and the minister had offered more prayers, they invited those present to help them in packing up the nursery room. They had boxes and labels and everyone pitched in to help undo the room. When they were finished they went off to a restaurant for a traditional closure.

People who have lost a child are often left stunned and bewildered. Even if there has been a lengthy illness preceding the death, nothing can adequately prepare a parent for the loss. We now know that grief comes in stages: denial, anger, mourning, and acceptance. We also know that caring for the body and sitting in vigil around the body is beneficial for the living. For parents to be denied access to the body of their child is a modern human tragedy. Any family who has had the opportunity to tend to the body of a loved one during the interval between death and the funeral will affirm its difficult but healing power.

One simple but beautiful example of a funeral service comes from Virginia Hine. She tells of a family who lost a two-year-old daughter to cancer. They had a conventional church service to which they added their own touches. The child had taken particular delight in helium balloons, so they filled the church with balloons. They tied them to the back of the pews and after the service they invited everyone to write, with magic markers, a short message to the child on their balloon. They then took the balloons outside and together let them go, watching them disappear out of sight but remain forever in their hearts. When simple symbolic acts are combined with a spiritual impulse they move beyond the psychological and into the realm of the soul.

·10·

CONSCIOUS DYING

MICHEL'S JOURNEY HOME

There is a lot of talk these days about conscious dying. Many people are now facing and going through their own dying process in an enlightened way. They are doing it with grace, dignity, and open-hearted communication with those around them.

The following account of one woman's dying process comes from my own experience and, due to its unusual nature, needs some background information. I live in New Mexico, a state that is known for its unique natural beauty and Southwestern lifestyle. It is a state inhabited by three distinct cultural groups. The original people, the Pueblo Indians, still live in their villages, often poverty stricken but made beautiful with adobe dwellings, ceremonial kivas, and plazas in which the people conduct traditional ceremonial dances throughout the four seasons of the year. The dominant Hispanic culture reaches back four hundred and fifty years. The Hispanics live on rich agricultural land along the rivers, where everyone knows that *agua es vida*. Their land was typically deeded to them from old Spanish land grants, and over the centuries they have passed it on to the next generation. Because of both of these traditions, it is still possible to bury loved ones on your own land and to maintain a family burial ground. The rest of us are known as "Anglos." The Anglos tend to live in big houses built on the mountainsides to afford everyone a great view of the wondrous sunsets that do indeed turn the Sangre de Cristos mountains blood red. The sense of community is strong here.

I live along the Pojoaque River, on land that can only be described as an oasis in the desert. I also live in a community with ten other people.

Our land is owned in common, while each house is owned privately, allow-ing each individual to sell their house and their share of the property if they so choose. We have no guiding teacher, philosophy, or religion. Our connection is to stewarding the land that we love. Our relationship with one another is one of loving good neighbors and extended family.

Six years ago, Michel, the woman who originally found the land and initiated the community, came down with cancer. She was determined to heal herself and put forth a valiant effort. She made the decision not to use chemotherapy but rather approach her illness through alternative healing practices. A few years into the illness it became necessary for her to sell her home here in order to meet her rising medical bills. Her friend Ella bought her house at a more than fair price, providing her with the much needed money. For the next two years, Michel traveled to healers and visited her children, grandchildren, sisters, and father. Michel was a charming, enter-taining, and willful woman. In spite of the cancer spreading in a most vicious way, she continued to hope for a miracle. Her determination and capacity to endure never ceased.

In the spring of 1995, Michel, now age 56, returned to the communi-ty for a visit. Her life was becoming more difficult; she needed a full-time nurse, was rapidly losing the capacity to travel, and was having trouble walking. She asked if she could return for the summer with the purpose of healing herself, or, failing that, dying and being buried here. Annie, a nurse practitioner with a private practice in town, who lives here, agreed to have Michel stay in her house, and Sandra, a very good friend of the communi-ty, agreed to come from the Seattle area and be a primary care giver. And so Michel returned, and with her came a flow of visiting hospice workers to help with her treatments, medication, and bathing.

Because Annie had only one bedroom, Linda, another member of the community, offered Michel the use of her guest bedroom. Meanwhile, Sandra, who had been in the process of deciding to move here and build herself a bedroom as an extension to Annie's house, decided that she would quickly build the second bedroom in order to give Michel room of her own and make things easier for Annie. The addition went up, and by the end of the summer Michel had a lovely new room. By the fall, Michel's condition was deteriorating. Community members were also experiencing exhaustion and burn-out as her care became more demanding. Annie rene-gotiated her contract with Michel, stating that Michel could say until

February. In the late summer, Becky, a hospice nurse from Phoenix who had cared for Michel there, decided to move here and be Michel's full-time nurse. Another community member, Cal, rented Becky her spare room. For the remainder of Michel's life, Becky, Sandra, and Annie would be her primary caregivers.

Michel's journey was not an easy one. She continued to hope for a cure in spite of the fact that the cancer had eaten through to the outside of her body. Another friend, Leslie, who is a videographer, came to interview Michel for a documentary that she was doing on conscious dying. She ended up virtually dropping her project, and took up caring for Michel as well.

Michel was an intelligent woman, and obviously a woman with a lot of charisma, who had a knack for drawing people into her life. She was well versed in alternative healing and New Age spirituality, and had also made contact with several American Indian medicine women who periodically visited and offered their wisdom and ceremonial skills. She was also visited by friends, children, grandchildren, siblings, and her father. On one hand this was wonderful; on the other it began to become a strain on the community at large, and especially for Annie in whose house all these guests congregated and stayed.

As autumn turned to winter, it became clear that Michel was in a state of denial about her condition. She could not believe that she was really dying, and it became more difficult to talk about conscious dying. Six months earlier, when she still maintained a hope of a cure, she spoke about what we should do if she should die. She wished to be buried here on the land, and she wanted to be buried sitting up, facing East. She wanted a simple service with prayers, chanting, and drumming. She also did not want any last minute medical interventions.

In December, the situation reached a crisis level. Michel was placed on ever-increasing doses of pain medication. She became bedridden and at times delirious; she required twenty-four-hour-a-day care. She was having visions of her deceased mother and friends who had passed over, but she did not want to go with them, she only wished to be healed. The women who were caring for her had reached a state of exhaustion bordering on breakdown. On the full moon we decided to hold a ceremony for the women, and we were to meet at six o'clock in the evening. Annie, Sandra, and Leslie arrived forty minutes late. Michel was in a crisis, her bladder was no longer working. We decided to pray, do ceremony, and ask for guidance

We lit candles and smudged with sage. We called in the Spirit of our different traditions and Michel's ancestors to bear witness to us. Then we began with a ball of yarn. The first woman to speak wrapped the string around her wrist, and when she was done she tossed it across the circle to whoever wanted to go next. The yarn went over and under, across, and back and forth as each woman spoke again and again, entwining us together as we spoke. We cried in the way only women can do, and we raged. It was deep and it was genuine. There was rage around the cancer, and there was anger toward Michel for not dying consciously. There was disappointment that her death was not going to be a glorious and transcendent moment. There was laughter at the audacity of our disappointment. How dare she not die consciously! There was real exhaustion and fragility. There was Michel in a crisis right now, and there was love. There were also life and death decisions yet to be made. We needed to figure out how to not only take care of Michel, but take care of one another as well. We came up with ways in which we could further support one another, and help ourselves and Michel.

At the end of the ceremony we were tangled in a spider web of yarn. As we disentangled ourselves from the yarn, we verbally released our attachments to Michel and asked that she might also have release. We then burned the yarn in the fireplace.

Then there was Michel. After the ceremony we went to Michel's room and gathered around her bed. She wanted to know what to do now, and what her options were. We all wept. Annie explained to her that her bladder was no longer functioning, and her options were to ride the pain and die, or go to the emergency room and get a catheter. Michel chose the catheter. Getting her into the car was not an easy process and having the catheter put in was very painful. In fact, over the next two weeks she would have to return to the emergency room three times in order to have the permanent catheter installed properly. Each time it was excruciating.

About this time people in the community began having dreams about when Michel would die. There was more disappointment around Michel's decision to have the catheter installed. She had said she would not go that route, but when her life hinged upon it, she chose medical intervention. By this point, she was on the equivalent of 15,000 milligrams of morphine a day. Friends who had died of AIDS had been on 10 milligrams of morphine in their final days. We began to realize that we were no longer dealing with our beloved Michel bur with a shell of who she was. There were, however, moments when the old Michel would emerge. One of these moments occurred on the Winter Solstice.

Winter Solstice is the day our community gathers together in the community house for a celebratory brunch, where we exchange presents and make prayer flags to hang around the land for the upcoming year. The prayer flags are made out of pieces of muslin cloth. We use magic markers and paints to decorate them, and write out our prayers for the year. While we were busy doing this, someone announced that a local woman who works in death and dying was coming out to visit Michel. No one really thought very much about it until she arrived with seven other people. We reckoned she was conducting a class and was going to show her students how to be with a dying person. Becky was with the sleeping Michel when they entered Michel's room. She tried to tell them that there were too many of them and that more than two people only confused Michel.

The show, as they say, must go on. The teacher and group brushed Becky aside and entered the room, whereupon the teacher began to rearrange Michel's altar. Becky, seeing this, replaced the items the way Michel wanted them, and was told by the teacher to leave the statue so that "when Michel awoke she could gaze upon it." Becky resisted the urge to throttle her. The group then began to meditate around Michel's bed, while the leader gently woke Michel up. After they left Michel asked, "Who were all those people? Did they expect me to die in front of them?" All of us, including Michel had a good laugh about it. I called it Death Tours USA.

There were so many crises before the holidays that we were sure Michel would not survive the New Year. because we were planning on burying Michel on the land we needed a coffin built and grave dug, a twelve-foot hole to accommodate her seated position. None of us had ever done this before, but we knew digging in frozen ground could be difficult. Our good friend Ramon built the box, and our neighbor Tony brought his backhoe over and dug the grave. Annie filed the appropriate papers with the county. In a sense, we were ready for the inevitable moment.

At any rate, Michel survived Winter Solstice, Christmas, and the New Year. My husband, Francis, asked her how long she wanted to stay around; her response was three or four more months. By the New Year,

Annie, Sandra, and Becky were on verge of collapse. Given the state of her body, no one but Francis could imagine that she could live that long. It did not seem humanly possible. Michel's capacity to endure the break-through pain was awesome—she rarely cried and more often simply winced in pain. She also somehow managed to maintain her warm personality. I have seen women with PMS more erratic and irritable than Michel on a bad day.

Come February, Annie told Michel that something had to change. Her family was contacted to see whether she could go to them; it proved to be a dead end. Plus, there was no feasible way to move a person in Michel's condition. Everyone felt awful. Michel called a friend and told her that Annie was throwing a dying person out. Finally, Linda came up with a brilliant solution to move Michel into the community house, set up the dining room as her bedroom, and have Becky and the other caretakers live in the bedrooms. Why we didn't think of this sooner only proves how stressed out everyone was. Annie would have her house back, and the ongoing visitors and helpers would be next door and not in Annie's space. It worked beautifully.

Over the next month we despaired as Michel stopped eating and rapidly wasted away to skin and bones. We realized that Michel had lost faith. She had so firmly believed in her capacity to heal herself—for that healing not to manifest was a crushing blow to her spirit. She had been so fixated on life, she could not entertain what the afterlife might be like, or that it even existed. There were, however, moments where she would drift in and out of this realm and report that it was very beautiful there. Yet she would not go or could not go. It seemed she had opportunities to cross over but always fought it off. In watching this, it appeared to me that during the dying process there are moments when we can surrender, or even will ourselves, over to a more merciful end. Barring that, we can only wait for Death to come and get us. All negotiations cease at that moment. As Seneca said, "those who do not go willingly, the Fates take kicking and screaming."

Michel did not go kicking and screaming. In fact, she never screamed. She coped with her pain in the most stoic manner. Near the end she began to wish for release and slowly, over a period of days, slipped out of consciousness. On the night of March 7, 1996, she quietly stopped breathing. Family members were immediately called and would be arriving the next day. She had been taking by then 22,000 milligrams of morphine a day.

Our agreement with Michel was not to touch her body for a couple of hours, and to leave her lie in quiet solitude. Our agreement with the state of New Mexico was to bury her as quickly as possible. Candles were already burning in her room and we lit incense. After a couple of hours we arranged her body to fit into the casket. We did not know how rigor mortis worked or how to position her in an upright, seated posture, except by placing a stool under her legs. We agreed to leave her in peace until the morning and then wash and tend to her body.

The next morning Annie and Becky cared for Michel's body, and when she was clean, she was carried in a blanket out to our ancient adobe chapel, where she was placed in her coffin. We used a shoulder harness and belts to strap her securely into a sitting position. The room was filled with candles, an altar, and flowers. We placed chairs for family members and friends, who began arriving that afternoon and evening to view the body. We would bury her at sunrise.

The following morning family and friends carried her coffin to the grave site. How we were going to lower the casket successfully into the ground was a question in all of our minds. We set up a large tripod made out of tipi poles, wrapped the casket with ropes and hoisted it up and over the grave. There was a moment in which the tripod began to fall and together we caught it and set it straight. Slowly we swung the coffin into position and lowered it into the grave. In keeping with the Hispanic spirit of our place, a local priest had specially blessed holy water to sprinkle on the ground, and we said blessings for Michel and the consecration of our cemetery.

We also smudged everyone and everything, and drummed and chanted as Michel had requested. Her family and friends made prayers, told stories, and wept. Ramona, a dear friend of Michel's led us in a rosary. I called in the Four Directions as Michel wished, and asked that each direction bear witness to the passing of this woman, this mother, this grandmother, sister, and daughter. And I asked that her journey be blessed. Together we sang more songs—the one I remember most was "Michel Row Your Boat Ashore, Alleluia." Afterwards we feasted; the day was glorious, and we gathered in small groups on the lawns, talking, telling stories, and relaxing.

In the days, weeks, and months following Michel's death, we rehashed all that transpired many times. Her death changed how most of us felt about dying, conscious dying, pain control, and our capacity to carry expectations. Each of us has our own particular view of the situation.

Annie realized that when she initially invited Michel to be here, she had no idea how complex the situation would become or how many support people, family, and friends would arrive on her doorstep. Looking back, Annie feels great gratitude at being able to have offered her place to Michel. Immediately after the funeral she felt as if she would never do such a thing again; six months later, she feels she would make herself available again to assist in helping a loved one die. She would also have much clearer lines of communication set up.

Annie also feels that her opinions on assisted death changed after the experience with Michel. She states, "In Michel's last three weeks, she was in a semicomatose state and racked with pain. There was no quality of life. When I saw the amount of drugs required to keep her alive, but still in pain, it seems that a little drug to die cannot be bad, but merciful. We need to think about our own dying and the reality of our death. We need to talk and feel what it might be like in order to do it as part of the practice of living. We need to prepare ourselves to have a good death."

For myself, I know now that death truly has is own time. I feel thankful that we managed to do the entire burial without professional help. It was not easy, but we did it. I used to think that pain control was essential, but after watching Michel I began to feel that it too has its limits in terms of serving the dying. The Michel we knew and loved disappeared somewhere along the line, and what was left was the morphine addiction that walked a very thin line in maintaining itself. Uncontrollable chronic pain is the body's way of telling us it is time to leave.

I was horrified by the group of "death counselors." There was no relationship, no real connection. The leader knew Michel was here and could have come out to visit Michel months earlier, taking time to cultivate a genuine connection with her. Coming in at the final hour, with a group of people is not acceptable at such an intimate time. I recommend being very cautious about letting such people into the field of your dying loved ones. It is essential to have a genuine relationship in place, then the dying person and family can mutually benefit from a good counselor.

Looking back on the experience, there was a lot to learn about the nature of forgiveness. Personally, I felt as though I needed to forgive Michel for living so long under such horrendous conditions. I also needed to forgive myself, take responsibility for carrying expectations around her death, and for my own experience of disappointment. I realize now that to project onto a dying person my ideas of how they should die is not only incorrect, it's stupid. All I can really do is remind myself to be compassionate and know that with each loved one's passing I ultimately confront my own mortality. I now know that even my own ideas of how I would like to die, or my preconceived ideas of how I will die, are probably erroneous. No one can possibly know how they will respond to their own dying until the moment actually arrives. I have seen wonderful, aware people have bitter, agonizing endings, and I have seen mean, angry people have a complete epiphany before they die. Each of us will cross that fateful bridge one day. My prayer is that we may do it with grace and dignity, surrounded by people who love us.

As for the community at large, the experience of Michel's death forged stronger bonds between us and our land. It was a very stressful situation, but we did stay in communication and do ceremony with one another. We especially felt the urge to protect the caregivers and make them take time off. We also decided as a group that from here on out, we would not accept any unusual requests; everyone gets buried in small wooden boxes, lying down.

·11·

TEENAGERS

Mad, Bad, and Dangerous to Know

OTHER TIMES AND OTHER PLACES

One of the great sorrows of the modern world is the absence of true initiations for our young adults. Throughout the world, traditional cultures still recognize and perform real rites of passage for their teenagers. The very word "teen" has two meanings according to the Oxford Dictionary. The first definition describes teen as 'harm inflicted or suffered; trouble, suffering, woe, anger, and wrath.' The second definition refers to someone from the ages of 13 to 19. Coincidental, but none the less interesting.

Traditional cultures in such places as Africa, Asia, the Americas, and Australia give full adult status to their children usually between the ages of 13 and 15. In general, initiations for boys occur more frequently than for girls, with cultures rooted in hunting and gathering initiating their young women with elaborate ceremonies, and cultures rooted in agriculture focusing their puberty rites on the boys.

Girls are welcomed into the community of adults as women themselves after their first menstrual cycle. Typically, they are provided with a ceremony that initiates them into the Greater Mystery of Life. The initiation of boys often requires a more complex ordeal such as the shedding of their own blood as they enter their manhood. Some anthropologists have suggested that the blood letting aspect of many male initiations is a form of mimicry symbolizing women's menstruation.

The use of mutilation and scarification is common in many cultures. Among the Maori, there is elaborate tattooing; in the Amazon, both boys and girls might have ear and lip plugs inserted to stretch the skin, thus making themselves more attractive. In Thailand and Burma, the hill tribes encircle the necks of young girls with rings of gold that eventually deform and elongate their necks. In Africa, some tribes scar the face, shoulders, backs, and arms in intricate patterns to increase one's beauty and power. African, Middle Eastern, and Australian traditions are also known for their genital mutilations, where adolescent boys' penises are either circumcised or subincised, and girls undergo clitoridectomies.

In the West modern young people have adopted both tattooing and body piercing as ways of distinguishing themselves, and as forms of sexual allure. They, however, rarely experience the support of their familial tribe; more commonly, the family is horrified that they have disfigured their bodies.

In many cultures, a girl's coming of age ceremony tends to be more celebratory in nature than the ordeals a boy goes through. Often all the young women who began their menstruation, or moon time, over the preceding year are presented to the tribe in a celebratory dance. Individually, as each girl has begun bleeding, the general pattern is for her to be cared for by the women in her family. In many cultures she becomes "taboo" during her moon time. Taboo means very powerful and very holy.

Among the Shasta Indians of California, each girl is given an elaborate ceremony that is also an ordeal. According to the account of anthropologist Roland B. Dixon, upon the onset of the first menstrual cycle a girl is immediately placed in a menstrual hut, her face painted with red stripes, and a visor of blue jay feathers placed upon her head. For the next ten days she is lovingly attended to by her mother and an old woman, usually her grandmother. They do everything for her, comb her hair, wash her face, cut up her food, and speak to her only in whispers. She is fed a restricted and specific diet and is given only warm water with a small amount of clay stirred into it to drink. She is not to hurry and not to get excited. Her job is to gather fire wood everyday for herself and everyone in the village. She is accompanied by several young girls, and if they meet anyone on the path the others turn aside, avert their eyes, and allow her to pass. Each morning the girl tells her mother any dreams that she might have, because she is now so powerful that these dreams are considered to be prophetic.

Every night there is a ceremonial dance. It begins with the girl dancing back and forth, to the east and to the west, as the onlookers sit in rows facing eastward. If she tires she has two men there to support her. As the days go by friends and relatives from neighboring villages arrive, painted as if for a war-dance. By this time the line dance has transformed into a "round dance" with both men and women participating. On the tenth night the dance continues until dawn at which time everyone stops for breakfast, then resumes the songs and dance until noon. The two men supporters then remove the girl's visor and throw it out of the circle to a man who catches it. Everything stops and the girl is taken by her mother to the river to bathe. The girl is dressed in her finest clothes and ornaments. She then returns to her people and everyone dances in celebration. When the dance ends, the mother brings out baskets filled with food—everyone feasts and then goes home. The ceremony is now complete.

The girl has been transformed into a woman before the eyes of her family and village. She has been initiated into the great mystery of the generations that came before her, as well as those who will issue forth from her womb. Her place is among the women, and she now has full responsibility as an adult woman and full respect. She will soon marry, bear and raise her children, and eventually will grow old in the company of the tribe. As a grandmother she will complete her obligations to past and future generations.

Puberty rites for boys can be much more demanding. Many cultures require a rigorous ordeal in which the young men symbolically die and are reborn as adult men. However, in some cultures, the dying may become more than symbolic, and a number of the boys may not survive the initiation. Among the Mende of Africa, if the boy dies during his initiation his name cannot be spoken again. His parents are told: "I am sorry to tell you that the pot that you gave me to fire is broken." There is no public grieving, rather it is as if the boy never existed.

In most male initiations there is usually a very dramatic separation from the mother and women in general. Sometimes the women wail as if the son is now dead, or the women will lie on the ground as the boys walk over them as if they were dead. This separation from the mother seems to be a key ingredient in male initiations. After the initiation, the boys, who are now men, live among the men and participate in the ceremonies, secret societies, and mysteries of manhood. In the modern world, many women who have been raising sons alone report that at around age thirteen it is time for the boys to go and live with their fathers. It seems both natural and necessary for young men to separate from their mothers and learn the ways of men.

In central Australia, the Aborigine Arunta men initiate their boys by capturing them and taking them off to a special camp. The mothers scream and impress upon the boys that they will never return to them. The boys then have their bodies painted and witness a special dance known as a *corroboree*, where the elder males chant the stories of the ancient heroes of the Dreamtime. Over a period of days the boy is initiated into tribal secrets and the ancient wisdom and history of his people. He is sworn to secrecy. During this time his nasal septum is pierced enabling him to wear a nose bone. Again there is more dancing and singing, and more lines of separation are drawn between boys and women.

As the ceremony progresses, it becomes more intense. When the sound of the bull roarers are heard it becomes time for the boys to be circumcised. The boy must be strong and show no fear or pain. The sound of the whirling bull roarer is the voice of the spirit who will help the boy heal after the ordeal. At this time he is also introduced to the *churingas*, sacred objects that are the dwelling places of the ancestors. He then remains in the men's camp until healed and ready for the next mutilation. Again in the company of only men, the boy's penis is subincised, or sliced open. With each phase and mutilation the boy acquires increased privilege and status.

Again the boy stays with men until healed. Then he is presented to the tribe, where the women snatch some of his hair as a reminder of his initiation. He is now able to sit among the elders and be present for secret male ceremonies. The ceremony still has a number of days to go until it is complete. The young man is now decorated and armed with a boomerang, which he throws toward his mother's ancestors' sacred place, or *songline*. He then goes into three days of silence in which he witnesses a number of performances that instill in him the deep history of his people. The final ordeal is for the young man to lie down upon the smoking wood of a fire and not get up until the elders give him permission. Now he has full status as a man in the tribe.

The previous ceremony is one of the more extreme puberty rites, but it is not uncommon. Genital mutilation occurs everywhere around the world. We circumcise our boys at birth; other cultures do it at puberty. In other cultures girls have their labias and/or clitorises removed as part of their puberty rites. An estimated 100 million women in Africa, the Middle East, Indonesia, and parts of Asia have had this rite performed on them.

They are mostly Muslims. The World Health Organization reports that tens of thousands of women die as a result of the procedure, and millions more live a life of agony. Many countries have outlawed such practices, but they still persist.

COMING OF AGE IN AMERICA

Coming of age in America is often just as perilous as having the penis subincised or having the clitoris removed. We cringe to hear of this type of mutilation, and yet what happens to many young people in the comfort of the modern world is equally horrifying. Without the wisdom of the elder community, young adults seek out their own rites of passage, often with disastrous consequences, and with no sense of the sacred or the greater good of the community.

Today, children murder both adults and other children. Gangs, which exist in over 125 American cities, recognize the importance of initiation, but of a profane kind. A gang initiation rite may require a young man or woman to randomly kill a stranger in a drive-by shooting or have sex with someone who has been diagnosed as being HIV positive. In parts of the country older men, sometimes family members, still insist upon taking a young man to the local brothel or introducing him to the "wonders" of a drunken stupor as a means of initiation. The tragedy of gang and "good old boy" initiations is that they do nothing to change a boy into a healthy young man. This type of debased rite of passage is symptomatic of the soul's deep longing for a proper, sanctified initiation that is community sanctioned, contributing to the common good and well being of the society at large.

Unlike traditional cultures where children are eager and ready to become responsible adults and parents at the age of fourteen, we in the West go through an extended childhood. The cycle of puberty rites was broken generations ago, and today we each bear the psychic scar of its absence. We find ourselves muddling through our lives as adults who still feel like teenagers. People who are fifty can be heard asking each other in jest, "What do you want to be when you grow up?"

In traditional cultures, children have responsibilities from an early age. One dear friend of mine, who is now 68, grew up on a farm and has had a very successful life. He speaks of the importance of integrating children into both family and community life. He recounts that when he was a child, age five, he had chores to do. One of his responsibilities was to gather kindling for the morning fire and stove. One morning he slept in and arrived downstairs to the family sitting around the table in the cold with no breakfast. He was terribly embarrassed by his forgetfulness, but also realized how important his job was. It never happened again. His story has stayed with me because the experience increased his sense of self worth. He was responsible for the hearth fire in his family's home. It was a real job, and if he did not do it, it impacted the entire family. When I think back to my own childhood, I can't remember ever having a job that felt important or critical to the well-being of my family.

In the past, and in the traditional cultures, there was not a protracted childhood as there is today. A child in our culture going through puberty can be given an initiation rite acknowledging their changing body and the transition into young adulthood, but we must also find a way to provide a real change in status. Otherwise the ceremony becomes a ritualized symbolic act that remains empty at its center and meaningless to all involved.

Change of Status and Phases of Initiation

Most children today do not, at age fourteen, leave the family home, get married, have children, and earn a living. In fact, young adults are increasingly staying in the family home well into their twenties. As adults, we need to think seriously about how to create and demarcate the transitions from one phase of young adulthood to another. We cannot simply have a child pass through an elaborate ceremony at age thirteen, as they would if they were born into an African tribe, and then continue to treat them like a child.

In creating rites of passage for teenagers there must be:
- A meaningful, family-sanctioned change in status
- Extended privileges
- Increased responsibilities
- Collaboration and negotiation

Creating a ceremony for a teenager can be a very delicate matter requiring sensitivity and collaboration. I have seen mothers become terribly disappointed because their daughters did not want to have a puberty moon-time ceremony—the women were most likely upset because they longed to experience the ceremony that was not held for them when they were the proper age. With the right approach, most young women and young men will be open to the idea of a ceremony, especially if it increases their privileges and status.

When approaching a young person with the idea of a rite of passage, conceptualize the rite of passage as a threefold event taking place over a period of years. The lines of demarcation can be drawn around a number of differing passages, each the crossing of new threshold.

Phase one: The physical passage from childhood to adolescents, such as menarche for girls and vocal changes and facial hair for boys, usually occurs between the ages of 12 and 14.

Phase two: The middle years, age 16 to 18, encompass graduation, driving an automobile, and perhaps a real vision quest.

Phase three: During the late teens the young adult prepares to leave home. For most young adults this phase usually involves going to college, getting a job, or joining the military, enabling them to become financially independent and move out on their own.

At each phase there is, of course, a change in status. If from the first ceremony the girl or boy is aware that this is the first of three, it establishes in their minds the journey of evolving into adults and that adulthood does not magically happen over night. It is a gradual transformation with ever increasing privilege, responsibility, and freedom.

With each phase, the ceremony can incorporate elements from the previous ceremony, perhaps with many of the same people present who recognize and acknowledge the shift in status and growth in the young adult.

FIRST-BLOOD RITES

Over the years many mothers and daughters have reincorporated the ceremonial marking of the first blood. The following components of the ceremony are those that I feel are either particularly powerful or beautiful. They emphasize the sacred aspect of the feminine and are empowering to the young girl, establishing increased self-esteem and self-respect for herself and her body. Together, the mother and daughter decide who to invite to the ceremony, usually friends and relatives. A place is chosen, perhaps in Nature, or at someone's home.

One such ceremony incorporated a number of very good elements into it, including the father. Carolyn and her daughter Tatiana created the ceremony together, with the help of Carolyn's good friend Jackie, whom the daughter always liked and thought was "cool." Jackie had offered herself to Tatiana as her confidant. Although Tatiana and her mother were close, both mother and daughter felt it might be better to have Jackie be a wise and older "girlfriend" to Tatiana. The day of the ceremony Jackie came over to the house and took Tatiana out shopping. They would buy grownup clothes and undergarments and have a nice lunch together. They agreed to discuss sex. They apparently they had quite a good and informative discussion about sex, periods, birth control, orgasms, babies, and men. Jackie let it be known that she was now Tatiana's friend, as well as a friend of Carolyn's, and that Tatiana could count on that friendship. She was being welcomed into the circle of adults.

While they were shopping Carolyn was busy decorating the house with red roses, lilies, and candles. Later that afternoon guests arrived, including two of Tatiana's girlfriends who had come of age and their mothers. There was a circle of pillows on the floor and an altar of flowers and candles in the center. The circle began with each of the women taking turns calling the names of their mothers and grandmothers: "I am Carolyn, daughter of Victoria, granddaughter of Isabel, great-granddaughter of Catherine, and mother of Tatiana." This affirmed the connection to the ancestors as well as the naturalness of womanhood. Then the women took turns sharing their own experiences of coming of age. Some of the stories were humorous and some of them were tearful. All agreed they could have benefited from a proper initiation. They encouraged Tatiana to be proud of her body and to respect it as a temple. Some of the women spoke of their experiences with anorexia and self-image. Others spoke about how important it is for a woman to cultivate good women friends, generate trust among women, and not abandon women friends when a man comes into one's life.

After the story telling, the women offered Tatiana gifts: a wreath of flowers for her hair, silk pajamas, a book on the Goddess, good quality makeup, and a cookbook. Because Carolyn and Tatiana had agreed that part of her new role as a young woman was to have Tatiana prepare dinner one night a week, the cookbook would come in handy. She would also be able to stay up later on school nights and be able to have weekend, night-time dates; previously she had only been allowed to go to the movies with a boy for a matinee. This was made public to the group.

Afterwards Tatiana went to her bedroom and put on her new clothes. Then one of the women skillfully applied the makeup to her face, teaching her techniques for highlighting, shading, and shaping her features. Afterwards they celebrated with a formal high tea. Later that evening Tatiana was taken out to a very good restaurant by her father, where they spoke of her hopes and dreams for her future, and how he might support her in achieving the life she desired.

RITES OF MANHOOD

One of my dear friends grew up in West Texas on a ranch. It is a *macho* world, cattle ranching, but interestingly the young men do go through an initiation. Scott described how there were a number of thresh-old experiences that he, his brother, and cousins had gone through in regard to the cattle round up.

Young boys under the age of twelve were not allowed to be on horse-back as the cattle were being driven into the corrals, even though they were quite accomplished riders. At that age, their job was to stand back and work the gates as the cattle were being driven into the pens. They could also haul firewood for the branding iron fire and run the branding irons to the men who were doing the branding.

Scott was brought up as a church-going Baptist, and it was during his first roundup that he heard the men in his family cussing. It was a family affair for the men, and women were not allowed to be anywhere around. There was a lot of ribald humor and teasing of the young boys by the men as they all worked together. Scott had never before heard men speak or joke like this before, and it was an eye opener. Around age 12 the boys could be on horseback, but were only permitted to hold the cattle in a cor-ner of the corral, or keep a calf and its mother separated. Older men, at least age 30, were the only ones allowed to wield the knife that was used to castrate the young bulls. The boys would now be offered their first prairie oyster, a bull testicle cooked over the branding fire.

Around the age of 18 the boys were allowed to rope and brand the cattle. This required manly strength and skill. The branding iron had to be hot, and the steer had to be held still long enough so that the branding iron was struck hard and fast, making sure the brand did not smear or end up in the wrong place. The teasing could get intense, especially if a young boy missed roping a calf a number of times. The men would try to push the boy to tears, and tears were unacceptable. Everyone was aware that the longer the teasing went on, the more difficult it became for the young man to successfully rope a steer. It was something to be endured until he proved himself.

Although this initiation does not contain any overt element of the sacred and is not necessarily viewed as an initiation, it did serve the function of a rite of passage into manhood. Like the Aborigine initiation, there are number of phases to the event, including the separation from the women, access to the private world of the men's lusty humor, and physical endurance. The young man could now be part of the adult world of men.

There are also remnants of old hunting initiations that continue throughout America. Scott reminded me about the honor of shooting one's first deer. Many boys across the country go hunting, and to carry your gun in the company of men and shoot your first buck is a traditional rite of passage. When Scott shot his first buck his forehead was marked with blood from the animal, and when it was gutted he was given a piece of the raw liver to eat. In England after a fox hunt, the tail of the fox is chopped off, and the bloody stump of the tail is used to mark the face of the newly initiated into the company of adults. These blood rites are ancient and can be traced all around the world, reaching back into the Paleolithic times of the cave dwellers.

Although many people might object to the killing of animals, there is a fundamental element of danger and ordeal that young men in particular require. Women often find this offensive and want to curb this impulse in their sons, but I suspect this is dangerous to the young men's psyches. If we, as women, do not support men in properly initiating young boys, we run the risk of emasculating the men in our lives. We can, however, encourage men to find more sacred and holy ways of introducing boys to manhood. Taking a young man to a brothel is not acceptable. Granted, boys need to separate from their mothers, but at the same time, they must learn to respect women and life in general. Otherwise, we end up with rapists, child molesters, serial killers, wanton destroyers of Nature, and a nation filled with disgruntled and violent males.

The amount of senseless destruction of life by young men and boys that greets us daily in the newspapers is a wake-up call to society. In the inner cities, where children grow up in a daily atmosphere of drugs, guns, and poverty, the laws of the jungle rule. Gangs often provide the first real sense of family, a place where people protect and care for one another. Gang members become a tribe inside the larger community, and they initiate one another into their private culture. It would be ridiculous to try to initiate these boys with a New Age type of ceremony. Likewise, the rites of passage that traditional religions offer are meaningless. We know that programs like "tough love" and Outward Bound can be helpful, but they still do not go far enough in addressing the deeper issues. Poverty and the lack of education are certainly factors, but senseless violence happens in middle class and rural areas as well. I cannot even pretend to hold a solution to the madness that has grasped the youth of America, but I cannot help feeling that the absence of powerful and meaningful rites of passage contributes to the violence. From conversations with young people, I hear of their despair about the future, and I recognize that they feel defeated in even trying to a make a go of life. Many cannot even imagine the planet being around by the time they grow up, so why bother? I remember an interview I read in which a nine year old "crack dealer" proudly showed off his limousine, gun, and several thousand dollars in cash. He coolly stated that he did not expect to be alive at age 18, but between now and then, he was going to have it all.

Men like Robert Bly recognize the tragedy of our younger generations, and the men's movement might be a source of help. Eliade, in his work *Rites and Symbols of Initiation*, described this process as "the benign intercession of elders." It seems essential that the men in each community take up the task of caring for the young boys. A community of elders, healthy men willing to step forth and seriously take on the role of initiators, could turn the tide. But first they must be willing to be adults themselves. The men's movement must first find a way to initiate one another and then graduate to create serious initiations in the real world of troubled young men.

LEAVING HOME

When a friend's daughter graduated from college she asked me to conduct a ceremony for her that would welcome her into the community of adults. On a Sunday afternoon she gave a party for Donna, who had agreed to be publicly acknowledged. We began by smudging everyone, and Jane, her mother, announced to the group that Donna was now a woman. She stated that everyone present was a longtime friend of hers and her family. In fact, they were all very good friends. She asked that the people present now create their own relationship with Donna, that they stop thinking of her as "my good friend Jane's daughter" and recognize her in own right. I did a modified version of the Birthing Way ceremony for Donna. Her mother brushed her hair and I washed her feet in a bowl of water scattered with rose petals. As I washed each foot I spoke to her about being an adult and the path that she would follow, wishing her a long life and good journey. At the end, those gathered told the stories of their relationships to Donna and invited her into their lives as an adult and as a good friend.

Donna's change in status as an adult meant she was capable of creating a career for herself. She could take the final steps toward leaving home and establishing herself as financially independent from her parents. To be acknowledged by the community at large meant that Donna could call upon them as colleagues and associates, as well as friends.

CONFIRMATION AND BAR MITZVAH

In today's world confirmation and Bar Mitzvah are perhaps the most common teenage initiation. Both ceremonies provide a way for children born into a spiritual tradition to claim their respective traditions as their own. In the Roman Catholic tradition, the ceremony takes place after the adolescent boy or girl has completed a course of study in which the articles of faith are examined and taken to heart. As part of the preparations, the confirmant asks someone of the same sex who personifies Roman Catholic beliefs to be their spiritual sponsor. They also choose a patron saint and adopt the saint's name. This saint is then viewed as a spiritual guide to be called upon in times of need.

The ceremony is usually conducted by a bishop during a special mass, and it is the time for the confirmant to make a public declaration of faith. Each confirmant and sponsor approach the bishop, the confirmant kneels while the sponsor places a hand on his or her shoulder. The confirmant then renews his or her vows and takes the saint's name. The bishop then annoints the confirmant with holy oil, slaps them lightly on the cheek, and says, "Peace be with you." Afterward there is usually a small dinner party and the sponsor gives a special gift to the young man or woman.

A Jewish boy or girl comes of age at thirteen and through the ceremony of the Bar/Bat Mitzvah becomes the "son/daughter of the commandment." Traditionally, it was a ceremony for young men but earlier this century a rabbi's daughter was initiated into the Bat Mitzvah. It is a time to demonstrate for the community how well he or she can perform traditional religious duties. Preparation often requires years of studying Hebrew, theology, and prayer. The ceremony takes place in the synogogue on the Shabbat after the child's thirteenth birthday. The young man studies Hebrew and in the synagogue gives his first public reading from the Torah, the sacred book of the Hebrews. In Reform Judaism girls are considered equal and they, too, are given the opportunity to pray in front of their spiritual community.

For the Jewish family and community, the festivities surrounding a Bar/Bat Mitzvah can be elaborate. The synagogue ceremony is usually followed by feasting and music with friends and family coming from thousands of miles away to honor and bestow many fine gifts upon the young adult. In return the initiate who can now read from the Torah is also expected to share in the responsibilities of the religious community.

THE VISION QUEST

During the last twenty years I have taken part in many different types of ceremonies and rites of passage. Obviously, some have been more powerful than others. A proper vision quest is, in my opinion, the most life-changing ceremony one can experience. It is unique in both its genuineness and its power. It is different from most other ceremonies in that it requires a seasoned and accomplished guide. It should not be undertaken alone or with amateurs. For everyone, and especially teenagers it provides an element of danger, a life and death situation. For young men, this risk seems to be crucial in order to confront their manhood.

In 1981, I was hired as a vision quest guide for an organization called Rites of Passage. The following year I became a training coordinator, teaching other people how to be guides. Over the next several years, I had the opportunity to act as a vision quest guide for several hundred people and to witness firsthand its powerful effect on contemporary people.

Rites of Passage is a non-profit organization, founded in Marin County, California, by Steven Foster and Meredith Little. The name was not chosen at random, but as a conscious effort on their parts to exemplify how modern-day people might experience change in their lives. The organization was the premier vision quest institute in the United States. It recognized the need for finding and developing ways in which contemporary people might symbolically discover how to make conscious the passages necessary in modern life, how to acquire new life status, and how to elevate a life crisis into a sacred moment, rather than let it sink into a psychological nightmare.

The vision quest, as conceived by Steven and Meredith, is based upon the initiation ceremony of the Oglala Sioux, an American Indian people. (The term "vision quest" was introduced by anthropologists studying the Sioux.) It was adapted to meet the needs of modern-day people and to provide a rite of passage for them. Today most people refer to this type of work as "vision fast" rather than "quest," in order to avoid controversy with American Indians. This seems highly rhetorical, because both Christ and Moses went fasting in the mountains seeking a vision. People everywhere have a right to seek a vision in Nature, and every culture has been doing it for tens of thousands of years.

With preparation, the individual journeys into the desert of Death Valley to spend three days and three nights alone, with no food and only two gallons of water. During this time, he or she sits inside a "medicine wheel," which they construct. This wheel represents the circle of their life and all they bring to it. There is real danger and risk involved. Many people have never been alone in the wilderness before, and many have never slept out in Nature. The forces of Nature are unpredictable. Weather might turn bad; rattlesnakes and mountain lions may appear; fear could turn into panic and panic into injury, putting lives at risk. Guides encourage the individual to accept the challenge, for as Steven says: "The greater the perceived risk, the greater the potential for personal growth and the more lasting the effects of the experience."

Ceremonial acts first affect the personal and then extend out into the culture at large. During the act of initiation, an individual undergoes a transformation from one stage of life to the next. The initiatory process among native peoples is always recognized and acknowledged by the family and other members of the community. The vision quest is one form of initiation, and a classic example of what Arnold Van Gennep described in *Les Rites de Passage*. In this ground-breaking book, first published in 1909, Van Gennep specifically describes a certain class of ceremony encompassing a variety of rites dealing with the crossing of boundaries, changes in time, and changes in personal and social status.

Van Gennep was the first person to break down ceremonial structure into a triadic movement. He saw ritual as having a beginning stage, in which the initiate severs from the world as he or she has known it and is seen to have crossed a boundary. This severance leads the person into what Van Gennep called the *liminal period* or *threshold experience*. During this phase the person is neither in this world nor the next. This is the initiation proper and is always characterized by danger and uncertainty. The final stage is integration back into the world, where the fully initiated novice returns with the status appropriate to his or her new stage of being. This new status is acknowledged by the family, friends, and society at large. All ceremonies of transition appear to follow this map, and ethnographic literature from around the world supports Van Gennep's insight into its structure. In essence, ceremony has a beginning, middle, and end. Even more importantly, there is a relationship between the symbolic and society.

Those who came to Rites of Passage were from all walks of life and from all over the country. During my first year, the program was divided into adult and youth programs. The adults came because they were in crisis: a marriage was ending, a line of work was changing, a new relationship was pending, or they simply had a sense that the ordeal of the vision quest would open them to something new and exciting. Some came as psychiatric referrals, some as executives whose companies were paying the bills, and some came to seek a vision. My job was to work with the adult program. The youth program was set up to work with teenagers, including at-risk youth. These young people were on the edge of being in trouble with the law. Often these youths were already in trouble with school officials and were funneled into our program via an outreach system we had developed, in which a slide show documenting the vision quest was shown in high schools around the Bay area.

Many of teenagers came because they wanted to face the challenge of the vision quest, some because they wanted out of school, and others because they wanted to be initiated into adulthood. In time we had graduating seniors participating as a rite of passage, and later we had their younger brothers and sisters, who came because they felt it was part of their family tradition to follow in the footsteps of their elder siblings. Eventually we even had parents joining in, saying that if their sons and daughters could do this seemingly difficult task and be so powerfully affected by it, they wanted to do it too.

During my second year at Rites of Passage, we combined the two programs into one, and to our delight it seemed to work even more effectively. The adults were inspired by the strength and courage of the youths, and the youths were fascinated by the fact that adults continued to face major life decisions and crises throughout adulthood. Most teenagers thought all their problems would magically disappear the day they turned twenty-one. All they could think about was how great it would be when they were on their own, with no one telling them what to do. It was my great joy to act as vision quest guide for a thirteen-year-old girl, her father, and a seventy-year-old man, all in the same group.

The vision quest is always conducted in a ceremonial manner with careful attention given to each symbolic act. Each vision quest is co-led by a man and a woman who share all responsibilities equally. Together the pair instructs the questers, acts as a support system, and works individually with each person to help them construct their ceremony. Each group has a maximum of ten people for every two instructors.

Enrollment in the vision quest program usually began with a phone call to Rites of Passage, and information was then sent to potential participants. Participants in the vision quest prepared at least a month beforehand, and some even prepared one year or longer before joining. There were four preliminary meetings before the actual vision quest, and it was at the first meeting that the act of severance would begin. The participants would prepared for the separation from family, home, friends, work, telephone, music, and civilization. Leaving their previous lives behind, they would soon be entering into the unknown liminal or threshold state. All four preparatory meetings were conducted ceremonially. We sat in a circle on the floor and lighted sage or cedar as a smudge (similar to incense in other sacred traditions). This simple act alerted the group that we were crossing over the threshold into vision quest time. In the center of the circle was a circle of stones, shells, bones, crystals, and wood. After a brief welcome, we invited people to choose an object from the circle and examine it. When each participant had chosen an object we invited each person in the circle to speak to the group about the object they had chosen and why they were doing a vision quest. Each one then described their object and how it represented them in their current stage. The descriptions were generally very revealing about who they were and why they were there. The use of the circle of stones as a symbolic metaphor would be a continuing theme over the next month, culminating in the building of a personal medicine wheel during the actual vision quest.

The first meeting was a time for introductions and the showing of a slide show illustrating the process of the vision quest with photographs of previous questers attending meetings, loading up the bus to depart, making base camp, going out to vision quest, returning back to base camp, and journeying home. The initial meeting was also a time for filling out release forms and questionnaires concerning health and general well-being. Through the questionnaire we discovered living conditions, relevant relationships, religious orientation, and medical histories. This provided us with important information regarding each person and how we might work most effectively with them. During the first meeting we provided a generalized idea of what our schedule during the vision quest time would be like, just enough information to satisfy the curious and still maintain some mystery.

Also during the first meeting we explained the format of the vision quest and what was expected of each person. As a group we would leave Marin County to spend a week in the desert of southern California. Each person was required to bring a backpack filled with whatever they felt was essential to their journey. Each would carry everything they brought on their backs. The following is a list of our recommendations:

backpack	bandanna
sleeping bag	water
sleeping pad (optional)	journal and pencil (required)
ground cloth or tarp	toilet paper
50 feet of rope	warm clothes, boots, cap
clasp knife	cup and spoon
matches	change of warm clothes

Three more meetings were held before leaving for the desert, each of these dealing with a particular topic.

The second meeting began in a similar manner as the first, sitting in a circle. Sage was lit and in front of us was the circle of stones, as well as other objects of the Earth. This time we addressed the fears of the group. Each object chosen would be described in terms of how it represented the individual's fear and anxiety about the vision quest. During these circles the leaders did not interrupt or comment on what was being expressed— we listened. We then began to explain the survival aspects of the journey—the kinds of equipment necessary and the reality of being in the desert for a few days or a week. We addressed the issue of rattlesnakes and what to do if bitten; how to protect oneself from the sun, rain, and lightning; and how to avoid hypothermia and heatstroke. The most important information concerned the "buddy system."

The buddy system was our built-in safety net. Each person had a partner, and together they kept one another well. We stressed the importance of this relationship and how we all feel it if someone gets hurt. The buddy system worked as follows.

The guides knew from maps approximately where each person was questing, but only the buddy knew exactly where their partner's site was. On the morning of leaving base camp to spend their time alone, buddies walked one another to their sites and dropped off their gear. They then chose a place halfway between the two places of power and built a stone pile. That first morning, one member of the duo placed a large stone or series of stones in a pile. The second person returned to the pile in the afternoon and added an additional rock. The following morning, the first person returned and placed his or her second rock. Although it was never stated, the stone pile was each person's connection to the rest of humanity, as well as a source of protection. Anyone who did not see a new rock placed by his or her buddy would immediately go to investigate the buddy's site. Otherwise, the pattern continued until the fourth morning, when the buddies met back at the stone pile and returned to base camp together.

In the event of an injury or accident, each buddy had the responsibilities of assessing his or her partner's condition and providing help in the form of shade, blankets, tourniquets, or splints. The buddy would then return to base camp to inform the guides, and emergency procedures would go into effect. One guide would go to the injured party, and the other would go for help if necessary. Over the years there were several thousand people who vision quested; we never had a serious injury or accident. The only snake bite that occurred was with a guide who was playing with a rattlesnake and was nipped as he set it down to release it. He felt a bit sick for twenty-four hours but did not require any unusual first aid.

The stone pile became an important symbol for every quester. Often people left "medicine" gifts—objects found in the desert, such as feathers and bones, or sometimes notes—for one another on the stone pile. People felt the deep responsibility of caretaking for another human being, and then a great relief that they had both survived. They knew with each day passed that their buddy was experiencing the sun, the hunger, the darkness, and the stars, and they knew that he or she was well. On the fourth morning, the partners were the first to give and receive the welcome of the hero/heroine back from the mythical quest.

The final preliminary meeting was devoted to last-minute questions about gear, where we were going, what time to meet, and what to do if you really do get bit by a rattlesnake. During this meeting we began to stress the re-integrative aspect of the quest. We called it "re-incorporation." We would explain to the group that the real vision quest began when they returned home to the world, that the act of having a vision is not enough, that it must be placed in context of the world and the rest of humanity. As Black Elk, an Oglala Sioux, said, "I think I have told you, but if I have not, you must have understood, that a man who has a vision is not able to use the power of it until he has performed the vision on Earth for the people to see." Of course, at this point, due to the anticipation of the vision quest itself, few of the questers fully understood this message. We made plans to meet the group one week later to depart for the mountains of Death Valley.

THE MEDICINE WHEEL

Each guide at Rites of Passage had the opportunity to work with a number of medicine men from the Native American community. None was as influential to us as Heyemeyohst Storm and his book *Seven Arrows*. He truly supported us in the work we were doing and offered himself to us as a consultant. His message was that he did not want us training people how to be Indians, but rather how to open themselves to the Earth and healing. He believed we are all the Earth's children. It was through him that we achieved a deeper understanding of the work and the importance of the medicine wheel as a map for finding one's self. During the third preliminary meeting, we explained the basic medicine wheel pattern and how it functions.

The medicine wheel is the alchemical circle of protection that surrounds a person while they quest. It is constructed out of stones and is about ten feet in diameter, large enough to lie in. Rocks are placed in the four cardinal directions: North, South, East, and West, and in the noncardinal points as well. Each direction has a particular quality associated with it, and with the placing of each rock the person is seen as invoking that energy into his or her circle. There is something universal about the concept of the four directions, but each culture differs in how it interprets each position.

To Native Americans, the stone representing the East is the stone of vision, insight, and illumination. It carries with it the spiritual aspects of the self and is represented by the color yellow and the element of fire; the power of the Eagle presides over it. The West stone is the stone of introspection. It is known as the "looks within place." It is the place of the shaman, the soul, and darkness. It is where physical healing occurs, and it is associated with the color black and the element of Earth; the Bear is its power animal. The third stone is the South and represents the emotions, water, the color red, and the ability to be trusting and innocent. The trickster energy of the Coyote sits here, as well as the healing power of plants. The final stone represents the North, where belief systems and mental activities are located. It is the place of the element of air and the color white, and the quartz crystal sits here as a transceiver of energy. The grandmother energy of White Buffalo Woman guides this direction, as does the power of the animal totems.

The non-cardinal directions represent particular powers of the Self as well as the four aspects of the spiritual warrior known as the Four Enemies. The Southeast is the place of the ancestors and the ability to love and accept oneself. For the spiritual warrior it is where fear is encountered through confronting the unknown. Fear is always defeated by first distinguishing real fear from imagined fear through the process of staying in the now. The Southwest is the place of the sacred dream where we experience our capacity to recognize the symbolic patterning that runs beneath the surface of our lives and to dream our dreams awake by manifesting our dreams in the real world. The enemy is clarity and in this sense it is a false knowing that perpetuates or verifies what we already know but does not open us up to new ways of viewing the world. In the Northeast is the karmic pattern that brings trials and tribulations, these are seen as "teachings." These repeating life lessons change when we gain the wisdom and understanding to break the pattern or karmic cycle. The enemy is power and the challenge is to move beyond our fear of becoming really powerful and at the same time not wield a heavy-handed form of power. The Northwest represents change and our emotional reaction to all that change brings. The enemy is old age and death. All life is viewed as a process in which change is inevitable. Coming to grips with our own death is the challenge of this direction.

The construction of a medicine wheel may take anywhere from one to three days. With the placement of each rock a person lays another piece of his or her psyche down on the Earth. The periphery of the wheel is seen as representing different aspects of the self and the Wheel of Life that surrounds us. It was suggested to participants that they spend part of their time actually sitting in each of the eight directions that compose the medicine wheel. The act of doing this would give them the opportunity to self-examine these different parts of themselves and to directly feel the power of the medicine wheel.

Participants often discovered that certain aspects of themselves were highly developed, while other aspects were practically non-existent or were functioning in their lives in painful ways. We emphasized the importance of fully developing all eight parts of the self and recognizing how they function together to create a whole person. The medicine wheel enables a person to journey into the center of one's life, where he or she commands self-authority and takes charge of his or her life. Primary emphasis was placed on developing the ability to be at the cause of one's life, rather than at the effect of it. It meant taking full responsibility for one's life.

In addition to constructing a medicine wheel, each quester was expected to keep a journal of his or her time. This began at the first meeting, and we hoped this process would last well into the future. During their time alone participants were encouraged to write of their experiences, their dreams, and their feelings. Because the quality of time becomes so dreamlike, we emphasized the importance of not assuming they would remember details. People were encouraged to dream and take note of the messages they might receive.

Participants were also encouraged to actively engage themselves in seeking a vision—to work towards that experience by creating ceremonial tasks in which they might gain insights into themselves. One of these tasks was to stay awake throughout the final night without a fire so that they might confront the darkness and the shadow elements that lurk there.

The final suggestion was that the questers open themselves to a new name—one that would always invoke the memory of this special time. This act required deeply listening to the forces of Nature and recognizing the connection of all life.

Throughout the three days participants were invited to speak out loud—to call their pleas out to the wind, the rain, and the animals that might appear—and to listen for a response.

TEENAGE INITIATION

One of my first groups with teenagers contained a young man from Berkeley High School. He was in his sophomore year and was a punk with hair style to match. At the first meeting, he picked up a rough piece of black obsidian from the circle of objects, and when it was his turn to speak he held the stone in his hands and said: "This stone is like me. It is hard, sharp, dark, and dangerous," whereupon he put the stone down. My heart leapt into my throat with a sense of dread as I thought, "This is going to be intense."

Philip came from a broken family. He never knew his father, and his mother was a liberal from the Sixties. She had encouraged him to do the vision quest because of trouble at home between him, his sister, and herself. He was willing to quest only because he could escape from his family and school for a week. Over the weeks that followed I came to see him as a conscious and concerned youth. He cared about the planet and about humanity. He also stated that he did not see much use in growing up because there probably was not going to be a world left anyway. His hard edge was his protection, and his lack of ambition was a serious problem related to his world view. I had questions myself about our future, and here was a young man that I was expected to guide into a vision of the future.

On the day when the group left base camp in search of their places of power, Philip headed out into the south in search of something magical. By this time he had endeared himself to the entire group, and I believe he also felt the strong connection we had made with him. When he returned that evening, he was grinning from ear to ear. He had found his place. As he was wandering around looking for it a butterfly had flown past, and he remembered to pay attention and read the omens of Nature. He changed his course and set off in the direction of the butterfly. Eventually he came to a spring, a small oasis in the desert that was not marked on the map. He was the envy of everyone in camp. He proudly said he would not need to carry extra water because he could drink from the spring and even bathe. He could hardly contain himself until the morning.

When the morning arrived he was up and ready to go. The day was beautiful, and this particular trip was blessed with glorious weather. People had warm sun and pleasant nights, everything was perfect. On the fourth morning, as the participants returned to base camp, Philip came in looking radiant. He said that when he returned to his place of power, he set up his camp and was lying around almost asleep when he heard a strange and frightening sound. He jumped up and noticed that in the rocks above him, about twenty feet away, there was a prairie falcon nest and the birds had come soaring in to roost, only to discover an intruder. He admitted to being rather scared, but decided to stay and work it out with the birds.

They would screech and fly around him, and he would make bird noises and be still. By the second day they had accepted him and he them. He felt this was a message to him to be strong and have faith. He watched the pair care for their young and stand guard over them, and he found himself wishing for his family. In our welcoming circle, he cried for his mother and sister and said that he had always been mean to his little sister because he had been jealous of her from the time she was born. Through watching the falcons with their family he realized "his family needed to stick together and take care of each other." He said his sister was really "okay" and that she obviously liked him, in spite of the bad time he gave her. He showed us a collection of feathers he had gathered from the birds and said that he could not wait to get home and give his mother and sister each a feather.

In his journal Philip wrote: "My life is ending now, I cry for myself and my boyhood dreams. Father, where are you? Bird, will you be my Father? I must father myself now and share in the responsibilities of life. I miss my sister and my mother. Please forgive me for being unkind. I feel like a bird hatching out of an egg and taking flight. My new name is Eyes That See.

·12·

WOMEN AND MEN

The Journey into Wholeness

If we are to resanctify ourselves, our families, and our communities, it is essential we reexamine our sexual politics. As men and women honor the sacred aspects of one another, a reconciliation takes place between the genders. Each in our own way travels through a cycle of inner births and deaths. Life-passages are not restricted to one sex or the other and do not magically go away when we reach the age of twenty-one.

Predictable moments of change come and go throughout the course of a life, and both men and women can be expected to experience a mid-life crisis. Whether they work outside the home or in it, are coupled or single, have children or not, the late thirties through the forties are a time for reevaluation. Job burnout, divorce, the death of parents, "empty nest syndrome," menopause, and psychological breakdown are a few of the catalysts to this reevaluation. The mid-life crisis provokes us to ask deep questions such as: Who am I?, How did I get here?, Where am I going?, and What am I doing? We begin to see more clearly what is working or not working in our lives, giving us the potential for redefining what is truly important and fulfilling in life.

Consequently, it is a perfect time for members of the same sex to seek out one another's company and elevate these transitory moments into something sacred. The ongoing women's movement and the emerging men's movement are actively addressing these needs. Inside a circle of one's own gender it is possible to create appropriate ceremonies that address male or female issues.

THE RITES OF WOMEN

The politics and consciousness raising of the women's movement gave birth to a feminine spirituality and an active ceremonial life. Women have been praying, chanting, and drumming together for the last twenty years. During that time they have helped to initiate one another into honoring their bodies and becoming psychically healthy, coming to terms with physical issues of size, shape, and early indoctrination concerning perceived beauty. In workshops women have gone into the old cultural wounds, and through ritual reenactment have dramatized various archetypes and their shadow aspects such as the virgin/whore, the nurturer/devourer, and the nice girl/bitch. Women have also created dramas around incest, rape, abandonment, the beauty myth, eating disorders, mothering, and, of course, our love relationships with men.

Women have also reclaimed their Blood Rites. Stories are shared of how they came into their menses to how they are coping with menopause. The creation of ceremonies for adolescent girls around their moon time is a popular activity, as so many women lament the fact of their own coming of age as a shameful time. The passage into menopause is also being ceremonialized, as women come to honor and respect themselves as wise women and crones who did indeed gather valuable wisdom and knowledge as they grew older. Many older women report a new found independence and freedom to be more fully who they are. As women age, they find themselves being less influenced by societal pressures to conform, hold their tongue, or maintain media images of beauty. Women who have toed the line and done everything right may yet become divorced or widowed, and through contact with younger liberated women discover themselves for the first time.

WOMEN'S ALLIANCE

For ten years I was part of an organization known as Women's Alliance, founded in the Bay Area, and headed by Charlotte Kelly. From 1984 to 1994, Charlotte organized a series of 10-day encampments for women. Held at Girl Scout camps, approximately 300 women from all walks of life gathered together to create ceremony and participate in healing, singing, drumming, art, and magic. The transformations that Women's

Alliance went through over the years, I believe speak as metaphor for what many women have experienced.

Over the years the camp had its ups and downs; in fact, there were times when I swore I would never return. In the early years Charlotte kept a tight rein on all of us, and it was a risky business. There were usually about a dozen teachers present for the length of the encampment. Over the years, speakers included such teachers as Joanna Macy, Clarissa Pinkola Estes, Colleen Kelley, Gabriel Roth, Luisa Teish, Deena Metzger, and many Bay Area activists, writers, and artists. Charlotte made a great effort to actively reach out to the black, Hispanic, and Asian communities by providing scholarships and bringing in women of color as teachers. We did not want the camp to be another stronghold of middle-class white women. As it turned out, the camp was a wonderful mixture of women of different races, sexual orientation, and every political and religious persuasion imaginable. The potential for ecstasy as well as conflict was always present, and through it all Charlotte endured as our angel and our target.

The first camp that I participated in featured a radical, separatist, lesbian feminist as a keynote speaker. Three hundred women gathered in a beautiful meadow to hear her speak. A few minutes into her talk I felt as if I was at a Nuremberg Rally, or in the presence of a Grand Inquisitor. As she gathered steam, she harangued the women about incest, rape, the patriarchy, and men. She lost all sense of time and went on for hours. About half way through her talk, women began to literally run screaming from the meadow to a nearby stream. A number of other teachers went to the aid of these distressed women and ministered to them, submerging them in the water, chanting and drumming, and soothing their injured souls. As women recovered, they too began to care for the ever growing crowd who had fled the meadow. The speaker was not at all alarmed by the women running screaming from the meadow; in fact, it seemed to spur her on, and she spoke right through the lunch period. When she was finished, she walked past the stream and on towards the dining hall, never stopping to help or inquire how or what the women were doing.

The other teachers were furious with her. We felt as if she expected us to be Red Cross workers at the scene of a disaster. When we confronted her on her tactics, and the women's response to her, she said "that happens everywhere I speak," and defended her position. Her message of abuse and dominance was not new information for the women, but the manner in which it was delivered was extremely patriarchal, like rubbing salt into old wounds. Her attitude completely lacked compassion, and rather than generate healing seemed designed to generate fear and loathing.

At another camp, we planned a number of lectures and panel discussions on sexuality. One teacher, Luisa Teish, brought an essay on temple prostitutes written by Deena Metzger; she anticipated handing copies out to the women as part of her lecture. The article was an intelligent and well-written piece, and certainly not a call for women to become prostitutes. The photocopied essay was to be distributed to the campers by Luisa the following morning. That night, two other teachers stole the papers from Luisa, because they did not believe it was an appropriate handout. Needless to say there was major scandal around it all.

It intrigues me how people can become the thing they hate in the culture at large. Just as the speaker who hated the patriarchy became the patriarch, the two teachers who were pro-choice advocates denied the rights of Luisa to intelligently talk about the sexual politics of temple prostitution. Furthermore they denied the capability of three hundred women to intelligently discern the content of the article.

In the evolution of the camp, there was a period where it seemed women expected high drama to unfold as a result of coming together in such large numbers. As women, we had never had such a forum at our disposal before, and many sensed the possibilities for genuine healing that would transcend the drama. As Charlotte took the initiative in creating a very active board of directors, she also began to let go of control. Her own evolution around the camp was most admirable. She began to invite teachers to camp three or four days early. Our task was to self-organize the camp. As teachers, we recognized that if we were united in our vision of the camp, it went smoothly. If we had a prima donna or dissension among us, it became like the pea under the mattress, and all the campers felt it. And once magnified through three hundred women, the pea could become quite large.

Charlotte's decision to let teachers organize the camp was one step away from letting campers organize it, and at the end of ten years Charlotte did in fact turn the camp over to the campers. The principle of self-organization was the most revolutionary example of freedom and trust I have experienced. The teaching staff had the opportunity to create the camp and choreograph the entire event as one large ceremony using a core of regular teachers and always a group of first-timers. Together, we saw what gifts and skills we carried, and from there began creating the flow of the camp. We also had the lessons of previous camps from which to learn.

In terms of organizing a conference, Charlotte broke all the rules by allowing speakers to organize the event according to who their colleagues were. It was a very radical experiment that worked beautifully. Conferences in general tend to be extremely boring, often with the same speakers, giving the same talk, year after year. There is nothing truly alive about them. Speakers arrive and are slotted into panel discussions, workshops, and a lecture while participants become passive receivers of "talking head" information. The free form model that Charlotte and Women's Alliance created is a very exciting form for conference organizers to consider.

Over the years we became very vigilant about ensuring that the participants' rights and responsibilities were fully respected. We also became very good at calling a spade a spade. In the Eighties, the camps had a lot of emotional content, as women freed themselves from past pains. In the Nineties, the energy began to shift. At a camp in Seattle, we decided to go beyond therapeutic process into a deeper ceremonial connection with the ancestral spirits, in order to get beyond the personal into an engaged relationship with the world.

During the opening ceremony a number of women became hysterical. The following evening, during a laying-on-of-hands healing ceremony, more women became hysterical. We called an emergency late-night staff meeting and decided to abandon the schedule. The next day we offered the campers an open microphone, so women could come forth to address whatever it was they thought was going on. This process lasted for two days and nights and what came out of it was very interesting.

In essence, women said they were tired of other women getting hysterical, especially if they knew the woman did this in every group she attended. One group of women who practice ceremony together told of their Solstice Celebration being ruined by a woman who routinely got hysterical at ceremonies. They felt it was inappropriate behavior, because the ceremony was for the common good, and not about the personal, or self-indulgent catharsis. They were fed up with this pattern.

Other women spoke about how they had never really considered the healing properties of ceremony. They had been taught by therapists to go into a cathartic response; healing was supposed to be a painful and lengthy therapeutic process, not a spontaneous ecstatic experience.

A number of options were suggested such as having guardians who would watch for those who were about to lose control and remove them from the group. This was immediately rejected because no one wanted to be the policeman. Another suggestion was to have a designated place where participants could go and scream with others to care for them. This was ultimately rejected. Women were tired of caregiving, and most participants felt it disempowered them by making women not responsible for their actions.

The women also expressed compassion for anyone who did suddenly find themselves going through an emotional upheaval and suggested that those in need feel free to ask someone nearby to help them. They did not feel comfortable with women making themselves the center of attention in an inappropriate context.

In retrospect, a large number of women were declaring themselves healed, and these women wanted to get on with such things as doing more ceremony for the greater good, taking on projects in their communities, or simply enjoying the company of other women who were not always in a state of crisis. The message was clear and it was said over a loud speaker in the presence of three hundred other women.

This was in 1993, and since then I have felt a shift happen in my own circle of women friends and with many women I meet. Women who identify themselves as healthy are having less and less patience with women who identify themselves as sick, weak, or victims. For twenty-five years women have been sympathetic to the suffering of other women, so much so that many women fell into the error of thinking women's groups were all about sharing the suffering, the pain, and the narcissism of processing the same story over and over again. I know both men and women who go from group to group with the same story, year after year, therapy after therapy, and somehow end up in the middle of the room, gathering energy from everyone present. Furthermore, the wounded victim stance, especially in middle-aged women, is not attractive to younger, more liberated women. Rather than seeing older women as wise elders who can be a source of guidance, these victim-identified women simply appear as the walking wounded.

SUBMERSION, THE UNDERWORLD, AND RESURRECTION

In an interview I did with Elizabeth Davis for her powerful book *The Women's Wheel of Life*, I talk about this process. Women who are self-identified as healthy have drawn a very permeable line saying "Look, you can cross over the line anytime you want. You can give one year, ten years, or a lifetime to the drama trauma of your story, or you can move on." We are all carrying trauma of one sort or another, but it is where we place our identity that is crucial. As a friend who was violently raped at age nineteen states, "I almost killed myself after the rape, when I woke up three months later, I said that's it. I gave those savages three months of my life; I am not going to give them anymore. It may sound cruel, but to spend decades of one's life identified as a victim, or to go to one's grave stigmatized by life's unjust ordeals is never to have lived at all."

Of course everyone goes through problematic changes; even healthy people have hard times. Healthy women are prepared to support one another through these changes, and even encourage a sister's descent into the underworld. A few years ago I fell into a serious depression that took me to the edge of suicide. I was living in London, and my life spun out of control into chaos and confusion. My women friends in the United States were well of aware of my state of mind, even though I was in denial. One day a good friend called and in the course of our conversation she kindly told me I did not need to be so proud or always be the strong one, that it was okay to fall apart. Her words were an instantaneous relief, I no longer had to maintain a false face of normalcy.

I cannot say that I went graciously into the underworld; rather I went kicking and screaming. I kept trying to create some semblance of order and control in my life, but at every turn I was defeated. The more I was defeated, the more depressed I became. The more depressed I became, the more I lost faith. The deeper my loss of faith became, the more despairing I grew. In my despair, I felt completely abandoned by everything I had previously relied upon. The Goddess, Shamanism, Buddha, the Christ Light all vanished from my world, and I was alone and alienated in a unfriendly universe. In the depths of my despair I had a recurring image of being alone in a large black sea, in which I was like a many-armed Goddess, madly flailing about in an attempt to stay afloat in an ocean of despair. It was both terrifying and exhausting. I found myself calling out for help against this psychic flailing. Out of the darkness a voice came and simply said: "Just drown, surrender, just let go and drown." And so I did. I let myself drown, but "I" did not die, yet something did.

I did not drown into a sea of bliss or even peace. The place I went to was beyond any emotional connotation, the only word that can describe it is emptiness. In the emptiness there was no need for effort, feeling, or even thinking. I stayed as if submerged in a void for quite a length of time. A few days later I asked: "What is this all about?" and I was told by an inner voice "this is the tempering." To temper is to bring anything to a proper or suitable quality by mingling its substance with something else, usually by immersing it while hot into cold water. A person can also be good-tempered or ill-tempered.

After this experience I mistakenly thought that I could immediately bob back up into my life. I soon realized the journey into the underworld and its total immersion into darkness is only half of the journey. My impulse to emerge too soon and get on with my life was strong, and yet another part of me said "Slow down, do not surface too soon, savor this journey." In actuality, I was completely at the mercy of powerful forces. The journey of descent and emergence lasted over eighteen months. It required me being present to the process, as well as learning how to read the signs and omens along the way. It was like learning to surf and ride the curl of the wave, or risk being pulled once again into the undertow. I had to stay behind my process, not get out in front of it.

The journey into the underworld was painful and initially shameful to me. I felt ashamed for falling apart, yet my friends were a great source of support. They supported me in getting better, but more importantly they supported my dismemberment and respected my ability to stay with the process and not name it or talk about it excessively. Sometimes it is essential to learn how to keep one's own counsel, especially through deep psychic upheavals. Naming things prematurely, or actively jumping in and fixing a psychic mess, denies the soulmaking aspect of the journey and can cripple the sojourner.

In retrospect I could see how women kill themselves, women like Virginia Woolf and Sylvia Plath. To know that something desperately wants to die, and to confuse it with your physical being can be a deadly error. The journey into the underworld as it comes to us from the epic poem of Inanna, the descent of Psyche or Persephone, or the crucifixion of Christ is about death and resurrection. It should not be cut short or literalized into an act of suicide. For many women the challenge of diving deep is not about experiencing the underworld, but how to avoid making it a permanent home.

As more and more women come into a healthy sense of their own power, they become comfortable with sharing who they are with the world. Women who support one another in being strong and vibrant are not afraid of honest communication or feedback. There is simply not time for niceties around things that are off. We owe it to one another to speak honestly, and we thrive in an environment where our sisters can tell us pointed things about ourselves. Being able to tell a friend how tedious it is to always experience her in real or imagined states of crises is a major step forward for all of us, for it stops our duplicity in the cycle of narcissism. It also liberates women to have an incredible amount of fun together, deeply serious fun.

Many women I work with report that when their lives begin to really transform, their women friends become intimidated or even jealous of their changes, especially if someone crosses over the line from victim to healed. I tell those women to find new friends. If your current friends require you to be suffering, narcissistic, and whiny in order to relate to you, something is wrong. There are a lot of healthy women who support one another in being their most radiant, powerful selves. They are not intimidated by another woman's beauty, or her gifts and talents. These women also know how to be supportive, honest, and creative. They are having a great time together, talking about topics beyond their personal stories. They also have the time and energy to collaborate on creative projects, as well as make a beneficial contribution to the world.

SUICIDE AND CEREMONY

During a week-long women's workshop, one participant told me she had attempted suicide a few months earlier. Sharon was a professional woman, in her late twenties, who found herself in deep despair over her relationship with her parents. She described them as: "very waspish and upper-middle class." They had never been willing to acknowledge the emotional side of life, and she had lived her life feeling incapable of communicating what was really going on with her.

Sharon had taken a knife and slit her wrists. She then dialed 911. After the ambulance ride and treatment at the emergency room she called her parents and her best friend to tell them what had happened. All three of them responded by refusing to believe that she was in a psychiatric unit or that she had attempted suicide. It took several minutes for her to convince them of the truth of the matter. She said this was a typical response because she seemed so normal and well-adjusted.

Sharon then decided to place herself into a private psychiatric care facility in the Bay Area. The hospital agreed to admit her only if her parents would take part in the process. She told me this was her real revenge on her parents, to force them at last to talk about themselves, along with the charged but denied emotional environment of the family.

When I met her she had returned to work and was taking antidepressant medication. She did not like the effect of the pills and had tried to stop on her own, but realized that her condition worsened. She took me aside one day at the women's gathering, and told me about the attempted suicide and that she had brought her "weapon" with her. It was a small buck knife with a four-inch blade. I asked her what she wanted to do with it. She wondered if we might do something ceremonial with it; so I asked if she was ready to give it up. She said yes.

The ceremony took place at night around a fire. All of the women came and sat in a circle. We burnt sage as incense, chanted, and then I asked Sharon to tell her story to the women, along with her hopes, fears, and expectations of what this ceremony might accomplish. She hoped that by sharing her story in a sacred context her shame might diminish and that somehow a curse could be turned into a blessing.

When she was finished, I said that all of us have weapons of one sort or another that we carry around and that each of us uses these weapons to murder our best impulses every day. I then brought out a large lump of clay and invited each woman to tear off a piece to fashion and shape into her own particular weapon of self-destruction. After we had finished working with the clay I asked everyone to share with the group what they had made. One by one the women told the story of their weapon and how they used it against themselves. There was a brain from a woman who denied her intelligence, a penis from a woman who used men, a large piece of cake from someone who was obese. When everyone had told their story I suggested that we take the opportunity to transform our weapons by returning the images back to the original lump of clay. Spontaneously the first woman smashed her weapon back into the mound of clay with force and said "Back to the Mother!" One by one the women returned their weapons back to the clay repeating the phrase "Back to the Mother" while the group chanted it with them.

When it was Sharon's turn she asked for help in removing the plastic handle from her knife. She wanted to burn the knife but did not want to put the plastic in the fire. We helped her dismantle the knife and she proceeded to smash the handle to bits. We all cheered. She then took the blade and spoke of the desperation of her attempted suicide and the desire for support she was learning and getting from other women. She tossed the blade into the fire with a final good riddance. I then asked the women to return to the clay and this time fashion a tool for themselves that would be useful in their lives as a way of transforming the weapon into something creative. The women then created objects of beauty and power for themselves. We left them to dry by the fire and took them home at the end of the week.

Sharon's tool was a heart with lips on it. She said that she was learning not to keep her feelings inside but to speak about her inner life. Prior to her attempt at killing herself she felt as if her soul was being asphyxiated. Now she was learning to express her deeper self and was realizing that her journey into darkness was not so solitary. She knew now that others had traveled similar roads, and it helped to be in the company of friends. Through the act of ceremonializing her crisis she began to recognize the gift of a dark night of the soul, and realized that even the horror of almost killing herself was an initiation into herself. She also saw the desperation of her attempt to manipulate her parents and began to assume responsibility for her own life. She could say now "no guilt, no blame."

I continued to see Sharon for several months, during which time we worked with her voice through chanting, and with ceremony, particularly in having her set up an altar and gather materials and objects for a Circle-of-Self Bundle. Sharon had begun a quest for life. She was not content with simply medicating the symptoms, she wanted to dive deeply into her own interior world and fully honor the transition she was making. She took the initiative to see an archetypal psychologist and eventually felt capable of cutting back her medication with the goal of stopping it altogether. A year later she was still in therapy, but was delighting herself with the richness of her inner world.

MAN'S RITES

The man of European descent comes into the world with a peculiar inheritance. He has a culturally bequeathed right to power, education, and success. This is both a curse and a blessing. Unlike women, who struggle to find their power, men struggle to experience their vulnerability.

For men, the process of discovering what determines a sense of healthy manhood is a quest into the past. It means revising the old myths of the hero and coming to grips with Goddess as well as God. This is a perilous journey, filled with double binds for many good hearted men. As men confront the paradox of manhood, they encounter a number of archetypal forms such as the father/tyrant, the lover/puer (eternal youth), warrior/murderer, provider/outlaw, and alchemist/scientist. Like women, men have created symbolic ritual reenactments around these contradictory energies. And like women, the journey has led them into ceremony and the search to properly initiate themselves into themselves.

As the men's movement gained popularity through such teachers as Robert Bly and James Hillman, there was a backlash from many women. Perhaps women felt threatened by men gathering together, doing ceremony, drumming, and learning to become vulnerable to issues of power, race, and homosexuality. Some women feared men would become even more dominant or more powerful and oppressive. The reality is men need to gather together to heal themselves of their cultural wounds. After all, the primary male icon of the last two thousand years has been the Son of God hanging, mortally wounded on the cross asking, "My God why have you forsaken me?"

Some men, in search of deeper meaning, offered themselves as hand servants to the Goddess movement. Although a seemingly beautiful gesture on the part of these men, it has had a high price. Many men lost the beauty of what a strong healthy male might be and found themselves rejected as lovers by strong women. This is not a new story. As late as the Roman Empire, men who were devotees of the ancient Goddess Cybele publicly flagellated and castrated themselves in her service. A few years ago there was a derogatory term for such men: *snag* a Sensitive New Age Guy. A cruel paradox in that women claim they want men to be more sensitive, but if men are too "nice" many women leave them for the old stereotype of the Marlboro Man. It is always tragic for either men or women to abandon their own strength and beauty in subservience to the opposite sex.

Through the men's movement, men can learn how to feel safe with one another. Men commit more violent crimes against one another than they do against women or children. Men know better than anyone how dangerous other men can be. Ever since the early days of patriarchal monotheism, men have been divided against themselves. When the art of animal husbandry was discovered, the ancient male bond of the hunter was destroyed. Animal husbandry requires knowledge of breeding, and breeding practices require one great bull to be singled out to inseminate the herd, while all other males are castrated or slaughtered. The shift men went through, from hunter to farmer, was as radical as what women went through in the shift from matriarchal to patriarchal societies. For men, this moment of animal castration set the stage for the Divine Right of Kings. It meant men were no longer part of a band of hunters, working in unison together, but rather one man was now dominant. In many cultures it literally meant the King had the right to every bride in the kingdom on her wedding night. The castration complex must surely lie in this mythic moment and not with fear of the mother.

For men, issues of trust towards other men are very real, not only on the streets or in business, but also in the sexual arena. Men can "cuckold" their best friend by having sex with the other man's wife. There is no complementary term for a woman whose best friend sleeps with her husband. To be cuckolded is extremely humiliating, as other men view the cuckold with a sneer or snicker. Ironically the shame lies with the husband who has been deceived, not with the deceiver.

Just as the women's movement has deepened, the men's movement has also grown in depth. After the initial headlines and media events around the Wild Man, men have settled down to do some good work together. Many men are now part of ongoing men's groups, where they actively support one another on their particular life's journey and learn to trust their brothers enough to be vulnerable. They too are learning how to heal themselves and one another of their wounds.

SEEKING DEATH TO FIND LIFE

The following account is how one middle-aged man came to grips with his demons through the process of the vision quest.

Stuart was a professor in philosophy at a New England university. He initially came to the Rites of Passage organization because his life was in a state of collapse. He was in the process of kicking a cocaine habit, his marriage was disintegrating, and his job was threatened. After his first quest he completed his rehabilitation for substance abuse, but was not able to salvage his marriage. He had returned to quest again, to deal with the issue of his pending divorce and to acquire strength to continue on his personal and professional path. He said he wanted to do a vision quest every year to keep himself awake. He asked permission to go out a day early, and since he already knew the structure, as a group we agreed.

The third night of this particular vision quest, the sky opened and the rain fell. Storms in the desert are often dramatic and this was no exception. We brief people about flash-floods and electrical storms, and how to protect themselves from such occurrences by avoiding ravines and staying off the tops of mountains. Stuart had chosen the peak of one of the Owl's Head Mountains. That night we could see him illuminated against the sky with every crash of thunder and strike of lightning. We prayed for his safety and for our own.

In the morning, when he entered base camp, we could not refrain from asking him how it was. He told us that he danced with death. The drugs, the ending of his marriage, the possible loss of his job were all part of his personal moment to live or die. He said that all of his life he had been courting a death wish and that he did not have the courage to simply commit suicide. Instead he chose ways that would undermine his life without really ending it. That night, alone on the mountain, he was determined to stay within his Medicine Wheel. He had constructed his wheel out of entirely black stones. It was a medicine wheel designed to invoke the darkness, introspection, and confrontation with death. When the storm came up, he felt as if "the Great Spirit had heard my cry, and paid me a personal visit." Lightning began to strike the mountain, as we had witnessed from base camp.

Before the storm he wrote in his journal:

"I have come here to meet my Death. Please let me die, my life is too painful. I want to be free. I want my bones to be picked clean by the vultures, and scattered to the four directions."

On the morning after the storm, he wrote:

"Last night I shook my fist at the sky. I dared the powers that be to strike me dead, I begged to be killed. When the first strike of light-ning hit, I was filled with the power to die. I called out, "Come closer death." Soon the second bolt hit and it was a little closer this time. I trembled inside, but was still bent on dying. When the third bolt struck, I fell on my belly and my whole body screamed NO! I knew then I could not leave my circle or I would surely be killed. The last strike had hit about 100 feet away and split a boulder open. At that moment I heard a voice that said, 'You must dance for your life.' I was so weak in the knees, I could barely stand. The fear was so great, but I got to my feet and I danced as the storm raged around me. It was absolutely crazy, there I was standing up on a mountain in a lightning storm, dancing for my life! The life I desperately wanted to end a few minutes earlier. I danced until the dawn came, I danced myself back into living."

WILD MAN MEETS THE GODDESS

The great gift of ceremony is that it allows us to find sacred ways for men and women to be together. In Chapter Seven I gave a number of examples of how ordinary people have found ways to make their relation-ships more sacred. There is a great longing in our culture between men and women. The desire to join together with another is a natural calling, but today there is a desperation in the longing. Both the women's and men's movement are striving towards creating healthier men and women. The work that can transpire in the company of one's own gender should enable individuals to more fully honor a potential partner. As each of us grows into wholeness, we automatically become more attractive.

A person who is filled with insecurities, needs, and narcissism only repeats previous failed relationships. I have watched many women and men who long for a permanent relationship choose the same inappropriate type of person again and again. What is amazing is how surprised they always seem when the relationship deconstructs, while everyone else has borne witness to its finality, like a slow train rolling down the tracks toward the end of line.

Some theorists claim we are always reproducing Mother or Father, trying to work out parental imprints through our lovers. Others see people imprinted on their first true love, hoping to recapture that magic moment. Scientists claim it is all a matter of smell, chemicals known as pheromones, or the addiction to neurotransmitters created as a result of experiencing the feeling of being in love. All of these theories probably hold some truth. Unfortunately they all ignore the complex psyche of any given individual.

Because this is a book primarily concerned with ceremony and the sense of the sacred, we won't go into a lengthy analysis of why differing dysfunctions manifest in our love relationships. I would, however, like to point out some of the fallacies or knots under which people seek out potential partners only to end with disappointment and mutual heartbreak. These descriptions may strike you as humorous, offensive, or simply too close to the bone. Do you see yourself here?

- I am naturally attracted to impossible and dangerous people, knowing my great Love for this type of person will change and correct all that is wrong with them. My Love will persevere and conquer all.
- If I am good enough, my partner will become stable, stop drinking, stop doing drugs, and become a model of success and kindness.
- My unrealistic expectations in changing your behavior eventually end in disappointment. By the initial act of being so accommodating to my partner's needs that I have given up all of my own interests, personal power, and integrity, I have now lost myself completely. I am filled with anger and resentment towards you.
- I will tell you I love you, and I will even live with you for a period of years, but we will both continually question whether or not we are actually in a "relationship." I will keep you guessing for as long as you can endure it and then be devastated if you leave me.
- If I am partnered, I become seen as healthy, normal, and sane. I am valuable as a human being, because I am complete as a result of being partnered. Not to be partnered is indicative of my own incapacity and failure as a human being.

- I gain status by being partnered with someone who is successful, rich, famous, or creative. Being partnered to someone like you proves that I am also healthy, attractive, and capable of success.

- I am currently not partnered, but according to self-help professionals I can attract the perfect person by making a list of every characteristic I could possibly desire in another human being. I am told to be as specific as my imagination will allow me. I can have everything I want in life, I deserve everything I could possibly want in life, and I can expect a miracle, especially if I post my list on my bathroom mirror.

- Hot sex is the most important aspect of a relationship, and I will suffer any indignity to have it. You can cheat on me, share me with others, talk me into group sex, or get me to indulge in esoteric tantric practices, where sex is performed under the guise of spirituality. You can also abuse me, beat me, and then make up to me in bed. Lots of fighting and threats of divorce create lots of opportunities for making up through hot sex.

- Because my partner is not fulfilling all of my criteria as the perfect mate, the grass sure looks greener over there. My well-being and self image has to do with how attractive I feel, and I feel most attractive when I am desired by someone from outside of our relationship.

- For my object of desire, I will become a chameleon. Whatever I think you want in a partner I will become—at least long enough to have you fall in love with me. I will misrepresent myself and my life style to seduce you. I will offer you whatever your heart desires—for a while. I don't really feel good enough about myself to show you who I really am, but after you really love me, I will slowly reveal my true self to you.

- I am secretly terrified of intimacy, but I have a really good horror story about my life. The story will enlighten you to all of my family history, traumas, failures, fears, disappointments, and pains. It will take quite a length of time to share all of this with you, and you will feel very special and helpful in healing me. However, when I have shared every single story and its smallest detail with you, and you are feeling intimate and vulnerable, I will lose interest in you. In truth, I will no longer have anything to share with you and will soon meet someone new with whom I can share all of my pain and suffering.

- Now that you have heard all of my stories, and I have revealed to you the depth of my injuries and insecurities, you dare not even think about leaving me. You now share in the burden and responsibility of keeping me from going insane or killing myself. Without you I am nothing.

- For me, partnership is about merging. I want a partner with whom I can completely merge. I love to get up in the morning, shower together, meditate together, and do yoga together. I want to create a joint career together, so we can be together every minute of every day. If you wish to see friends without me or go for hike alone, I will be offended and hurt, because obviously you are rejecting me and my love. Your parents made a terrible mistake in giving you your Christian name; I would like to change your name to something that is more suitable, more to my image of who we should be. I will take care of you, cook for you, and be an ardent lover, I am an old-fashioned kind of girl.

Unfortunately, these behavior patterns are all too familiar. We either know people who relate this way, or have participated in one or more of the above knots ourselves. People who are successful in maintaining a long-term, fulfilling relationship have found other ways to relate to themselves and their partner.

Happy, healthy long-term relationships are a rarity, but they do exist. Patterns of behavior also exist among the couples I know who have good marriages. A happily married psychiatrist described his own process of coming to grips with his unrealistic expectations. In his youth he was attracted to strong women who could fulfill and complete him. He would become so needy towards the woman that she would leave him in order to save herself. Through therapy and meditation practices he eventually made conscious his underlying pattern and was able to consciously move beyond it.

Individuals who have done their homework around themselves and are living conscious lives as relatively whole people attract other whole people. These people are not interested in merging, changing, or fixing their partners. There is a level of acceptance towards themselves, and towards their partners. They have realistic expectations of one another, and often clear overt agreements around the arrangement of their lives. Compromise is done under a clear light and as an act of love, not as manipulation. Hidden agendas around negotiations are doomed to failure as they breed disappointments and resentments. Explicit compromises that are mutually beneficial to the relationship allow each person to express a sense of appreciation for the other's sacrifices in the relationship.

Every solid couple I have talked with said they do not do therapy with one another. This, they warned, is deadly. Never fall into analyzing one another; therapy and counseling can be helpful, but it should be done with a third party.

Couples need sacred time together. More than anything else, a spiritual way of being acknowledges something greater than mundane reality, allowing a relationship to exist in a larger framework. When the relationship is placed in the light of something larger than the personalities involved, a new level of truthfulness is attained. Truth and trust go hand in hand. Placing a relationship under the auspices of Truth assures each person of trust. If I am not truthful with you, how can you trust me? Having a shared spiritual connection, whether through organized religion or a marriage bundle, is important, but it must be a private reality to really work. Participating in public spiritual exercises is not the same as having an intimate and sacred connection.

Creating time together in which the higher self can be presented to the beloved naturally calls us into ceremony. If each person has answered the question "In whose Light?" then as a couple each can recognize and honor the guiding light of the other, and it need not be the same guiding light. Knowing that my partner is present to me from his higher self, and me to him, permits us to unashamedly, and even humorously, acknowledge the God and Goddess within one another.

Hopefully, men's and women's groups will truly expand or raise consciousness. Drumming, singing, and chanting leads both groups into recognizing the need for rites of passages and ceremony. The ceremonies created today are more powerful than the pageantry of twenty years ago. Group ceremony works deep within the mythic mind, provoking each person towards self examination. The more each of us can see through old patterns of behavior, the more we can move towards wholeness. As we move towards wholeness, we approach the possibility of bringing men and women together. My vision is of a sacred event, a ceremonial honoring of one another. Past attempts have focused too much on exposing the mutual pain. Matters of the heart are delicate moments in our lives, and should be treated tenderly and in a sacred way.

·13·

CELEBRATING COMMUNITY

THE SPIRIT OF PLACE, PILGRIMAGE, AND POWER

We began our quest for the sacred with the story of Psyche and Eros, noting how through the Anima Mundi we begin to discover how our individual soul touches the Soul of the World, and how this world soul envelops us as human beings. We are all returning home after being away for a very long time. The moon and stars and the heavenly bodies illuminate the night sky and point out both our special place in creation and our insignificance. The longing for Nature and its wildness is an emotional calling. To hear the howl of the wolf, the roar of the grizzly bear, or to wish for the return of the buffalo is a desire that overrides any perceived danger. Our National Parks are overwhelmed with unprecedented numbers of visitors, people thrilled at the sight of herds of deer, elk, moose, and buffalo. The return of eagles, hawks, and condors from the edge of extinction makes us gaze upward in wonder as they ride the currents of wind above us. Walking in an aspen glen, a maple forest, or a pine wood awakens in us a sense of childlike awe. Journeys to the ocean, where we might see whales and dolphins or perhaps even swim among them, bestows upon us a communion of kinship. Hiking along a mountain stream and glimpsing an otter swimming home with a brown trout in its mouth takes one's breath away.

The numinous quality we experience in Nature pierces us with its beauty and its sacred simplicity. From our self-centered perspective we think we must save indigenous cultures, habitats, and animals, never realizing that the natural world, its people, and creatures may in fact be calling us to them with the hope that we might save ourselves. Native peoples everywhere are continually praying for the civilized world to transcend its rational knowing and find a way for its scientific knowledge to be transmuted into a wisdom for living in balance and harmony with the rest of creation.

If we are to have a meaningful ceremonial life, one in which celebrations, initiations, rites of passage, and Nature are included, we must have a sense of place. Ceremonial form rises up out of the land in which people abide. By listening to the land and the voices of its multitudes of species an internal synchronization begins to take place. The monthly arc of the moon and the rhythmic seasonal changes reverberate inside us. To gather together with friends and families for celebratory days is a natural evocation, and out of these events a sense of ceremony begins to emerge.

By fully inhabiting the place in which we live, we become attuned to the land. Coming to know one's place can be a journey in which the entire family can participate. It can begin by exploring the local history, myths, and legends of the land and it inhabitants. Often this means discovering who the native peoples were before the coming of the settlers and how their stories speak of the land. There may be particular geological formations, rivers, valleys, mountains, and rocks that have traditionally been recognized as places of power. Some of these places may be places of solitude and renewal, others may be haunted by the past, especially if there have been massacres or battles which have occurred there. It is a meditation practice to go to local power places and simply sit in the presence of the soul of the land. Often images and dreams will come to reveal some hidden aspect of the place.

Traditionally, places of power are approached on foot with incense or smudge, prayers, circumambulations, offerings, and requests for healing. In cathedrals we frequently light a candle and pray. In Nature, bring an offering of some kind to the spirit of the place and speak out loud your prayers. These offerings can be food, feathers, crystals, or hand-crafted objects made with a prayerful intention. Here in New Mexico, it is common to find offerings at traditional natural holy sites, such as sacred mountain tops. A prayer arrow, which is a stick wrapped with yarn, in which one's prayerful intentions have been wound, and then decorated with feathers is a common offering of native peoples. It is important not to remove or disturb other peoples offerings, and children should be taught to respect others' gifts back to the land.

All of creation is sacred, and yet some places are filled with a sense of power or spirit. The archeological remains of previous cultures stir our imagination and awaken our souls. The pyramids of Egypt, the Druidic standing stones of Stonehenge, Machu Pichu in Peru, or the Mayan pyramids of the Yucatan are a few of the wonders of the ancient world. The temples of India, France's Chartres and Notre Dame Cathedrals, St. Peters Basilica in Rome, Jerusalem, and Mecca demonstrate an unbroken chain of religious use and continual pilgrimage on the part of the faithful. Natural wonders like the mesas and canyons of the American Southwest, the Himalayas, Ayers Rock, the oceans, rivers, and springs call people to them. All of these places, historic and natural, invite us to embark on a pilgrimage, to go beyond being a tourist. The conscious act of making a pilgrimage to a holy place puts us into contact with the lineage of all who have made the pilgrimage before, as well as the spirit of the place. Respect for local custom, dress, and behavior is part of the process. Whether we are making pilgrimage to exotic places in distant lands, or discovering the holiness of the landscape in which we live, the act of entering into relationship with the spirit of the place is the same. It is cultivated through time and space.

If we are to know our place intimately, we must comprehend the mythic and spiritual aspects of the place and acquire an adequate understanding of its physical realities. Again, the entire family can participate is answering such questions as: Where does our water really come from? Where are the head waters of the river? Where does our garbage go? How many species of animals or birds live here? Who migrates through our territory? What is the state of our soil, air, and water? Where does our electricity come from? Answering such questions is part of the process of cultivating a relationship with the land on which we live.

If we are to break out of our dysfunctional Industrial Age patterns, it is essential that we create new socio-ecological ways of being. We can no longer treat only the identified patient in the family, or even the family itself. The pathology that afflicts the modern world requires us to think in terms of whole systems. In the forefront of pattern thinking is Bill Mollison and his Permaculture system. In his book *Introduction to Permaculture*, Mollison states: "We ourselves can cure all the famine, all the injustice, and all the stupidity of the world. We can do it by understanding the way natural systems work, by careful forestry and gardening, by contemplation and by taking care of the Earth... Only those who share their multiple and varied skills, true friendships, and a sense of community and knowledge of the Earth know they are safe wherever they go.... There is no other path for us than that of cooperative productivity and community responsibility."

NATURE'S PLANETARY HOLY DAYS

The ceremonial Wheel of the Year is an ancient calendar connecting us into the old seasonal cycles familiar to pastoralists, farmers, and hunter-gatherers. It is part of a European tradition, and although we now celebrate Christianized versions of the old cycles, the original ceremonies dealt more openly with our connection to the Sun, Earth, and Moon, animals, and the rhythms of planting and harvesting.

In pre-Christian times the four seasons were marked by the Spring Equinox (March 20–23), the Summer Solstice (June 20–23), the Fall Equinox (Sept. 20–23), and the Winter Solstice (Dec. 20–23), all of which were holy days of celebration. The equinoxes are the only two days of the year in which day and night are of equal length. It is a time of harmony and balance, planting and harvesting, a time to balance the inner and outer, as well as the feminine and masculine. Modern day ceremonialists often incorporate eggs into their Equinox ceremonies. In New York City many people take to the streets, and at the exact moment of the Equinox balance a raw egg on end. An egg will only do this on the Equinoxes. The Spring Equinox is a time of return, when new seeds come forth, and the land is renewed from the sleep of winter. Today, the Equinox is celebrated through the holy day of Easter, the rebirth of Christ and his resurrection. Easter Sunday falls on the first Sunday, after the first full moon, that follows the Spring Equinox. Passover is also determined by the Spring Equinox. It celebrates the passing of the darkness of slavery and the return of freedom.

The Summer Solstice was known as *Litha* in pagan times. (The word *pagan* or *heathen* has been misappropriated over the centuries. Originally the word *pagan* simply meant a peasant or rustic, who was not a practicing Christian, Jew, or Muslim—someone who practiced the old Nature-worshipping ceremonies of our collective past. *Heathen* was a term for people who lived on the heath, or wilderness area outside of cultivated villages and towns. Today, a neo-pagan movement is gaining popularity as a way to connect with the Earth, and to practice shamanism and white magic. Paganism absolutely should not be confused with any brand of Satanism, because paganism is the precursor to the Judeo-Christian world—it has no concept of a Christian devil. Modern day pagans pray to both Goddess and God, often finding their roots in the ancient Celtic and Druidic traditions of Europe.) The Summer Solstice is a time for celebration, bonfires, flowers, and the breaking of bread together. It is the longest day of year and the shortest night. The Earth is at its fullest as the Sun King pays homage to the Queen of Summer. Energetically it is like an Earthly full moon, heightening feelings of goodwill, radiance, and the hope of a bountiful harvest to come.

The Fall Equinox, known as *Mabon* in ancient times, is the season of harvest. Altars contain the fruits of the harvest and the seeds of next year's food. It is the gathering time for corn and grains, a time to separate the wheat from the chaff. The forces of day and night are in balance, but the night is about to grow longer than the day. It is a time of thanksgiving and making preparations for the coming descent into Winter. As we sow, shall we reap, and self-reflection and introspection are natural turns of mind in this season.

Winter Solstice is the Yuletide, the longest night of the year, the darkest hour before the yearly dawn. It is like an Earthly new moon. It is the birthday of the Divine Sun King, who the modern world knows as Christ. Ceremonially it is a time of darkness and returning light. The darkness should be dwelled in and experienced, a time to appreciate introspection and to look deep within to the soul. Modern day rite-makers often light candles and bonfires, symbolizing the return of the light from the extreme of darkness. The traditional yule log was the ceremonial fire lit on Christmas Eve to insure the rebirth of the light.

THE CROSS-QUARTER DAYS

In the Wheel of the Year, the equinoxes and solstices are like the cardinal directions on a compass. In the non-cardinal directions are feast days known as cross-quarter days. They occur half way between the days that mark the four seasons.

The ending of the year, on October 31, is known as Samhain or All-Hallows Eve, popularly known as Halloween. Hallow means to make holy or sacred, to sanctify or consecrate. It is the time of honoring the dead, and in many countries is known as the Day of the Dead. Halfway between the harvest ceremonies of the Fall Equinox and the dark of the Winter Solstice, Samhain and the following day, known as All-Saints' Day, celebrates the ending of the year and the birth of a new beginning, recognizing that even though the fields lie fallow the potential for life is present.

On February 2, the feast of Brigit takes place. Brigit was an ancient Irish Goddess, whose priestesses kept an ever-burning fire lit at Kildare. But Brigit can be traced back to Rome and the Middle East, where she was known respectively as Juno and Tanit. She has always been recognized as the Triple Goddess, and even in her Christianized form as St. Brigit, she was part of a triad with St. Patrick and St. Columba. February 2 became Christianized, too, and today Candlemas is a feast day for the purification of the Virgin. In terms of the Wheel of the Year, Candlemas is like a waxing moon, gathering energy as the light slowly grows out of the Winter Solstice, preparing for the coming Spring. The seeds that have lain dormant through the Winter have begun to tremble in the Earth and will later sprout into new growth and life. The potency of Candlemas is symbolized by the lighting of candles and self-reflection that generates inspiration towards creative acts to come.

Halfway between the Spring Equinox and Summer Solstice lies *Beltane*, or May Day, on May 1. Beltane does not have a Christian equivalent, perhaps because of its sexual nature. Throughout northern Europe, May eve bonfires would be lit on the hill tops while the people would leap through the flames, dance, sing, and "spend all night in pleasant pastimes." Marriage bonds were temporarily forgotten, and love making in the fields was thought to encourage an abundant harvest. On May Day, a Maypole would be decorated with flowers and multicolored ribbons, and people would dance and weave themselves around the Maypole, wrapping the pole with the ribbons. Everyone, including the Church and the Puritans was aware of the sexual significance of the Pole. The Church, as early as the seventh century, objected to the ceremony, and as late as the seventeenth century, people were lamenting the new puritanical laws against May Day. It was not until Cromwell and the Reformation that the Beltane fires burned no more.

Until recently, all that has remained of this ceremony has been the naming of a May Queen or homecoming King and Queen. The high school prom itself must be remnant of this festival. Over the last few years I have been aware of a number of Maypole celebrations where people properly wrap the pole in many colors. The participation of children and adults is a joyous sight as they sing, dance, and feast together. The reviving of this custom reminds people of the possibility of a sacred marriage between men and women, as well as the joys of family and community life.

Lughnasad is the old word for the feast day of August 1, also known as *Lammas*. It is the cross-quarter day between Summer Solstice and the Autumnal Equinox. In England, Lammas is the beginning of the harvest festival, when the first wheat is baked into bread and consecrated as the host for the Mass. Lammas means the *loaf mass* or *bread feast*. The name Lughnasad comes from Lug, the Celtic God who was the mythical founder of Lyons and London, whose temple stood on Ludgate Hill. Lug was married to the Moon Goddess in England, and in Ireland he was married to the local Earth Mother. Lug was Christianized into several saints: St. Lugad, St. Luan, and St. Lugidus. Lammas is an early reminder of the coming harvest and subsequent turn to autumn and winter. The ceremony honors the first dying away of the old Sun King in the form of the first cutting of the wheat. Altars are decorated with wheat, corn, and grain. Baked bread or gingerbread cookies shaped as humans are used as offerings in a contemporary way to celebrate the Bread Feast.

BUILDING COMMUNITY THROUGH CEREMONY

Ceremony is a sacred way to create community. Traditionally we gather our friends and family together to celebrate obvious rites of passages such as a birth, marriage, or death. These are rare moments in our secular world, when we grant ourselves permission to be in a prayerful space with one another. By observing the seasonal cycles or monthly lunar phases, we not only increase the opportunity to gather together in a sacred way, but begin the process of finding ourselves in sync with the natural cyclical rhythms of the planet and cosmos.

Unlike rites of passages, full moons, solstices, or equinoxes do not focus on any single individual or family. Instead, the planetary holy days are a time for community gathering and celebration. People from all walks of life, the churched and the unchurched, are responsive to such ceremonial events, and women especially love the idea of holding women's circles on the full moon.

Deciding to host a ceremony on one of the above described holy days is perhaps the easiest way to begin to put into practice the theory of a sacred ceremonial way. Working together with friends to create such an event is a great way to learn to implement the elements of the sacred. In my work over the years as a ceremonialist, I have created ceremonies on these days in a number of ways. Initially, I began by inviting friends, and I am still amazed by the number of people who show up, especially when it requires them to buy an airline ticket in order to participate. As I and my circle of friends became more confident, we began to offer Solstice or Equinox ceremonies as public events, and always for free. I still hold the personal belief that planetary holy days should be celebrated with family, friends, and when possible, with the community at large. These days should not become part of our secular world, to be turned into a "workshop" where people are expected to pay a fee in order to attend. As a teacher and workshop leader, these days are part of my give-away to my community.

Before going public with a ceremonial event it is a great help to have a ceremonial circle of friends who provide a number of skills and talents such as music, singing, art, dance and story telling. Contemporary ceremony has gone beyond the High Priest or Priestess role into a collaborative adventure, and this process aids us in learning how to resocialize or retribalize ourselves in the company of others. When we model for others our process of creating and facilitating a ceremony together, we become an inspiration.

When we find ourselves with a proper network of ceremonial friends, and we decide to put on a public event, there are a number of ways to go about it. The easiest way is to simply place an advertisement in the local paper or put up flyers around town giving the time, place, and whatever items people might want to bring (especially if participants are expected to arrive with something special to give away or exchange). Bookstores are another valuable community resource. Often small bookstores or art gallery owners are more than happy to sponsor such community events.

WINTER SOLSTICE CEREMONY

For a number of years I lived on the north coast of California, in the Point Reyes National Seashore. Together with ceremonial artists Robert

Ott, Colleen Kelly, and my husband Francis Huxley, we decided to organize a Winter Solstice ceremony for the community. We placed a small ad
in the local newspaper announcing a free Winter Solstice ceremony to be
held at Abbots Lagoon Beach.

On the solstice, as people arrived, we were already busy scraping a
large labyrinth pattern onto the sand. These labyrinth patterns—found
throughout the world in art and architecture—are an intricate number of
winding passages leading to the center. People readily joined in to help
with the preparations. They scraped away the sand and made a three-foot
wide passageway that would be the labyrinth. Others gathered white shells
and rocks and laid them down in a line separating each passageway. There
were about 100 people, including small children and the elderly. We had
various props with us for the ceremony, and we set these up. When the
labyrinth was complete, we gathered everyone together into a circle to
explain what we would do.

In the center of the labyrinth we lit a fire and made a simple altar
with crystals, shells, and a pair of scissors. At the entrance to the labyrinth
we placed unlit torches. Our intention was to honor the dark time of year
and the return of the sun. We began by smudging the entire circle. Next,
we handed out two pieces of paper to everyone and asked them to spend a
few minutes in silent meditation reflecting on what they might want to
give up or give away from the past year. This was to be written on one piece
of paper. The other piece of paper was for writing down what they wanted
to do in the next year that might be beneficial for the world. We asked
them to think of it as a New Year resolution to take home with them.
Francis then told the story of the myth of the labyrinth, and how it was
used in ancient Greece and throughout Europe.

Each person would have the opportunity to dance into the center of
the labyrinth while the rest of us chanted and drummed. At the entrance
they were handed an unlit torch to carry into the center where they would
offer their give-away to the fire out loud. There, they would find a pair of
scissors, and they could cut a piece of their hair to be offered to the fire as
well. Once they had made their offerings they were to light the torch and
carry the light of the sun out of the labyrinth of darkness.

It took at least ten minutes to dance into the labyrinth. The dancers
were sent in a few minutes apart; we waited while each person had their
time in the center. People took their time in the center seriously; some

knelt down, others stood with their arms uplifted, each made their vow. The dance in and out was done with a minimum of awkwardness, and some people were obviously thrilled to be on stage.

The fact that it was free and for the local community gave people the chance to meet and talk, often for the first time. It was important for us that cleansing and purification be a part of the event. When everyone had been into the center we held hands and returned to the center as a group, snaking our way in and out again. We ended by being in a large circle around the labyrinth, singing, chanting, and dancing, while in the sky above us a large cloud formation appeared in the shape of a white crane. Our final act was to erase the labyrinth from the sand and to leave the land as we found it.

As a community event, it was very powerful and it spoke to a need inside the people. The community had recently survived a devastating flood, in which we had witnessed the enchanted landscape turn deadly. The ceremony became a way for people to make peace with the land. It was also important to us, as the organizers, that the vows taken be concerned with something larger than the self. We wanted the event to be seen in the larger context of community, and I believe the ceremony was a success. We heard later from a number of people how important it was for them to get rid of "stuff" from the past year in a public, but yet private way. It added power to their process. In the months that followed we met people on the streets or in the market who conveyed how important the ceremony was to them. They often told us how they were manifesting their vow out in the world.

This ceremony incorporated a number of elements of traditional ceremony and yet was very much of the moment. There was the purification with the smudge, the lighting of the fire, crossing the threshold into the labyrinth, the personal offering or give away, a taking of a personal vow, chanting and dancing, and general celebration of the Winter Solstice day. As a ceremonial event, it cost virtually nothing, outside of the announcement in the paper. Most importantly, it was a healing experience for the community at large.

Events like these can be created in every community. The more we experience our interdependence, the better, for all of life thrives on being in relationship and in community. Grass-roots ceremonial connections through our church, schools, or circle of family and friends increases our capacity to be intimate with others and brings a sense of the sacred into our everyday life.

MILLENNIAL DREAMING

As we approach the year 2000 there is a quickening of the world pulse. The end of a thousand-year cycle is always a time of prophecy, hope and despair. The prophets are already among us preaching about the Apocalypse, the Second Coming, the Rapture, the coming of aliens, the collapse of the environment, and the Age of Aquarius. As part of a larger Earthly cycle, the millennium has historically been a time of endings, and a time to make preparations for salvation. According to salvationists, it will be enjoyed only by the faithful, and when it does come, it will completely transform life on Earth.

Recently, I saw a bumper sticker which said: "Jesus is coming—look busy." Between now and the year 2000 is a time to prepare for the next cycle of life. From the present moment it is difficult to anticipate what state the world will be in circa 2000. God willing, most of us will still be around to celebrate the coming of a new thousand-year cycle. I have already heard talk of planetary wide celebrations, perhaps through satellite technology, with downlinks hooking up power places and religious leaders, broadcasting into communities around the world. Pilgrims are already booking hotel reservations at sacred sites, such as the pyramids, or Stonehenge.

Obviously it is a time to celebrate, and a perfect opportunity for community celebration. We can also begin to dream the new millennium now, especially if we reflect on where the past thousand years have taken us. As a result of science and technology, we are living in a global village, and the world has become very small. We can travel to the most distant places in a day, and from the comfort of our homes we can witness, via satellite, the plight of our neighbors. Those of us in developed countries share a burden of suffering with those less fortunate, knowing that "there but for the grace of God go I."

Through self-reflection and community awareness we can begin to take a more active role in deciding how we create the world of tomorrow. This book has been a call to bring the sacred back into our ordinary lives through new and reinvigorating ceremonial practices. The variety of revitalization movements afoot provide a number of contexts in which we can participate with others from our community. To want to make the world a better place for future generations is a calling that is easily scorned. The feeling of approaching a moment of radical change is pervasive throughout the world. Some envision political upheaval, collapsing economies, or sudden and devastating ecological changes. Already various forms of psychic house cleanings are taking place; therapy is being criticized by therapists, science is being forced to reencounter the mystery of life, religions are required to adapt to the times in which they currently exist, and economies based upon the myth of infinite resources are facing the realities of widespread environmental degradation.

All of this coexists with great hopes and dreams for the world. There is a strong desire to experience our lives more meaningfully. Seeing ourselves in the context of the great wisdom traditions of the planet, and the Perennial Philosophy, which reminds us of who we are, is part of our revelatory process. By staying alert and aware, and by refusing to go unconsciously into the tumultuous times in which we live, we can create lives that are worth living.

BIBLIOGRAPHY

Abram, David. *The Spell of the Sensuous*. New York: Pantheon Books, 1996.

Adlington, William. 1556 translation. *The Golden Ass of Lucius Apuleius*. London: Simpkin Marshall.

Bellah, Robert N. *Habits of the Heart*. New York: Harper and Row, 1986.

Berry, Thomas. *The Dream of the Earth*. San Francisco, Sierra Club Books, 1988.

Blofeld, John. *Compassion Yoga*. London: George Allen & Unwin, 1977.

Cohn, Norman. *The Pursuit of the Millennium*. New York: Oxford University Press, 1970.

Davis, Elizabeth and Leonard, Carol. *The Women's Wheel of Life*. New York: Viking Arkana, 1996.

Delbanco, Andrew. *The Death of Satan*. New York: Farrar, Straus, & Giroux, 1995.

Eisler, Riane. *The Chalice and the Blade*. San Francisco: Harper and Row, 1987.

Estes, Clarissa Pinkola. *Women Who Run with the Wolves*. New York: Ballantine Books, 1992.

Fox, Matthew. *Creation Spirit Duality*. San Francisco: Harper, 1940.

Fox, Matthew. *Original Blessing*. Santa Fe, New Mexico: Bear & Co., 1983.

Fox, Warwick. *Toward a Transpersonal Ecology*. Boston: Shambhala, 1990.

Frazer, James George. *The New Golden Bough*. New York: Criterion Books, 1950.

Getty, Adele. *Goddess: Mother of Living Nature*. London: Thames & Hudson, 1990.

Halifax, Joan. *Shaman*. London: Thames & Hudson, 1982.

Hillman, James. *A Blue Fire*. New York: Harper Perennial, 1989.

Hillman, James, and Ventura, Michael. *We've Had a Hundred Years of Psychotherapy*. San Francisco: Harper, 1992.

Huxley, Francis. *The Way of the Sacred*. London: Aldus Books, 1974.

Huxley, Julian. *Religion Without Revelation*. London: C.A. Watts & Co., 1967.

Kipnis, Aaron R. *Knights Without Armor*. Los Angeles: Jeremy Tarcher, 1991.

LaBarre, Weston. *The Ghost Dance*. London: George Allen & Unwin, 1972.

LaFontaine, J.S. *Initiation*. London: Penguin Books, 1985.

Lasch, Christopher. *The Culture of Narcissism*. New York: W.W. Norton, 1978.

Liptik, Karen. *Coming-of-Age*. Brookefield, Connecticut: The Millbrook Press, 1994.

Lovelock, James. *The Ages of Gaia*. Oxford: Oxford University Press, 1988.

Mahdi, Louise Carus, Steven Foster, and Meredith Little. *Betwixt and Between*. Lasalle, Illinois: Open Court, 1987.

Mauss, Marcel. *A General Theory of Magic*. Boston: Routledge and Kegan Paul, 1972.

Maybury-Lewis, David. *Millennium*. New York: Viking, 1992.

Meade, Margaret, and Calis, Nicolas. *Primitive Heritage*. New York: Random House, 1953.

Mollison, Bill. *Introduction to Permaculture*. Australia: Tagari Press, 1991.

Neumann, Erich. *Amor and Psyche*. New York: Bollingen Foundation, 1956.

Noble, Vicki, ed. *Uncoiling the Snake*. San Francisco: Harper, 1993.

Peck, M. Scott. *People of the Lie*. New York: Simon and Schuster, 1983.

Pipher, Mary. *The Shelter of Each Other*. New York: Putnam, 1996.

Roszak, Theodore. *The Voice of the Earth*. New York: Simon and Schuster, 1992.

Schaef, Anne Wilson. *Native Wisdom for White Minds*. New York: Ballantine Books, 1995.

Seed, John, et. al. *Thinking Like A Mountain*. Philadelphia: New Society Publishers, 1988.

Sheldrake, Rupert. *The Rebirth of Nature*. New York: Bantam Books, 1991.

Shepard, Paul. *Nature and Madness*. San Francisco: Sierra Club Books, 1982.

Snyder, Gary. *The Practice of the Wild*. Berkeley, California: North Point Press.

Spretnak, Charlene. *The Politics of Women's Spirituality*. New York: Anchor Books, 1982.

Stone, Merlin. *When God Was A Woman*. San Diego: Harcourt, Brace, Jovanovich, 1976.

Thrupp, Sylvia L., ed. *Millennial Dreams in Action*. New York: Schoken Books, 1970.

Walker, Barbara G. *The Woman's Encyclopedia of Myths and Secrets*. San Francisco: Harper and Row, 1983.

Wall, Kathleen, and Fergeson, Gary. *Lights of Passage*. San Francisco: Harper, 1994.

Resource Directory

Chanting tapes: Adele Getty, Lou Montgomery
Video: Sacred Sites of England
Montgomery Media
P.O. Box 8164
Santa Fe, NM 87504

Vision Questing: Steven Foster, Meredith Little
School of Lost Borders
P.O. Box 55
Big Pine, CA 93513

Earth Lodge:
Nancy Goddard, Colleen Kelly
301C Main St.
Sebastopol, CA 95472

Community Development:
Community Matters
P.O. Box 14816
Santa Rosa, CA 93513

Permaculture Institute
P.O. Box 3703
Santa Fe, NM 87501

INDEX

Pilgrimage, 189–91
Place, spirit of, 189–91
Plants, 46–48
Plath, Sylvia, 177
Platon, Nicholas, 22
Plutarch, 15
Power objects, 92
Prayer, 89, 103–6
Pregnancy, 130–33
Psyche and Eros, 9–16
Puberty rites, 147–50

R

Rationalism, 31–37
Reformation, 32–33
Relationships, 100–101, 102
  ceremonial connections,
      107–17, 126–29
  divorce, 124–26
  ended, 122–29
  trust and, 118–19
  women and men, 184–88
Religion, science and, 36–37
Revitalization, 62, 76–78
Rippo, Tony, 106
Rites. *See also* Ceremony
  of men, 181–82
  of teenagers, 146–69
  of women, 171
Rites of Passage, 158–64, 183–84
Ritual, 81. *See also* Ceremony;
  Rites
Rome, ancient, 26–27, 28–31
Rorty, Richard, 39
Roszak, Theodore, 6
Ryle, Gilbert, 32

S

Sacred
  awakened within, 79–94
  changing relationship to, 18–20

sense of, 1–2
severance from, 33–34
technicians of, 45–46
St. Catherine of the Wheel, 30
St. Francis of Assisi, 16
Scaef, Ann Wilson, 130
Science, fundamentalism and,
      35–37, 77, 103
Scientific rationalism, 31–37
Self, extending circle of, 95–106
Shamanism, 49–61
Sharing, 89–90. *See also*
  Community
Shaw, George Bernard, 69
Sheldrake, Rupert, 5–6, 32, 37, 79
Shepard, Paul, 28
Silence, ceremonial, 91
Singing, 52–53, 90–91
Snake, Rueben, 53
Solstices
  summer, 192–93
  winter, 141, 193, 196–99
Sontag, Susan, 41
Soul, 16
Spring Equinox, 192
Stark, Rodney, 29
Stillbirth, 134
Stone, Merlin, 68
Storm, Heyemeyohst, 58, 164
Storytelling, 8–9
Suicide, 130–31, 177–81
Summer solstice, 192–93
Swedenborg, Emanuel, 69

T

Taboo, 92
Talking Stick, 115–16
Teacher plants, 46–48
Teenagers, 146–69
Teish, Luisa, 173
Tens, Isaac, 52
Thales, 4, 49

About the Author

Adele Getty holds a degree in environmental science and an M.A. in psychology. She has been working in the United States and Europe as a cultural ecologist lecturing and giving workshops. In 1982 she began working as the training coordinator for Steven Foster's internationally known organization Rites of Passage (now renamed the School of Lost Borders), which is dedicated to exploring modern day initiation rites and vision quest work. In 1988 Getty was a keynote speaker at an international conference in Oslo, Norway, entitled *Civilization in Transition*, which was sponsored by the Norwegian government and members of the Nobel Prize committee. She has been active in the women's spirituality movement in the United States and is listed in *Who's Who of International Women*. Author of *Goddess: Mother of Living Nature*, Getty has also been published in an anthology of women writers entitled *Snake Power*. She has appeared on television in Europe and on National Public Radio in America. Getty lives in Santa Fe, New Mexico, with her husband, British anthropologist Francis Huxley.